ターミナル

TERMINAL ISLAND
Lost Communities on America's Edge

LA
THE PORT
OF LOS ANGELES

TERMINAL ISLAND
Lost Communities on America's Edge

Naomi Hirahara • Geraldine Knatz

Eric Lynxwiler, Photography Editor

Design by Amy Inouye

Foreword by William Deverell

Afterword by George Takei

ANGEL CITY PRESS
LOS ANGELES PUBLIC LIBRARY

This watercolor of the squatter town on the East Jetty was dated March 12, 1902, but it was not signed. Prominent in the painting is Idah Strobridge's Wickieup (the long white structure on the right, a haven for artistic women in East San Pedro), which may indicate a connection between the painter and the island's resident bohemian community. In 1902, however, a Los Angeles art school advertised sketching classes on Terminal Island, so this colorful piece may be the work of someone who visited the island to study art.

Overleaf: On a moonlit night, squatters' homes are strung like an archipelago along the East Jetty in this early twentieth-century photo.

Opposite: Standing on the bridge at the Japanese garden at Mildred Obarr Walizer Elementary School in Fish Harbor: from left, Tadashi Ito, Koo Ito, teacher Annie Garcia, Masashi Ito, teacher Margaret Savage Dever, Teruko Ito, Kiyoshi Ito, and Principal Burton E. Davis. Circa 1936.

Front cover: Artist and writer Olive Percival, a frequent visitor to Terminal Island in the early 1900s, captured two important elements of East San Pedro—sea and home—in this captivating cyanotype. 1906.

Translation, front cover: Terminal, the abbreviated name for Terminal Island.

Back cover: Home life on the island ended with the U.S. military's forced removal of all residents in February of 1942. The Japanese American households suffered the most, since many of their men had already been arrested and incarcerated.

Translation, back cover: Lost Communities on America's Edge.

To the people of the lost communities.
You are not forgotten.

目次

Contents

序文

Foreword

by William Deverell

History is a great tool for excavation. When wielded with skill and dexterity, history unearths the past, lifts people and pathos into view, offers ideas and explanations to fathom mysteries, and then finds safe places to store discoveries and theories. That deftness is well in hand here—the authors of *Terminal Island: The Lost Communities of Los Angeles Harbor* have gone deep into our shared regional past, carefully unpacking and peeling back time's layers, and they've found a safe, beautiful place both to reveal and care for their findings. In these pages are many lives, many eras, many individual moments and events, all somehow knotted by place, all looped together by the necklace woven of the fascinating history of the littoral zone that makes up the Los Angeles Harbor and one fascinating island in it.

There is much to learn here. Expert on their topics, Geraldine Knatz and Naomi Hirahara fill this book with insight. Long-lost Terminal Island and harbor denizens wander its pages as if sent from a central casting call for salty characters or the far West's counterpart to Marlon Brando's Terry Malloy. Railroads and railroaders come, adding a waterfront chapter to their technological conquest of western spaces and western commerce. The army and the navy show up, push a lot of earth and sea around, and re-make space and the economy in the doing. From the world over arrive the fishermen, only to find the boundlessness of the Pacific often countermanded by the sheer pettiness of simple hate and prejudice exhibited by their neighbors, and by laws sprung of fear and meanness.

Alongside the pain that careful histories inevitably illuminate, there are other threads pulled from the Terminal Island past. What is especially impressive here is how Hirahara and Knatz, in text and amazing images curated by Eric Lynxwiler, address the island and the entire reach of the harbor region as a place of breathtaking coastal beauty *and* the site of ruthless industrial

Bathers at the beach in front of the bulkhead at the Terminal Island bathhouse. 1905.

ambition. It's both, it long has been both, and that intertwining is not about to go away. If anything, this book reminds us of two very important features of the Los Angeles Harbor: it is a thing and a place created at the intersection of nature and culture, and it remains very much so today. The terms may change, the balances may tip here or there, but the inevitable pairing will endure.

The best histories uncover or rethink what has not been known or has not been as well understood as it might be. And the best histories, with grace and subtlety, show how past and present have a seam, an ineffable connection, a relationship that stands. Authors Knatz and Hirahara pull back time in the pages of *Terminal Island*, and they show us in their excavation an island and a harbor profoundly different from what exists today. Place names are no longer what they were, and they have changed more than once. It all looks different than it did—very different. And yet, Hirahara and Knatz know that the past endures, that its traces are everywhere. Harbor landscape and street names reach back fifty, eighty, a hundred years or more. Decisions made for railroads still provoke consequences in the modern era of cars and containers. Heartaches born of exclusion and internment cross generations, cross the harbor's water, cross even the ocean.

Terminal Island. Not "terminal" as in "mortal" (though there is that history there, too, as with anywhere, in lives individual and collective), but terminal as limit, boundary, an end point. The name credits the ambitions of railroaders, both to stop their iron at the coastline and to use their railroad as the terminus of grander railroad visions stretching the length of the continent. This book relates that history well, the history of the island as a tiny finale of westering and all

that it entailed. But there's irony here, too, irony that our authors allow to speak quietly for itself. Lives begin on Terminal. Lives are renewed on the island, dreams recast. The tiny communities of the island—East San Pedro, Terminal, and Brighton Beach—become home to travelers from all the world. Some come as seasonal visitors from nearby Los Angeles locales. Some come from Japan, or Scandinavia, or Italy. They may stop on Terminal Island—it may be the concluding site of a long or not-so-long journey. But newness and beginnings are here every bit as much as endings.

Here we meet the tourists, the scientists, the artists, and those turn-of-the-century Southern Californians who constituted the counterculture of their day, circa 1900. Idah Meacham Strobridge, bohemian and bookbinder extraordinaire, forged personal and artistic ties that united Terminal Island with the emergent Arroyo Culture. That could not have been easy—that required a cultural bridge to span distance and different points of view, but she did it. Here, too, is the irrepressible writer, reformer, booster, and bon vivant Charles Fletcher Lummis, coming regularly to the ocean from his handmade Arroyo-stone home, El Alisal. On the island, right against the ocean, Lummis became a squatter in his other house, his beloved Jib-O-Jib. There, he and his family retreated on weekends, catching fish from their porch, and interacting with all those locals, visitors, part-timers. Artists mingled with writers, military men exchanged ideas with scientists, Los Angeles swells came in the summer, Chicago tourists came in the winter. It was scenic, and it was a scene.

Kobei Tatsumi came, too. And so did Kihei Nasu. And so many other Japanese fishermen and settlers. With them and their families came a deep and lasting

Japanese imprint on Terminal Island culture, on the political economy of the region, on the very language and linguistic tendencies of the place. One of the magnificent achievements of this book is that the authors have woven the complex stories of the island's small population waves and changes by introducing us to real people and real lives. All is not renewal and rejuvenation, to be sure. Foreigners—Japanese as well as Europeans and Eastern Europeans—faced trouble in depressingly familiar fashion. And with the Second World War, that trouble multiplied a hundredfold for the Japanese and Japanese Americans living on this side of, and right next to, the Pacific Ocean.

Then there's the harbor itself, that place and space that wraps Terminal Island in its embrace: the remarkable harbor, the harbor as economic engine for Los Angeles, for California, for the West, for the nation. The harbor shows up first more as a dream than a reality, a dream tied taut to engineering and fiscal imperatives, and a dream that takes a long time to come true. This book's dialed-in examination of the creation of the harbor makes for a great capsule study of western American economic, political, and environmental development.

Credit again to the authors: in a book in which well-considered biographies drive the story, the Los Angeles Harbor is nearly a biographical subject itself. It is not because of its harbor that Los Angeles is where it is. Los Angeles came into being by virtue of its proximity to that modest riparian feature of the landscape, the Los Angeles River. But if we ask why Los Angeles is *what* it is, we must credit the harbor for a great deal. Ask about Los Angeles growth and metropolitan clout, and its harbor looms in view and emphasis. The harbor's very creation ushered in the modern period of Los Angeles.

That transition from what was to what could be, so ably symbolized by the Los Angeles River's engineered exit into the Pacific Ocean through the harbor region and right past Terminal Island itself, urges us to study the harbor, its history, its denizens, its human and environmental complexities and frailties. This is a superb companion to that obligation, a wonderful instance of the insights that come from adroit use of history to dig and thereby discover.

The harbor is connected to Los Angeles by a thin municipal boundary line known as the shoestring. We could suggest that the historical line is as lean. The harbor often skates free from historical perspectives on Los Angeles, for reasons not especially apparent (and this is *especially* true in the case of a place like Terminal Island, which gets doubly forgotten). The harbor is a region filled with people proud of its history, people who know a great deal about its history, and people who know that this or that self-styled school of metropolitan history knows precious little about the harbor.

We can hope only that this book starts to "thicken" that historical shoestring that connects the Los Angeles past to the harbor and island past. There's fun and, yes, sorrow in these pages, fun in the discovery of things and people and events unknown, and sorrow in the same. But we can hope that the novelty wears off in the future, that the harbor or the island's history loses some of its exoticism, but never its message. Here's the place to start in words and pictures, and we can thank the authors for their efforts at pushing L.A. and harbor together, as they are and should be. Here's an idea: read the book twice, first for its surprises, then again for raising familiarity with its themes and personnel. Both reactions are warranted.

San Pedro was drawn by J. Ross Browne, an author, illustrator, and a confidential agent for the U.S. Treasury Department who was assigned to inspect customs houses. This period illustration of Deadman's Island appeared in a six-article series titled "A Tour through Arizona" and was published in *Harper's Monthly* from October 1864 through March 1865.

Isla de la Culebra de Cascabel y Isla de los Muertos

An 1880 painting of Deadman's Island shows the jetty connecting Rattlesnake Island and Deadman's Island, and small structures on the breakwater. Timm's Point on the San Pedro side of the channel is visible in the foreground.

Isla de la Culebra de Cascabel, the Isle of the Snake of the Rattle, Rattlesnake Island. It was one long, sinuous strip of sandbar, essentially devoid of vegetation, not wider than a quarter mile. Formed by the action of wind and waves that tossed the sediments flowing into Los Angeles Harbor from the San Gabriel River after heavy rains, the island was named for the snakes that washed down with the rains.

There were no identified Native American sites on the island, although the Gabrielino population had villages on the mainland. The large amount of shellfish found at these mainland sites indicates that the native islanders likely used the bay and the islands for collecting food.

Because the island was not significant enough to be a landmark for mariners, early explorers Juan Cabrillo and Sebastián Viscaíno made no mention of its existence in the logs of their journeys to San Pedro Bay. José González Cabrera Bueno's chart of the coastline drawn from Viscaíno's explorations only noted a small unnamed

island, which later became known as Deadman's Island. Located just off the southwestern tip of Rattlesnake Island, Deadman's Island was tiny compared to Rattlesnake Island, but its tall, conical shape, about forty to fifty feet high, made it noteworthy. Richard Henry Dana must have been similarly unimpressed with Rattlesnake Island, as he only remarked on Deadman's Island in his 1840 tome, *Two Years Before the Mast*:

> The only other thing which broke the surface of the great bay was a small, desolate looking island, steep and conical, of a clayey soil, and without the sign of vegetable life upon it, yet which had a peculiar and melancholy interest to me, for on the top of it were buried the remains of an Englishman.

Deadman's Island, however, was always shrouded in mystery as thick as the fog that made it perilous to mariners. Dana alluded to the mystery concerning the first burial, a captain of a merchant brig, likely a whaler. Dana

View of Deadman's Island with the rocks of the East Jetty in the foreground. After the first burial of a white man, around 1810, the island was called *La Isla del Muerto*, the island of the dead man; later, more burials forced a change to *Isla de los Muertos*.

Opposite: This painting by Joe Duncan Gleason is titled *Dead Man's Island Seen from Timms Point, San Pedro, in the 1870s*. In 1953, the Los Angeles Harbor Department commissioned Gleason to paint six historical harbor-related scenes. Most historical texts on file at the Harbor Department Archives use the spelling Timm's Point, which is used in this book, but the island was named after Augustus Timms.

was vague about how he died, but suspected poisoning. Others said he was hanged by a mutinous crew. In 1901, the *Los Angeles Times* reported that a cave-in at the island exposed a coffin with a skeleton inside. Four boys from Los Angeles, boys brave enough to venture to the island, discovered that coffin. It held a man about thirty-five or forty years of age, and an old rotting rope was still tied around his bones between the head and the rib cage, the rope thick enough to be used for a hanging. The boys may have found remains of the same mysterious body Richard Henry Dana alluded to six decades before.

There were plenty more reasons to name this mass of land in honor of death. Black Hawk, the last Native American to live on St. Nicholas Island, was buried on Deadman's Island. The British brig *Boxer* also buried a number of its crewmembers there, all dead from an unnamed disease. Six U.S. marines from the USS *Savannah* killed at the Battle of Dominguez Rancho in 1858, the grieving widow of Captain Parker who gave up all hope when he was lost at sea, and a castaway who made it to shore alive but who couldn't take another breath, were also in graves on the island. In 1927, the graves were disinterred in preparation for the removal of the island. Twenty cadavers were found at that time, most close together, but three separated from the rest. That threesome contained what was left of a blond woman and two cavaliers in Spanish conquistador boots, one skeleton still with a sword at its side. Then, during the island demolition, two redwood coffins and three additional skeletons were found. Deadman's Island, indeed. Deadwoman's, too.

Even festivities on the island had whispers of death. The first Independence Day event that occurred on either island was in 1853. Although July Fourth had been celebrated in Southern California as far back as 1828, this 1853 fiesta was most unusual for its location: the summit of Deadman's Island. Captain Juan Capistrano Sepulveda and an entourage set off from his huge Palos Verdes rancho, bound for San Pedro. Upon arriving, the entire group boarded a boat, ferried over to the spot that would one day be Wilmington, loaded a cannon on the boat, and sailed for Deadman's Island. The cannon was fired from the highest point on Deadman's Island to salute the dead marines buried there and to dispel any ill feelings in the hearts of Mexican-born Californians. The cannon, called the Old Woman's Gun, has a permanent home at the U.S. Naval Academy Museum at Annapolis, Maryland.

Mariners who viewed the rocky outpost of Deadman's Island on the way into the harbor conjured legends that made a trip to the island a ghoulish and exciting adventure for tourists.

The remains of bodies were found buried on Deadman's Island. As a burial place, the island was cloaked in mystery and myth. From time to time, as graves became exposed, the remains were removed to other Los Angeles cemeteries. The remaining bodies were exhumed from their graves prior to demolition of the island.

The 1859 U.S. Coast Survey by W.M. Johnson and Charles Bache mapped both Rattlesnake Island and Deadman's Island. In 1860, San Diego-based shore whalers Henry Johnson and Captain Hart opened up a shore-whaling station on Deadman's Island, which they operated successfully for two years. During the 1865–66 season, Jack Smith and J.K. Phillips opened a business there, but the company dissolved after catching only a few whales. Then, from 1866 to 1867, Captain John Brown who captured whales from his ship, the *Ned Beale*, used the island for processing blubber.

Rattlesnake and Deadman's Islands were physically joined together, linked by a rock jetty and later combined into one land mass that ultimately succumbed to the march of progress inevitable in Los Angeles Harbor— but not before six decades of residential occupation. The residential communities that began on Rattlesnake Island changed as the island changed, grew larger as the transportation options to the island increased, and evolved as the nature of the island evolved. That evolution drove some residents away, but at the same time, it drew others to the island like a magnet.

The First Residents
of Rattlesnake Island

Native Americans probably took advantage of the abundant shellfish on Rattlesnake Island, although no evidence of permanent Native American habitation has ever surfaced. The mainland surrounding the harbor had few permanent residents during the first half of the nineteenth century. During the Gold Rush, easterners who crossed the Isthmus of Panama took steamers up the coast, stopping at San Pedro. Some, like Phineas Banning, would stay near the harbor and make it their home. There was little reason for anyone to consider moving to the island, especially since there was no natural freshwater supply.

As the surrounding communities of San Pedro and Wilmington developed in the latter half of the nineteenth century, the curious ventured to the island. They could wade across the harbor channel or row to the island in small boats since the water between Rattlesnake and the mainland was often as shallow as one foot. It was an irresistible place for fishermen and adventurers (including children who liked to explore), and there was always plenty of driftwood and lumber washing up along the island beaches that could be used to construct shelters or small cabins. But still, the lack of freshwater made it difficult for anyone to live there permanently.

In the 1870s, however, hardy souls looking for peace and quiet took refuge on the island. To these individuals, carrying freshwater to the island was no obstacle in their quest for solitude. Most of these early residents who lived this hermit lifestyle were fishermen, many of whom had discovered the island while in the harbor, working from their boats.

One such fisherman-turned-hermit was "Old Bob Brown." Brown moved to Rattlesnake Island about 1879 and took up residence in a wood shack, when no more than four other houses existed on the island. He lived with his cats, which were observed swimming out to meet his boat when he returned from fishing. According to a story about Brown published by the *Los Angeles Herald* in 1904, the antisocial codger would begin his day killing rattlesnakes. Known to be a drinker, Brown had a broad view of ownership and took what he needed to survive. This activity often landed him in the San Pedro jail. Like other recluses in the harbor area, Brown moved from place to place on the island as development set in. The article about Brown piqued the interest of at least one artist, who was attracted to the harbor's picturesque settings. A few months after the article appeared, noted California Impressionist Granville Redmond ventured to the island and started a painting of Brown's hovel. The artwork captured the hermit's collection of trash, boxes, and tattered canvas alongside his dilapidated houseboat. Brown became "angry as a bear," but Redmond, who could neither hear nor speak, survived the encounter and vowed to finish the painting the next day.

Tommy Leggett was another early resident of Rattlesnake Island, a solitary fellow, perhaps, but certainly not a hermit like Old Bob Brown. Leggett enjoyed people, was well loved, and often shared his bounty of fish. An 1885 map of Rattlesnake Island surveyed by

Tommy Leggett, fisherman and early resident of Rattlesnake Island, photographed by Helen Lukens Jones. Circa 1900. The daughter of Theodore Lukens, mayor of Pasadena, Jones became a well-established photojournalist publishing in *Out West* and other magazines of the day. After her second marriage in 1906, the photographer used the name Helen Lukens Gaut.

This late nineteenth-century drawing shows civil works improvements made by the U.S. Army Corps of Engineers along both sides of the Main Channel into Wilmington Harbor. The Corps began with the East Jetty in 1871. This drawing was made to show how the harbor would look once the outer harbor breakwater, begun in 1899, was complete, although it depicts an early scheme in which the breakwater had an opening near its western edge at San Pedro.

Terminal Island: Lost Communities on America's Edge

G. Hansen and A. Solano (available at the Huntington Library in San Marino, California) identifies a few structures along with names of the occupants. On the north side of the island is a small structure labeled simply "Legget" [sic]. Squatting in ramshackle cabins in various places around the harbor, first on Mormon Island, then Rattlesnake Island in the 1880s, Leggett moved to Timm's Point in San Pedro. When he was evicted from Timm's Point in 1899, he went back "home" to Rattlesnake Island, now renamed Terminal Island.

Another early settler of Rattlesnake Island was Captain William Wallace Barce. He came to San Pedro Bay in the early 1860s. In 1882, he was the government inspector and would report the number of vessels, cargo types, and tonnage for Wilmington Harbor. Captain Barce had a ship-repair facility on Rattlesnake Island; in February of 1884, the *Los Angeles Times* reported that the tugboat *Alpha* was repaired at Barce's shipyard. Little else is known of his operation on the island.

Women also went to Terminal Island, although their residencies were likely short-term and likely for the purpose of giving comfort to lonely mariners. On January 21, 1888, the *Los Angeles Herald* carried a story about Susan B. Webber, who was charged with assault with intent to kill Miss M.A. McGoon. The two women were fighting over the key to a house on the island.

Other names appearing on the Hansen and Solano map include William Jones Marines, Captain Edward Johnston, Dan Barker, Joseph Bresh, E. Peterson, Henry Welbel, John Harmon, Green Stram, and two individuals identified only by their last names, Schub and Tweed. Other details of those earliest days are left to the imagination.

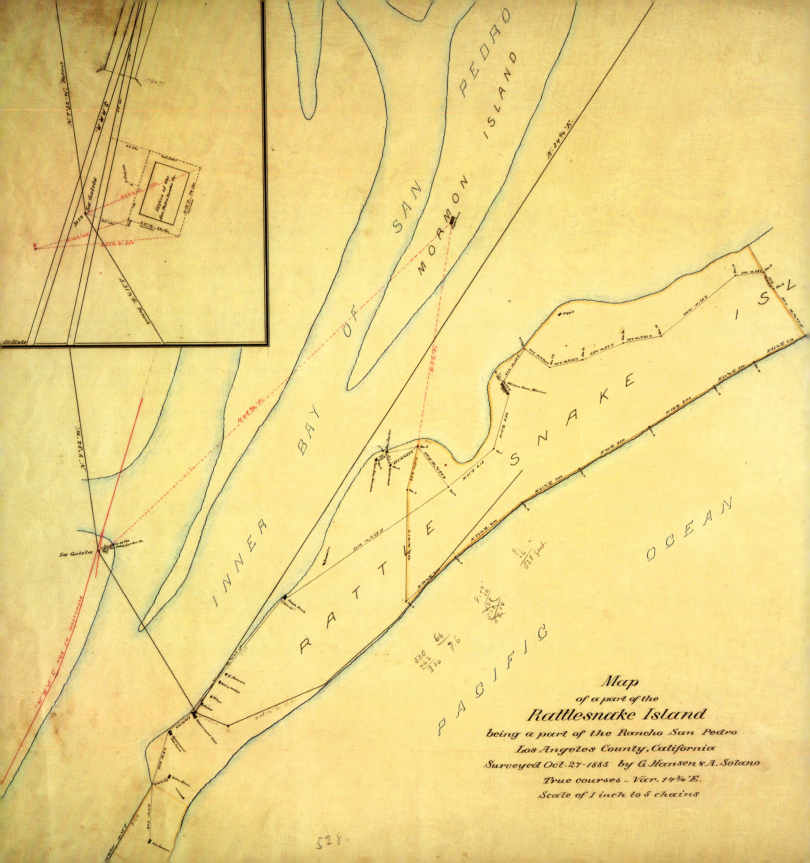

SAN PEDRO ISLAND

BAY OF SAN PEDRO

MORMON ISLAND

INNER BAY

RATTLE SNAKE IS L

PACIFIC OCEAN

La Goleta

Map
of a part of the
Rattlesnake Island
being a part of the Rancho San Pedro
Los Angeles County, California
Surveyed Oct. 27. 1885 by G. Hansen & A. Solano
True courses — Var. 14¾° E.
Scale of 1 inch to 5 chains

528.

The Army Moves to Rattlesnake Island

The *Los Angeles Star* drew attention to the need for a survey of the harbor. As early as November 1858, the newspaper called for the construction of a breakwater between Deadman's Island and Rattlesnake Island. Pressure to improve the harbor facilities intensified as Los Angeles took steps to support the construction of the Los Angeles and San Pedro Railroad, which linked the city of Los Angeles to Wilmington by rail, adding another option to the old-standby wagon, in 1869. Los Angeles business leaders such as Phineas Banning, Don Benito Wilson, Judge Robert M. Widney, and Dr. Joseph P. Widney recognized the need for more adequate harbor facilities and began to pressure the Army Corps of Engineers to undertake a study of harbor improvements. A very shallow entrance to Los Angeles Harbor forced incoming ships to anchor in the bay and transfer goods and passengers into smaller vessels, called lighters, which could navigate the shallow depth. This major limitation to navigation meant Los Angeles would never become an important port.

In 1871, U.S. Congressman Sherman D. Houghton of San Jose, California, pressured congress for an appropriation of two hundred thousand dollars to start the necessary work. He was successful, and that same year, the Corps of Engineers began its first civil works project in Los Angeles Harbor. The project was designed to deepen the harbor entrance by building a one-and-one-quarter-mile jetty from the western end of Rattlesnake Island to Deadman's Island.

Although the first federal investment in San Pedro Bay occurred on Rattlesnake Island, the purpose of the project was to improve navigation to the inner harbor at Wilmington, not to promote development on the island. Inadvertently, however, this early civil works project began a process of stabilization and creation of land that increased the size of Rattlesnake Island, which enhanced prospects for colonization and development there.

The engineering principle behind this first federal project was fairly simple. If the Army Corps could succeed in focusing the ocean currents between two rock jetties—one on the east side of the channel and another on the west—the action of the tides would naturally remove sand, effectively deepening the channel. It was anticipated this natural scouring action of the tides would increase the depth of the channel from two feet to ten feet. Soon no one would be able to wade from San Pedro to Rattlesnake Island.

The East Jetty was constructed of timber and rock in three sections. Closest to Rattlesnake Island was a section of single-timber sheet pile (a row of timber piles adjacent to each other that formed a wall called the "single works"), followed by two rows of wooden sheet pile (the "double works"), and the last two thousand feet, which terminated at Deadman's Island, was rock. The demarcation between the different sections of the breakwater was significant because the Army Corps tolerated people living on the single-works portion of the breakwater but not on the double works.

An 1885 map of Rattlesnake Island shows notations for buildings and the names of some residents. One denoted "Legget" [sic], indicating where Tommy Leggett lived on the island in the late 1880s.

The jetty construction work was very labor-intensive, and the number of workers camped on site quickly grew from 30 to 150, all working under the orders of Army Captain Clinton B. Sears. In early 1872, with the expectation that the labor force would grow to two hundred, the men spent five weeks building cabins on the island for housing. The army contracted for four thousand gallons of freshwater to be brought in daily, and a large water tank was constructed. Since the population of San Pedro and Wilmington combined was only 942 in 1870, the influx of 200 construction workers was more than the local community could sustain. Army Corps engineers not only had to manage construction of the project, but also provision the workforce and provide for their living arrangements. At one point, the number of workers employed on the project and living on the island was reported to be as high as six hundred. Thus, the workers on this first federal construction project formed the first real residential community on the island, albeit a predominantly male population.

The relentless force of the Pacific Ocean made it difficult to protect the integrity of the East Jetty. The Army Corps was anxious to create conditions whereby sand would accrete along the jetty to fortify it. When that did not happen quickly enough, a series of spurs or rock groins were added perpendicular to the jetty to intercept sand. The groins did not completely stabilize the jetty, so trees and grass were planted with limited success. Unintentionally, Corps engineers were creating waterfront property attractive for seaside living. By 1876, nearly forty acres of land covered with sand dunes and bearing beach vegetation had been created.

The Army Corps worked for ten years on the East Jetty, and in 1881 they sought funding to continue the deepening of the Los Angeles Harbor channel to fifteen feet. Thus, army engineers became a permanent part of the island's landscape. The 1885 Hansen and Solano survey indicates the presence of two large structures, one identified as a "government house" and the other as a "government test house," although both were often referred to as warehouses by the army officials. More significant, however, was the effect of island living on the project workforce. After the need for workers decreased, some of the workers stayed on the island, becoming the first residents of a community that would become known as East San Pedro.

In 1888, San Pedro's population was more than five hundred people, and the populace voted to incorporate as a city. The incorporation of San Pedro did not include the community of East San Pedro or any part of the island. The citizens of East San Pedro wanted to be part of San Pedro. So, in June, another election was held that would have annexed Rattlesnake Island to San Pedro. The *Los Angeles Herald* reported that the results were disastrous for those in favor of San Pedro annexing Rattlesnake Island. Only 23 of the 142 votes cast supported the idea. The people of San Pedro lacked the foresight to anticipate that seventeen years later they would be embroiled in litigation over their desire to annex East San Pedro.

Frank Merwin, a machinist living on Terminal Island, poses near the arch at Deadman's Island. Circa 1900. It was possible to walk through the arch at low tide.

The Lure of Deadman's Island

In its early days, Rattlesnake Island was a recreational spot for those who loved the outdoors and nature. It was a tourist destination with no hotels; no accommodations existed for the well-to-do tourist from Los Angeles. Access was limited to small boats, so there was no efficient way to get proper construction materials to the island, and even if a hotel had been built, there was no good way to keep it adequately supplied. But the island still attracted local visitors and those from Los Angeles because it was a nearby getaway on a hot day.

In 1888, Rattlesnake Island and San Pedro were deemed by the *Los Angeles Times* to be interesting places to visit, despite being "rough looking." Visitors could watch fishermen haul in their beach seines and observe the death struggles of sharks and rays caught in the nets. The island was touted as a place for the naturalist. At night, the glow of phosphorescent sea creatures painted the ocean waves like a "sheet of glimmering undulations." A plug was also made for the student of anthropology, since, as the *Times* went on to note, one could find some of the hardiest specimens of man known to exist in the "boozing pens."

The ocean conditions that made the construction of the East Jetty so challenging for the Army Corps created a boon for beachcombers, shell collectors, and bathers. Both Rattlesnake Island and Deadman's Island turned into a shell hunter's paradise. Teachers took their students to the islands to collect shells, since more could be found along the islands' beaches in thirty minutes than could be collected in other coastal spots in a week. The top of Deadman's Island was loose, sandy soil that contained fossilized seashells. The shells were washed down with the rain and fell into the rock pools below. Shells housing living organisms could be found alongside fossilized cousins among the rocks surrounding Deadman's Island. The ocean waves that hit the beach brought to shore numerous varieties of shells, some considered to be among the rarest that scientists in the United States had ever seen.

In the late 1880s, a group of Los Angeles–based shell enthusiasts, many of them women, began to collect and study the shells from Los Angeles Harbor. Those shells attracted Mrs. Martha Burton Williamson to both Deadman's and Rattlesnake Islands.

An 1873 photograph looks southeast over the cluster of structures at Timm's Landing and captures Deadman's Island in San Pedro Harbor. Timm's Landing, often referred to as Timm's Point, became the location of the Southern Pacific Slip (Berth 73).

The East Jetty is photographed from Deadman's Island looking toward Rattlesnake Island. 1898.

A member of the Agassiz Society, Williamson was preparing a catalog of California seashells for the Smithsonian Institution. She was well-known in literary and club circles in Los Angeles and a frequent speaker at society meetings, where she shared her careful research on both history and science. Her research on the island must have begun shortly after she arrived in Los Angeles with her family in 1887, because by 1892 her Smithsonian paper on San Pedro Bay was already published.

The efforts of these female shell-hounds were duly noted, and in fact, their results came as major surprises to the leading male scientists, some of whom had been studying the distribution of mollusks along the West Coast since 1870. This was because Deadman's Island's geological formation provided the opportunity to collect fossils from the various strata exposed: the Quaternary on top, the Pliocene and Pleistocene nearer its base. Williamson delighted the Los Angeles Friday Morning Club in June 1892 with her tales of conchological lore and her devilfish specimen collected from Rattlesnake

Island in summer 1891. The women were excited to see an actual specimen of something they knew only from Victor Hugo's terrifying description of a devilfish, a.k.a. an octopus, in *Les Travailleurs de la Mer* in 1866. At the close of the session, Williamson was asked back the next day to continue the discussion with the club's science committee.

The first commercial structure built on Rattlesnake Island for recreational use was a bathhouse. Its builder, Michael Duffy, also operated a ferry service between San Pedro and the island. Having ferryboats to carry supplies gave Duffy an advantage for his island business. Duffy was already in the bathhouse business in Santa Monica, where he had constructed the town's first bathhouse in 1876. His bathhouse on Rattlesnake Island, built around 1881, appears on the 1885 Hansen and Solano survey. Although a description of the bathhouse on Rattlesnake Island was not available, his Santa Monica bathhouse consisted of two narrow structures with sixteen dressing rooms, each with a bath and shower plumbed with freshwater. For twenty-five cents, a swimmer or sunbather could rent a bathing suit and a dressing room.

Duffy began the ferry service to Rattlesnake Island to encourage use of his bathhouse. His "resort" also included a café so island visitors could enjoy the beach while taking refreshment. For the first nine years, Duffy pulled his flat-bottomed ferryboats across the channel using a pole, then switched to motor launches. He named his boats after his children: *Blanche, Dora, Ina, George,* and *Elsie.* Each boat carried thirty to forty passengers until he added the *Orient,* which held one hundred people. Although Duffy had no competition in the early years, it was not clear how successful his enterprise

was. His name appears on the 1886 Los Angeles County delinquent tax list for his properties in both San Pedro and Santa Monica. After the Southern Pacific Railroad took over the waterfront property in San Pedro and the Terminal Railroad took over the island side, Duffy was forced to enter into contracts with the railroads to maintain access for loading his passengers. Captain Duffy and his family operated the ferry for twenty-six years until he lost the contract in a competitive bidding process in 1906.

With limited access to Rattlesnake Island, it was very difficult to draw tourist business, and it was even harder to convince people to set up permanent residence. That all changed once a railroad arrived. By late 1891, the Los Angeles Terminal Railroad completed its line from Los Angeles to new stations on Rattlesnake Island, ending the line at a station called East San Pedro, so named because it was directly across, or "east," from the city of San Pedro on the mainland. Twice a day trains made the fifty-minute trip from downtown Los Angeles to Long Beach. So passengers could reach Rattlesnake Island from Long Beach, the Terminal Railroad constructed a trestle bridge from Long Beach to the eastern side of Rattlesnake Island; with that addition, it took just another ten minutes to reach the last stop, the East San Pedro station. For the first time, people could access the island without a boat. That the rail access came from the city of Long Beach rather than San Pedro would figure into later annexation battles over the island.

In 1892, the Los Angeles Terminal Land Company, a subsidiary of the Los Angeles Terminal Railroad, purchased portions of Rancho San Pedro, including Rattlesnake Island and all the marshland adjacent to it,

Deadman's Island, near San Pedro, Cal.

Women who climbed to the top of Deadman's Island in 1906 stand by the marker placed by the U.S. Navy.

Left: Postcard. Circa 1890. The large rocks in the foreground are part of the East Jetty. Visitors to Deadman's Island used a ladder to climb to the summit of the island.

To reach the bathhouse constructed by Michael Duffy on Terminal Island, people could take one of Duffy's ferryboats from a landing near downtown San Pedro. Circa 1900.

"MIKE" DUFFY.

Michael Duffy operated a ferry service from San Pedro to Terminal Island until losing the concession in 1906. The genial Irishman then entered politics and was elected to the San Pedro Board of Trustees in 1907. His published platform included "giving the Southern Pacific a franchise for an elevated railway to the moon" and "assessing all single members of the Fire Department 100 dollars if not married within 23 days after the election." His platform appealed to many, and he bested a field of fifteen opponents to win the seat. This caricature was made of him in 1909 during the campaign by the City of Los Angeles to annex the harbor area. Duffy supported the annexation.

Right: People climbed to the top of Deadman's Island for viewing and treasure hunting. Who made the ladder is unknown, but it deteriorated after this photograph was taken. Circa 1910.

The Bushnell family, year-round residents living in a house named Sleepy Hollow, enjoy a mild January day in 1905. Mormon Island is in the background.

Terminal Island: Lost Communities on America's Edge

Terminal Island,   Bath House,

In the early 1890s, the Terminal Railroad Company began constructing this bathhouse and other amenities to serve the island's increasing number of visitors.

the area known as "the salt flats," and the inner harbor areas in Wilmington and Long Beach. The purchase price was three hundred dollars, paid to the heirs of the Dominguez family, plus an amount sufficient to retire three notes on the property valued at forty thousand dollars each, held by Los Angeles developer Daniel McFarland. The Terminal Island Land Company undertook the development of a wharf at East San Pedro, and the name of the island was changed from Rattlesnake Island to Terminal Island.

By 1893, there was significant construction happening on the island in preparation for commercial operations. The Los Angeles Terminal Railroad Company built a wharf and brought in tugboats to handle its own lightering and towing activity. The Ganahl Lumber Company workers were leveling sand dunes and stacking lumber while a pile driver worked at their wharf. The Marriner Brothers were finishing their wharf to handle coal. And pipe was being laid to bring freshwater to the island from San Pedro. The Bouton Water Company was formed in 1894, specifically to supply water to Long Beach, Terminal Island, and San Pedro from wells on Bouton's land north of Long Beach.

Passenger service was initially the railroad's primary business, and special excursion trains were often added to handle peak crowds. To lure visitors and encourage use of the line, the Los Angeles Terminal Land Company built a pavilion, bathhouses, and two hotels, the Terminal Tavern and the Brighton Beach Hotel. The railroad frequently operated at capacity, borrowing cars from other rail lines or using gondolas with bench seats and overhead canopies.

At the turn of the twentieth century, there were three distinct communities on Terminal Island: East San Pedro, Terminal (sometimes called Terminal Beach), and Brighton Beach. Terminal was about a mile farther east from East San Pedro, and Brighton Beach was yet another mile east, closer to Long Beach.

The land company also offered oceanfront lots that were prime for custom construction in Terminal Beach and Brighton Beach. Wealthy Angelenos built stately homes facing the surf. At the same time, an eclectic community of bohemians thrived in East San Pedro, where writers, artists, and scientists escaped the city. Many were squatters who settled on the East Jetty and enjoyed an idyllic lifestyle of no rent and all-you-can-eat fish, not unlike the hermits who had come before them.

In 1899, passengers arriving at the East San Pedro Station of the Los Angeles Terminal Railway could spend the day at the beach and return to Los Angeles on the evening train.

36

Albert H. Slade painted this scene of Terminal Island after the Terminal Railroad reached the island. At the time, Slade was living in Ventura but likely visited the island as a tourist. The painting captures multiple activities happening on the island in the 1890s—recreation, railroading, and lumber operations.

A.H.Slade.

Bohemian Los Angeles Comes to the Harbor

In East San Pedro, squatters built their homes on pilings where sand accreted along the single works, a row of single piles supporting a wall constructed by the U.S. Army Corps of Engineers.

East San Pedro was the first area on the island with permanent residents, many of whom were the East Jetty construction workers who stayed on after their work was finished. People who moved to East San Pedro, onto the East Jetty, or on the sand alongside it, were squatters in the truest sense of the word—these folks occupied land, never paid for it, built their homes on the property, and assumed they had the same property rights as homesteaders. So many squatters took advantage of this opportunity that East San

Pedro was soon known as "Squatter Town" (or "Stilt Town," since many of the homes were actually built on stilts above the water).

A prospective resident could stake a claim and generally would meet with no resistance to building a house on the property. The U.S. Army Corps of Engineers was tolerant of the squatters who resided on the single-works portion of the East Jetty. If settlers formally wrote requesting permission to stay, the Corps often provided residents with letters indicating no objection

to the settlement. The army prohibited squatters from occupying the double-works portion of the breakwater, primarily because the army had retained that area for its own use.

Many squatters built their homes from driftwood or lumber that was lost from cargo ships and washed up on the beach. Lumber terminals were being developed on the island, providing a source for those inclined to purchase new wood. And it was likely that lumber used to build the cabins for the construction workers on the jetty was recycled into these newer homes. Early pictures of East San Pedro show homes of similar shape and size—simple wood structures with porches and railings, elevated on stilts or pilings to avoid flooding. There was no sanitation system, and the toilets would discharge waste below the house into the mudflats or tidewater below. Some structures could rightly be classified as "shacks." Even if the inhabitants could afford to invest in improving their properties, they chose not to because they did not own the land and many knew

At the Terminal Railroad Station (later the San Pedro, Los Angeles and Salt Lake Railroad) in East San Pedro, visitors could catch a ship to Catalina, or take the S.S. *Harvard* on a trip as far north as San Francisco.

Left: Photographer Olive Percival captures the picturesque vistas of East San Pedro and the harbor that was so attractive to the artistic community. 1906. Percival noted in her diary that she was proud of her photos of San Pedro, but also indicated that she struggled and never attained commercial success.

A fisherman squatter sits in front of his home in East San Pedro in this photograph by Helen Lukens Jones (later Helen Lukens Gaut).

that they could be evicted at any time. A. Bert Bynon described East San Pedro in his 1899 history, *San Pedro, Its History*:

> The buildings of East San Pedro are of the cheapest character consisting almost entirely of laborers and fisherman huts, generally built on

piles driven into the bay or perched upon the government breakwater.

Once there was a supply of freshwater to the island, the idea of homesteading on the newly created tidelands or on the jetty took hold. The community was an eclectic group of Italians, Spaniards, Frenchmen,

The buildings or shacks found in East San Pedro were typically fashioned from scrap lumber and built on sand that accumulated along the East Jetty. Circa 1905.

Scandinavians, and Slavic people. But now, in addition to mariners, longshore workers, and fishermen, others began to move to East San Pedro. Some moved there because they worked at the newly built lumber terminals on the island or because they worked for the Terminal Railroad. The island also appealed to a group of educated people who were unconventional in their thinking and lifestyle. They were an artistic and literary bunch from Garvanza, an area along the western banks of the Arroyo Seco just northeast of Los Angeles, and they were part of the bohemian culture that developed in Los Angeles as progressivism took hold.

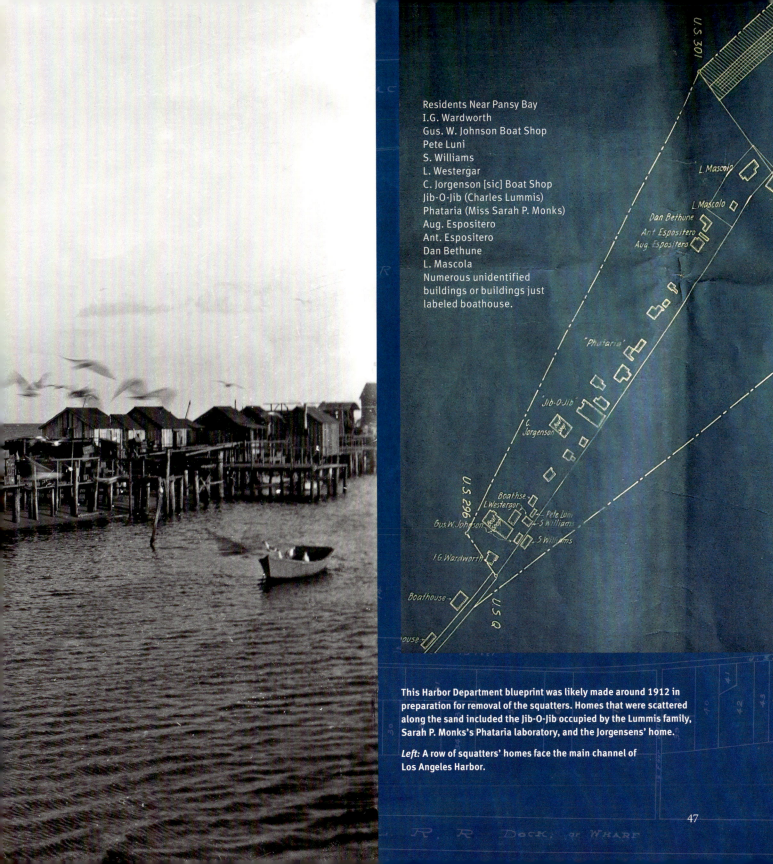

Residents Near Pansy Bay
I.G. Wardworth
Gus. W. Johnson Boat Shop
Pete Luni
S. Williams
L. Westergar
C. Jorgenson [sic] Boat Shop
Jib-O-Jib (Charles Lummis)
Phataria (Miss Sarah P. Monks)
Aug. Espositero
Ant. Espositero
Dan Bethune
L. Mascola
Numerous unidentified
buildings or buildings just
labeled boathouse.

This Harbor Department blueprint was likely made around 1912 in preparation for removal of the squatters. Homes that were scattered along the sand included the Jib-O-Jib occupied by the Lummis family, Sarah P. Monks's Phataria laboratory, and the Jorgensens' home.

Left: A row of squatters' homes face the main channel of Los Angeles Harbor.

Charles Lummis—journalist, city librarian, and founder of the Southwest Museum—built his home, El Alisal, in the Arroyo Seco, which became the nucleus for the Los Angeles bohemian culture that prospered from the 1880s to 1920s. The artists and writers who took up residence in the Arroyo Seco lived within walking distance of one another. They were drawn to the natural environment they found in the Arroyo. There they could reject the industrial expansion that was introducing conveniences such as indoor plumbing and modern utilities, in favor of building their homes themselves, often with materials that were readily available.

The bohemians who came to Los Angeles Harbor adapted easily to the alternative lifestyle of East San Pedro. The primitive living conditions in Squatter Town were in keeping with their own values. And because art and writing did not pay well, they also liked the fact that land was free, building materials could be scavenged, and, if they were lucky, they could catch their food. On the island, life was rich with nature, and it was cheap.

Local artists in Los Angeles were struggling for recognition, so they were also struggling to make a living. Since many Angelenos were transplanted easterners, they had brought with them their own bias in favor of European art from their tours abroad. But, as those transplanted easterners began to enjoy the spectacular vistas of the western United States, their respect for local art developed. Native westerners, for the most part, didn't go to Europe to buy art for their drawing rooms, so they were more open to art that celebrated the land around them. Art appreciation groups such as the

This bird's-eye view of the waterfront of San Pedro and Terminal Island illustrates how the streets, blocks, and lots originally were laid out by the Terminal Railway. 1897.

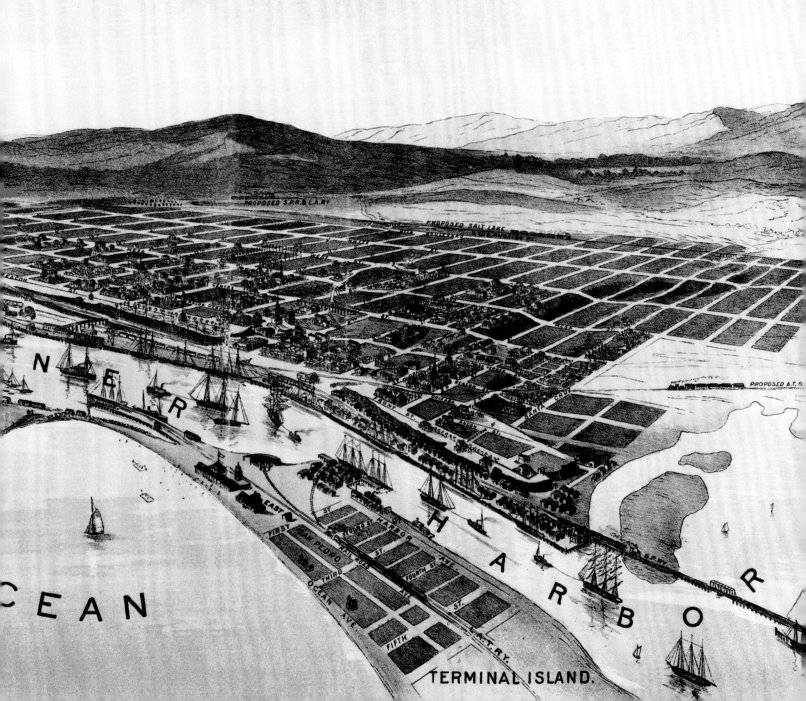

TERMINAL ISLAND.

Ruskin Art Club and the Friday Morning Club hosted exhibits of local artists, whose depictions of western scenery became known as "impressionistic realism."

When Theodore Roosevelt became president in 1901, he espoused the view that art should reflect the soul of the nation and chastised the wealthy for their homage to the European masters. Now buying local art was patriotic. Californians began to turn their parlors into "living rooms" filled with local art: Native American baskets, rugs, and other crafts reflecting the aesthetic reform of the Arts and Crafts movement.

When Lummis took over as editor of the journal *Land of Sunshine* in June of 1895, he expanded its content to include historic preservation, conservation of natural resources, western life, and history. He also used its editorial section to comment on significant local and state issues. The previous editor, Charles Dwight Willard, was secretary of the Los Angeles Chamber of Commerce, so under his watch the journal had been geared to L.A. boosterism. The magazine provided Lummis a unique opportunity to promote his progressive ideals and to connect with artists and writers who shared his views. (Lummis continued as editor and changed the name of the journal to *Out West* in 1902.)

In this era, many women sought outlets for self-expression outside the home, throwing off the restrictive bonds of Victorian social customs and morality, along with gender norms. Many women turned to art, writing, or the study of nature. In 1897, a woman living alone on a Nevada ranch sent Lummis some of her writings about life in the desert. Lummis encouraged her writing to such an extent that she sold her ranch, purchased a lot near Lummis and constructed her home and bookbinding shop, Artemisia Bindery, on East Avenue 41. Her name was Idah Meacham Strobridge.

Above: This photograph, titled *High Life and Low Tide at San Pedro*, was featured on a postcard, but the shacks and boat in the foreground are across the channel in East San Pedro. April 19, 1908.

Squatter homes lined the shore in East San Pedro, a place that was often called Stilt Town because many of its structures were built on pilings.

Olive Percival took many photographs of East San Pedro in 1906 including this one of the Wickieup, the women's literary and artistic retreat created by Idah Strobridge on the East Jetty.

Inset: Portrait of Idah Meacham Strobridge. Circa 1895. She was born in 1855 and died in 1932.

Idah's Wickieup: The Women's Retreat on the Old Breakwater

Idah Meacham Strobridge is credited by San Pedro historians Anna Marie Hager and Everett Gordon Hager with introducing the Arroyo Seco bohemians to East San Pedro. Strobridge had endured years of hardship and tragedy before she turned to a literary career. Although born and educated in California, she was living in Nevada when the sudden loss of her husband and sons forced her to make her living as a mining superintendent and ranch operator. She loved the desert and quickly adapted to the solitude, as she spent much time on horseback handling what were then traditionally male chores that were necessary for her own survival. When she moved to California in 1901, she took up a very different sort of life, a life focused on making her bookbinding business a success. Because her writing emphasized the Southwest, Strobridge became friends with many authors. She ventured to Terminal Island and became a squatter on the East Jetty, a choice she made that reflected her values. She created a retreat for artistic and literary women in East San Pedro that she called the Wickieup, a reference to the Native American lodges in the West and Southwest that are also called wigwams. She invited women to come and spend time there, in an environment that was supportive of their life choices for self-expression.

Strobridge described the Wickieup to a reporter from the *Los Angeles Herald Examiner* in 1904:

> An existence wholly away from those conventional things hampered by man is what I long for. It is the life on the desert wholly apart from everything of pretense. I cannot give it up

entirely and so I have furnished in fitting manner the "wickieup" my substitute for the desert.

Strobridge wrote two of her Sagebrush Trilogy books about life in the Southwest while living in the Wickieup: *The Loom of the Desert*, published in 1906, and *The Land of Purple Shadows*, published in 1909. These books were illustrated by artist Maynard Dixon. Dixon met Strobridge sometime in 1899, undoubtedly introduced by Lummis, since Dixon illustrated an article she was doing for the *Land of Sunshine*. Dixon and Strobridge shared a love of the desert. Dixon designed the cover and frontispiece and did three illustrations for *The Land of Purple Shadows*, a collection of stories that reflect many experiences of Strobridge's own life. The first book in her trilogy, *In Miners' Mirage-Land*, was illustrated by a young painter named Joe D. Gleason. In 1904, Gleason had just returned from studying at the Chicago Art Institute and was considered a rising young artist. He was only twenty-four years old when Strobridge asked him to do the illustrations. It is probable that Strobridge introduced Gleason to the harbor area. Gleason went on to become well-known for his paintings of Los Angeles Harbor, and began signing his paintings with only his middle and surname, "Duncan Gleason." Gleason would go on to become so revered for his maritime works that the Los Angeles Harbor Department commissioned him to do six paintings in 1953.

Strobridge was not the first of the Arroyo Seco crowd to visit the harbor, nor the first woman. Another female writer, Olive Percival, wrote in her diary that she had gone to San Pedro with a friend named John Gilmore to get abalone in August 1895.

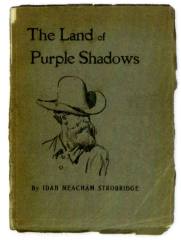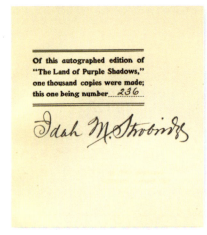

Idah Meacham Strobridge bound, numbered, and autographed a thousand copies of each of her three books. Highly prized by collectors, they include stories of life in the Southwest. Joe Duncan Gleason illustrated the cover of *In Miners' Mirage-Land*, and Maynard Dixon was the cover artist for *The Land of Purple Shadows*. The books sold for $1.75 when they were originally published.

Lovely moonlight night, harvest moon rose red from the dull gray lines over the harbor. Many different kinds of craft, all casting dark wavering shadows on the water. Music from the pavilion, songs from the rowboats, floated over the water. . . . I retired around mid-night. Arose half past 2 and found my way to John's cottage. He was sleeping soundly. A three-mile walk to Point Fermin upgrade in the cool gray light before dawn. . . . On the way home stopped at the ruins of the old adobe custom house of which Dana speaks in his *Two Years before the Mast*. Had luncheon on Dead Man's Island.

One might imagine that Percival was concerned about seeking out a man in his cottage at two in the morning, waking him, and then spending hours walking around the harbor in the dark, unchaperoned. Victorian standards were still in place for most women. Not for Olive Percival. In fact, her diary entry shows concern only with a specific method of collecting abalone:

I do not like to lie flat on a slimy rock over which the waves occasionally break, and put my hand in the dark cold waters up to my shoulders and feel around the rock for sea animals of any description or value. It would have been not so creepy perhaps in broad daylight.

Percival clearly represented a new breed of woman. She worked for a living. She bought land in Garvanza and built her own home. Percival continued to visit the jetty for many years, often accompanied by fellow writer Amanda Mathews Chase. Although she had opportunities for marriage, she instead elected to care for her mother. She kept extensive diaries, which detail many of the challenges she faced—particularly financial—to maintain a household for her mother and herself. Percival was focused on making ends meet.

Strobridge, in contrast, was of sufficient means to help others. Her Wickieup was cheerful, homey, and artistic. She introduced many literary figures and artists to the picturesque setting of the harbor through her invitations to the Wickieup. In fact, she also issued an invitation to Eva Lummis's entire Spanish class for a moonlight picnic at the Wickieup.

But her greatest help to others was as Idah Meacham Strobridge, Publisher. Initially a self-publisher, she became the only woman in Los Angeles to publish her own work *and* make a financial success of it. *In Miners' Mirage-Land*, published in 1904, helped establish her bookbinding business. She struggled as an independent woman to survive in a man's world, but that struggle seems to have motivated her to help other women once she was a success. She published the work of Amanda Mathews Chase, who frequently accompanied Olive Percival on her trips to the Wickieup. Mathews Chase had spent four years in Mexico, learning the language and studying people of lesser economic means. She chronicled her experiences and her research in the book Strobridge published, *The Hieroglyphics of Love: Stories of Sonoratown and Old Mexico*. The *Los Angeles Times* noted that the book, published in 1906, was the first written by a woman *and* published by another woman.

In May 1909, Strobridge, who was also an art collector, exhibited her entire collection at The Little Corner of Local Art, a studio that adjoined her Artemisia bookbinding workshop in Garvanza. Included among these paintings were the works of artists who retreated to East San Pedro to paint. While it is not possible to identify all the paintings made by these bohemian artists while at the harbor area, some are obvious by their titles. In this exhibit was Carl Oscar Borg's *Street in East San Pedro* and *Reflections*, described as boats in the golden glow of twilight. A painting by Charles Sumner

Olive Percival, who appreciated the Japanese aesthetic, hangs lanterns in the garden of her Arroyo Seco home that she named Downhyl Claim. She collected Japanese prints and hosted a young Japanese author, Adachi Kinnosuke, in 1899. Later, she protested the California Alien Land Law of 1913 that discriminated against the Japanese. Her support of the Japanese led some of her friends in the Friday Morning Club to accuse her of being un-American. Circa 1920.

Ward was also shown in her collection called *From the Window of the Wickieup*. The painting was described as having sand in the foreground and a strip of pale green sea beyond.

In addition to Borg and Ward, other artists who spent time in East San Pedro were Norman St. Clair, Ralph Mocine, L. Maynard Dixon, John M. Donovan, William H. Cole, Lillian Drain, and Granville Redmond. Gutzon Borglum was reported by Anna Marie Hager to have been one of the painters who worked in the harbor. Borglum, who went on to carve the faces on Mount Rushmore, socialized with Los Angeles notables who had houses on Terminal Island.

Impressionist painter Granville Redmond must not have been deterred by his unfortunate encounter with Old Bob Brown (see page 21), the hermit of

Rattlesnake Island, because he returned to the island to live with his wife and daughter, Jean. Redmond and his family lived in a converted trolley car close to the water. The description of his dwelling sounds like East San Pedro, not the wealthier enclaves of Terminal Beach or Brighton Beach. Both Redmond and his wife could neither hear nor speak, but Jean had no such challenges. The only time Redmond was known to make a sound was one day when walking with his family on the island, his daughter skipping ahead. Redmond felt the vibration of an oncoming train and, with fear for his daughter's safety, "issued forth from his mouth a cry like a wild beast." Living so close to Terminal Railroad tracks would surely strike fear in the hearts of any parent, but Redmond reacted without the benefit of hearing the train's roar. Fortunately, his other senses were so highly developed that he was able to feel that train on approach long before his daughter was aware of it.

Another member of the Arroyo group, Ralph Mocine, who had supplied the illustrations for Amanda Mathews Chase's book *The Hieroglyphics of Love*, showed his painting *Late Afternoon, San Pedro* in the annual Southern California painters exhibit at Blanchard Galleries in November of 1908. Lillian Drain exhibited her *San Pedro Harbor* at the first exhibition of women artists in Southern California held in February of 1909.

While local legend has linked Jack London to the artistic community in East San Pedro, there is no evidence that he ever wrote in East San Pedro. Stories that his yacht the *Snark* had languished in the west basin of the port for decades proved to be untrue. Jack London may have visited the resorts of Terminal Island. However, in the summer of 1903 during the height of the bohemian period in East San Pedro, London had separated

Artist Lillian Drain outside Idah Strobridge's Wickieup gestures to Mike Pacetti in this photograph taken by Olive Percival. This is the only photograph found to date of any artist at the Wickieup.

Opposite: Olive Percival wanted to produce exceptional photographs and felt that these cyanotypes of East San Pedro were some of her best work. Here, squatters have tied their boats to the pilings holding up their shacks.

from his wife, and for a period of time worked as a foreign correspondent, landing in a Japanese prison while covering the Russo-Japanese War for the *San Francisco Examiner*.

Although London didn't live or work in East San Pedro, his wife retreated to Idah's Wickieup. At the time Bessie London came to the Wickieup, she was under a terrible strain. Her three-year-old child Joan was sick, and Bessie had struggled for years trying to make ends meet for the London family. She may have been disappointed about her husband's sale of the rights to *Call of the Wild* for only two thousand dollars. Unlike Idah's other guests, Bessie did not come to write or paint; rather, she needed a period of rest and recuperation by the seashore. London arrived in East San Pedro with Joan and eighteen-month-old baby Bessie in February of 1904. While she was in residence at the Wickieup, a reporter visited her. When asked how she felt about her husband being in a Japanese prison, she replied that she felt his life was in no danger. Bessie London rested at the Wickieup for about a month and then moved on to stay at a home in the Arroyo Seco.

Looking south to the main channel, a photographer captured Los Angeles Harbor on a moonlit night. Circa 1900. Wilmington Transportation Company ferried passengers to and from Catalina Island on the *Falcon*, which can be seen in the distance, steaming into the harbor.

Squatters also used the East Jetty to establish their businesses. Warren B. Hipple, a machinist, and Al Larson, a boatbuilder, owned complementary businesses, so the fact that their lots were adjacent was a plus. They both squatted on the East Jetty and built substantial buildings for their enterprises. Eventually they were evicted by the city.

The Making of a Community

As the population of squatters in East San Pedro grew to three hundred, businesses also moved to the breakwater to support the residents. By 1899 a saloon, store, post office, and a fish market, as well as establishments catering to the tourist trade had moved in, also as squatters. The residents undertook what was necessary to make the jetty a self-sufficient place to live and work. They ingeniously connected their shacks by a network of boardwalks and built a road they named United States Avenue that extended from the Salt Lake Wharf between the east- and west-facing rows of squatter shacks. Building a community was a mutual goal among the inhabitants, one that would set a strong spirit of camaraderie on the island for many years to come.

Old railroad cars were often used for living arrangements on Terminal Island. Artist Granville Redmond, his wife, and daughter lived on the island in a converted trolley. This photograph was taken at Zinc Station on the north side of the island, where the railroad treated its timber pilings in a zinc solution.

A school opened on September 18, 1899, with Miss Alice D. Higley of Pasadena chosen as the teacher. Mrs. Lucie Laubershermer's cottage was rented as a temporary schoolhouse, at least while steps were underway to procure a permanent building. A census of children on the island indicated that the school would have forty-seven pupils. The cottage was located on Railroad Avenue, at the southeast corner of Fifth Street in Terminal. In 1902, the citizens of Terminal Island pronounced the school had its best year ever, under the management of Miss Celia D. Cady. By 1904, the population had

expanded so greatly that the school could hold only half the pupils on the island. The voters of Terminal approved a five-thousand-dollar bond measure to support the purchase of land and the construction of a new school.

The Terminal Island School was built at 121 Railroad Avenue at Seventh Street, near what is now the east end of the Vincent Thomas Bridge. This school served all the children from East San Pedro, Terminal Beach, and Brighton Beach. Children could walk to school barefoot because the island was mostly sand. In addition

Terminal Island: Lost Communities on America's Edge

Wilmington Transportation Company donated the S.S. *Warrior*, which was then modified to serve as the Bethel Seamen's Institute Mission, a refuge for aging mariners. San Pedro Historical Society member William Olesen wrote about a visit with its captain, Charles Farr, at the mission in 1921. Later, Farr was forced to move inland, after the ship fell victim to the channel widening.

to the school, the island had its own library, described by Charles Lummis in his diary on September 11, 1909: "Through a maze of lumber yards to the little reading room in a rooming-house. . . . They don't do anything but the latest novels there."

In 1902, the Seamen's Friend Society of Southern California established a nondenominational mission for seafarers to be located in East San Pedro and operated

The interior of the Bethel Seamen's Mission reflects its earlier life as the S.S. *Warrior*, but it was outfitted to host twenty seamen comfortably. Circa 1900.

by Captain Charles Farr. Along with Captain Farr, Curtis W. Wilbur and George W. Parsons ministered to the fishermen, although it was often noted that it was not the odor of sanctity that pervaded the old Bethel, but the odor of fish. The Banning family donated the old hull of the *Warrior*, which had been used to ferry passengers and freight to Catalina Island. Farr beached it behind the Salt Lake Railroad wharf, put a roof on it, and created a reading room for seafarers. By 1909, the Bethel Seamen's Institute, as it became known, under the presidency of Curtis W. Wilbur, had successfully developed the mission into a place with numerous amenities for the mariners and fishermen. That same year, Wilbur was part of a delegation of Los Angeles Chamber members who welcomed members of the Japanese squadron to San Pedro. Wilbur went on to become the secretary of the navy in March 1924 under President Calvin Coolidge and served until March 1929.

Squatters took advantage of sand that was captured by perpendicular rock groins built by the Army Corps of Engineers to stabilize the East Jetty. While some lived right on the jetty, many squatters nested on the sand at Pansy Bay. This photograph looks east toward San Pedro. The pavilion that was once in Plaza Park appears in the background. Circa 1900.

Charles Lummis and his Jib-O-Jib

The most famous squatter in East San Pedro was Charles Lummis. On Tuesday, October 8, 1901, Olive Percival stepped off the streetcar at Avenue 66 in the Arroyo Seco. She immediately got the news from her mother—who was chatting on the same streetcar with Lummis's wife Eva—that the couple had purchased the Longs' house on the old breakwater in the harbor. The source was good enough to add credence to the gossip about one prominent Los Angeles man who had taken possession of a lot in East San Pedro for no money. Nobody could confirm if Lummis was at the heart of the gossip, and it didn't matter. Word had spread quickly; over the weekend there had been a small stampede of squatters who wanted to grab a lot for free in the summer of 1901, including a Mrs. M. Burton Williamson. Some squatters may have paid others for their houses, rather than build them, but *nobody* paid for the land. One day that would be a problem, but not in 1901.

No one has chronicled the life of a squatter in East San Pedro more extensively than Lummis. Lummis is described today as a "salvage ethnographer" because he sought to record the disappearing way of life he found in his travels through the Southwest. His diaries are rich in detail about his daily life on the island and the lives of his neighbors on the jetty or "old breakwater," as it was becoming known since the new breakwater construction started in 1899. His diaries for the years 1908 and 1909 were frequently written from his home there.

Lummis named his home in East San Pedro the "Jib-O-Jib." The name must have been well-known, because the blueprints in the holdings of the Harbor Department identify Lummis's home as the Jib-O-Jib.

Lummis did not live on the East Jetty itself like many squatters, and his diary often referred to walking over to it. Lummis built the Jib, as he lovingly called it, near a perpendicular extension the Army Corps of Engineers had built off the old breakwater to capture sand. This sand accumulated and created a small bay, which became known as "Pansy Bay" or "Sea Pansy Bay," named in honor of a jellyfish that is leaf shaped and lives on sand or mud. (This colonial organism is made up of many individual polyps like a coral. Sea pansies are bioluminescent when they are disturbed, so their presence in the bay may partially account for the numerous reports of bioluminescence from people living on Terminal Island.)

Lummis and his children loved the Jib, so they spent nearly every weekend there in 1908 and 1909. Most of his diary detailed his daily attempts to outsmart the fish that would turn into the evening's supper. In a letter to John Cotton Dana in 1908, he outlined his strategy:

> The tides run up under the house and we catch good big fish, like halibut or rock bass from the back porch. A bed spring with a cowbell on it holds each line. When the back doorbell rings, we stampede out to give a glad hand to our finny guest. It is remarkable how easy fish learn good manners.

Lummis's hand-drawn floorplan of his house lays out what some might call a shotgun-style house: eighteen feet wide by about forty-four feet deep, one end facing the channel of San Pedro harbor and one end facing the breakwater. Like many of the homes, a porch extended around a portion of the house that varied from four feet to six feet wide. The homes were built on pilings allowing

Street. 15 feet

the tide to run up under the house, a necessity when toilets emptied directly under the house.

On the weekends, Lummis reports his children would spend their days in the water. He would lament as the weekend drew to a close, "It is rather disgusting to have to go back in the morning." He said of his home El Alisal: "Incredible as it may seem, this isn't as restful as the Jib-O-Jib. The Pacific has about as many waves as people that wash against us . . . but I like their sound better. The air is also better . . . down there where the sharks are."

Lummis endeavored to escape from the city every Friday on the 3:25 train, at times with his children in tow, and would note other regulars on the cars heading to the island, who often joined him for revelry at the Jib, like on August 15, 1908, when he met the Norman St. Clairs. On Monday morning Lummis would return to the city.

The Autry National Center (which includes the Southwest Museum Lummis founded) has a poem that Lummis penned expressing his passion for his beloved Jib-O-Jib, or as he calls it, *The Good Old Jib-O-Jib*:

The floorplan of Charles Lummis's Jib-O-Jib in East San Pedro shows that homes faced the ocean on one side and the harbor's main channel on the other. Note that swimming took place on the opposite side of the toilet and fishing area.

Opposite: The front of the Jib-O-Jib. Charles Lummis and his children would scramble over the rocks to reach the ocean to swim.

Opposite Inset: Charles Fletcher Lummis was the center of bohemian culture in the Arroyo Seco area of Los Angeles and in East San Pedro. Circa 1910.

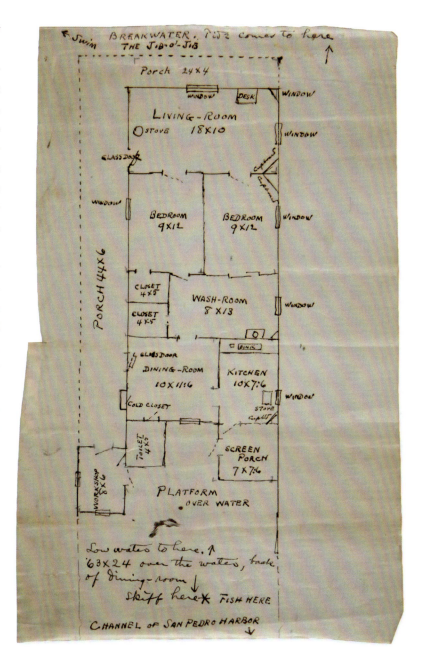

The Good Old Jib-O-Jib

Oh some are for the Country Clubs,
And Tennis is their fad—
And some they golf away like dubs
And many are auto-mad.
But they may be dad-binged, for me,
(I never learned to fib)
It's tennis off, and to hell with golf,
And me to the Jib-O-Jib.

—

A little shack at the Jetty's back
And the tide beneath the floor
And the ripples lap and the wavelets tap,
And the salt breeze whispering o'er;
And neighbor fishers and all well-wishers
And our hearts and tongues are glib
It's go as you please, and up to your knees
In the easy old Jib-O-Jib.

—

There's Brownie-Brown, who cannot drown
And Quimu that climbs the wall
And little Marie, like a star to see,
And the Old Man bossing 'em all
And a halibut on the hook has got
And a sculpin is ringing the bell
Oh, it's us ad lib at the Jib-O-Jib
And the rest may go to—San Francisco.

Sometimes the staff from the Los Angeles Public Library would join him for an afternoon at the beach. Idah Strobridge was a frequent visitor, and would often come to listen to the Lummis family play instruments.

Lummis wrote often of his children, his friends and neighbors, including the hermit fisherman Tommy Leggett (who became known as Uncle Tommy to him), and the Jorgensen family. Carl Jorgensen was a fisherman and boatbuilder known for his temper. Lummis remarked on how people feared Jorgensen, but that his wife and two sons were earnest, likable, hardworking people. Evening time was for sitting out on the porch and singing or playing music until all hours of the night, or a nightly row out to the beacon light to fish.

> The Jorgensens slipped out with their boat early this morning and went fishing for fun . . . a most extraordinary procedure for these hard workers. They got a dozen big fat albacore and came back with them this evening. Jorgensen salts them down, and they beat codfish out of sight. He gave me two big fresh ones to take home; and the whole neighborhood can have baked fish tomorrow.

There was a constant need to guard against the dreaded teredo, a marine borer from the mollusk family that is often called a shipworm. Resembling a worm fitted with two bivalve plates, the creature can bore through wood, causing terrible damage to wood pilings and other wooden objects. Teredos were so destructive—and prevalent—that East San Pedro squatters whose homes were on pilings had to take special precautions so their entire houses wouldn't collapse into the sea due to a teredo infestation. Lummis and his children would collect pilings from along the East Jetty and drag them back to the Jib to use as firewood, or if the piling was sturdy enough, to replace ones under their home that had become riddled with worm holes.

> I dragged the various wet piles out to the back platform and split up those that were good only for firewood and have three splendid ones that will do to replace pilings under the house when needed. . . . As I suspect it is now. Our big piles to which the *Lum* [Lummis's boat] is always moored fell down while we were away, eaten off by the bloody teredos.

Lummis expressed his concern for his friends and neighbors, especially Tommy Leggett. Lummis described "Uncle Tommy" as one of the "gentlest, most unselfish, and most lovable of neighbors." Leggett lived by his wits and sustained himself by the bounty of the sea. At night he would take his boat out for a ten- to twelve-mile run, dragging his nets, getting back early the next morning. He scraped by, earning a few dollars here or there, selling fish and investing it in nets. The Department of Fish and Game wasn't impressed; the agency issued a complaint against him in February of 1900 for fishing without a license. Didn't the department understand that loners like Leggett couldn't be bothered with fishing licenses?

Lummis's diary refers to Leggett's cough, his loss of weight, and the "cure" he was taking that Lummis feared was worse than the cough itself. "Poor old Uncle Tommy looks pretty rocky but promises to come up this week." Lummis convinced his friend to move away from the water for health reasons. While a guest at the Lummis home in Garvanza, Leggett turned up in the society pages of the *Los Angeles Times*. It must have tickled him: a poor old hermit of Rattlesnake Island landing in the *Times* society pages. There was Leggett, along with Miss Idah Meacham Strobridge, Mrs. Norman St. Clair, and others who were being entertained by Mr. Arthur Elliott, a member of the Ethel Barrymore Company, all at the Lummis home.

Leggett was not getting any better, however, and returned to the harbor. Lummis recalls coming home on Friday, May 21, 1909, to find Leggett wandering around in the tall grass, where Lummis stopped and photographed him. Leggett died in his cabin on the night of July 14, 1909, amid his nets and fishing gear he so dearly collected. On Sunday, July 18, Lummis and other squatters returned from a meeting regarding the railroad situation and decided that they would make an inventory of their friend's possessions.

> It was like hunting a miser's treasures, only more interesting because it was for love and friendship. We dug everywhere through the squalid old rooms, under the beds and up under the rafters and found every scrap of paper we could and found the unknown address of his sister back in Ohio. . . . Then we made an inventory of the 14 new nets and 33 old nets and the various other possessions of the poor old man and appraised them and Miss Brown made a list which we will all sign in the morning. . . . It felt something like piracy . . . but we all feel better that we have discharged our plain frontier duty to our Old Friend. The sharks won't find it so easy to gobble everything he has left.

Leggett is buried in an unmarked grave at Harbor View Memorial Cemetery in San Pedro.

The Marine Biological Laboratory: The Big Fish That Got Away

The Marine Biological Laboratory on Terminal Island was a scientific field station established in 1901 by Professor William E. Ritter, the chairman of the biology department at the University of California at Berkeley. The scientist had begun the department's off-site research operation in Northern California in the 1890s, with a small tent station in Pacific Grove, near Monterey. Not wanting to compete with Stanford University's Hopkins Marine Station that was also located in Pacific Grove, Ritter looked to Southern California for a location.

In 1893, Ritter moved his tents to Catalina Island in Avalon Bay, and there he became enamored with San Pedro as the ideal location for a marine research station. Two years later, Ritter set up tents again, this time at Timm's Point for several weeks in the summer. In 1901, Ritter expanded the facility by taking over the Duffy Bathhouse structure and established what he called the Marine Biological Station at Terminal Island. There were two buildings. One was a long structure with individual rooms for the use of the scientists, a small room

In 1902, the Marine Biological Laboratory at Terminal Island operated under the direction of Professors C.A. Kofoid and H.B. Torrey. Torrey described the island as "packed full of novel and exciting experiences." Kofoid worked with W.E. Ritter to ensure permanent establishment of a marine biological research station in Southern California.

Michael Duffy leased his ferryboat *Elsie* to William Ritter for use by his team of scientists from the Marine Biological Laboratory who collected specimens. 1901.

for storage, and a long room for the library. A larger building held classrooms, storage, and accommodations for additional scientists and fifteen students. Ritter had the lab equipped with a freshwater and seawater piping system. He also hired one of Michael Duffy's boats, *Elsie*. Duffy's daughter, Elsie, apparently came with it as boat operator, since records obtained from Scripps Oceanographic Institution Library indicate that Elsie Duffy received a payment of $140 per month for her launch and labor. The exposure to academicians from the prestigious U.C. Berkeley must have kindled a spark in Miss Duffy, who had just graduated from Long Beach High School. After working that first summer

for Ritter and his scientists, she was off to U.C. Berkeley. Her father was chastised by a member of the San Pedro Board of Education, Joseph A. Atchison, who complained that Duffy was wasting his money because Elsie Duffy would probably get married. Miss Duffy returned to teach Spanish at San Pedro High School. She was a favorite of the students and never married.

Ritter had the responsibility of funding the laboratory and received donations from Henry O'Melveny, William G. Kerckhoff, Herman Henry Kerckhoff, Jackson A. Graves, Isaac Newton Van Nuys, James Horton Shankland, Jacob Baruch, Harris Newmark, Mrs. Hearst, the Los Angeles Terminal Railway, William

R. Rowland, J.E. Plater, the Banning Company, Hans Jevne, Miss M.M. Fette, R.H. and W.J. Variel, Leslie R. Hewitt, Russ Avery, C.M. Wright, the E.K. Wood Lumber Company, and Standard Oil Company. The scientific staff included Calvin O. Esterly, Charles Atwood Kofoid, Frank Watts Bancroft, and Ritter himself—names now known to students of marine science. The only female staff member was Alice Robertson, who was in charge of the collections. Of the seven independent scientists conducting research at the lab, remarkably, three of them were women: Ida Oldroyd, Sarah P. Monks, and Gulielma R. Crocker. The fourteen students were mostly teachers from the area high schools and colleges, including Martha Burton Williamson.

The Marine Biological Laboratory operated on Terminal Island for two years. In 1901, Professor C.A. Kofoid, who was in charge of the field office, was interviewed by San Diegan Dr. Fred Baker, who insisted that San Diego was a better location for the marine station.

Sarah P. Monks named her squatter shack Phataria, in honor of the Latin word assigned to the genus of starfish. In this photo, the name can still be seen on the fence, missing its last two letters.

Baker brought together San Diego interests under the auspices of the Chamber of Commerce to facilitate the move of the Terminal Island laboratory to Coronado Island for the 1903 research season. A committee of fifty businessmen from Los Angeles under the chairmanship of William Graves sought to raise twenty-five thousand dollars to try to keep the permanent laboratory on Terminal Island. Then, Baker created an association called the Marine Biological Association of San Diego with siblings Ellen Browning Scripps and Edward Willis Scripps as board members and the lab's principal funders. With significant funding from the Scripps family, and Ritter's concern that outer harbor breakwater construction begun in 1899 would mean that the harbor would become too industrial, the lab was moved to its permanent location in La Jolla and eventually renamed the Scripps Institution of Oceanography.

When the lab closed on the island, scientist Sarah Monks, who had been an independent researcher at the lab, stayed and became a squatter—by far one of the most well-educated squatters in East San Pedro. A teacher, naturalist, and scientist, she graduated with distinction from Vassar in 1876 and was inducted into Phi Beta Kappa. When she moved to California, she taught at the Los Angeles Normal School, and she then studied at the Woods Hole Oceanographic Institution in Massachusetts, before doing her research studies at the Terminal Island lab.

She called her squatter shack a "place of study," naming it Phataria after the genus of starfish that she used for her research. Monks would often pop over to Charles Lummis's Jib-O-Jib, and also spent time with Olive Percival and Idah Strobridge. Her work on regeneration of the arms of starfish was published by the

Academy of Natural Sciences in Philadelphia in 1903. Her research interests were many, and on January 28, 1906, Monks had a special article on the "worker's page" of the *Los Angeles Times* about how the yucca plant could be used for surgical splints and other purposes.

Martha Burton Williamson, who had been a student at the Marine Biological Laboratory in 1902 and went on to study biology at University of Southern California in 1904, was already very familiar with the island before she came to take a class at the laboratory. She had spent time collecting shells there when it was still known as Rattlesnake Island. Williamson, a malacologist, was devoted to the study of mollusks (she was so devoted, in fact, that from 1893 to 1898, she was secretary of the Isaac Lea Chapter of the Agassiz Association, a national group of malacologists). At the time she enrolled as a student in the Marine Biological Laboratory, Williamson's "An Annotated List of the Shells of San Pedro Bay and Vicinity" had already been published by the United States National Museum of the Smithsonian Institution. Her paper is the earliest known scientific writing specific to San Pedro Bay published by a woman.

Williamson and Monks each sensed that being a squatter on the island could be a very temporary situation unless they protected their spots—in writing. In 1904, Williamson wrote directly to Captain C.H. McKinstry, the Corps of Engineers officer overseeing San Pedro Harbor, formally requesting to build on the breakwater, and then followed up with a visit to his office. Williamson received the same response all squatters did who wrote asking about their rights. McKinstry sent a carefully worded reply indicating no action would be taken by his department to remove her cottage.

A few years later, Monks took a similar approach. In 1907, she was one of the many squatters who directly contacted Captain Amos Fries, the army engineer in charge at Los Angeles Harbor, trying to solidify their claim to their land. She wrote a letter asking for his assistance in protecting her laboratory on the breakwater:

San Pedro, California
December 23, 1907
Captain A.A. Fries

Dear Sir:

Enclosed please find a letter to the Secretary of the Navy in regard to my cabin on the East Breakwater. My cabin is named Phataria. It is a place of study, not a money-making place, and I shall be pleased if you will help me in any way

Sarah P. Monks, left, leans over the railing at her laboratory, Phataria, in East San Pedro. February 22, 1910. Monks was a poet and naturalist and is credited with discovering the phenomenon of regeneration in starfish. She taught for twenty-two years in the State Normal School and authored a textbook on physiology.

to get a more permanent right to this site. . . . Some of the owners of cabins had their cabins surveyed and hired lawyers to send petitions to Washington claiming that it is the right way to gain permission, but it seems to me that all letters and petitions should go to you.

There is no one in Washington who knows me except Dr. Dall and Marcus Baker. . . . I may not learn anything of economic use in regard of the process but I hold it is a good thing for many people to study more destructive animals with the hope that someone may learn a way of destroying the destroyers. So the undisputed right to that bit of tide and tideland will be of great service to me and I will devote the piles and much of my time to Limnoria and Teredo.

Thanking you in advance,
I am respectfully yours,
Sarah P. Monks

Monks knew that the wood-boring teredo was the scourge of the Army Corps of Engineers and that keeping wood structures from being destroyed by them was essential to operations in the marine environment. She also was not above name-dropping people she knew in Washington D.C.; both Dall and Baker were affiliated with the Smithsonian and founders of the National Geographic Society. Captain Fries received a number of

Sarah P. Monks, third from left, retired to a big red house at 223 Fifteenth Street in San Pedro. Her home was a veritable cabinet of curiosities, its shelves lined with collections of starfish, sea urchins, sea mosses, shells, minerals, and geological specimens, all neatly arranged. Her stairs held human skulls. In her yard, she kept her collection of snakes in jars of formalin.

these types of letters from the squatters and his replies were standard:

The United States has control over navigable waters of the United States and over tidelands below high water line for commercial and navigation purposes, but with the exception of special cases does not own these lands; they have been ceded to the state shortly after California was admitted into the Union. The land occupied by you at East San Pedro, popularly known as No Man's Land, comes in this category. The United States, however, claims control over the land in order that no obstructions may be placed in the way of the harbor improvements now going forward at San Pedro.

You will not be disturbed in your possession of the area now occupied by you at San Pedro, so far as the United States is concerned, unless it should later develop that your building should be an obstruction and detrimental to the harbor improvements now in progress at San Pedro. This, however, can give you no immunity from ejection suits which might be started by the corporation claiming control of the land under a lease from the City of Long Beach which lease it is understood was confirmed by the state legislature at its last session.

But Monks's letter must have struck a chord with the captain, as he added to his letter: "On account of the work you are doing in the cause of science, I trust you will be allowed to remain in undisputed possession of the land now occupied by you."

The Tentacles of the Octopus Creep Nearer

The Charles Lummis family lived on the breakwater when the cities of San Pedro and Long Beach were fighting over control of Terminal Island. Every Monday, Lummis went for a dip in the ocean before taking the train back to Los Angeles. Unfortunately, one Monday he stepped on a "stingaree." Neighbors commiserated with him, as many had also been stung, some even landing in the hospital as a result. When stepped on, the venomous barb of a stingray can cause illness, muscle cramps and, rarely, more serious consequences. Lummis blamed his own misfortune on the port development activities that were going on.

It's all that damn dredger which is sucking these beasts up from the inner harbor and vomiting them forth into our bathing place. This is the first time we have encountered them. After this, we will take our baths in boots if nothing else besides the usual smile.

The City of Long Beach annexed Terminal Island in August 1905 in a highly contested election, rife with charges of fraud by San Pedro that Los Angeles residents with summer homes on the island had stuffed the ballot box. There had to be some reason why citizens from Los Angeles changed their voter registration to their island address so they could vote, they argued. In what must have been a bitter pill for San Pedro to swallow, after winning the annexation election, Long Beach changed the name of East San Pedro to West Long Beach.

It was not long before actions by the City of Long Beach revealed one of the hidden motivations in the annexation election. A few short months after the Long Beach annexation, the City of Long Beach issued a forty-six-year lease to the San Pedro, Los Angeles and Salt Lake Railroad, formerly the Terminal Railroad. The lease allowed the railroad to fill in the water area to create new land, including the area where squatters had already settled, and the railroad began a concerted effort to drive the squatters out. The following year the City of Long Beach approved a fifty-year lease to Pacific Wharf and Storage Company in East San Pedro, which also threatened the squatter town. John T. Gaffey, a board member of Pacific Wharf and Storage, was one of the many capitalists who worked behind the scenes to the ensure the Long Beach takeover of the island and the subsequent favorable lease to the company. The *Los Angeles Times* editorialized that the men of the Pacific Wharf and Storage Company were investing little of their own capital and obtaining land valued at one million dollars. Votes from officials working for both these companies were among those contested in a legal battle between the two cities. The collusion was blatant— Long Beach even had legal assistance from the railroad in arguing its case in court against San Pedro.

Both the San Pedro, Los Angeles and Salt Lake Railroad and the Pacific Wharf and Storage Company were given permits by the Army Corps of Engineers to construct a bulkhead or retaining wall. Material from the army's dredging was pumped through a pipeline to the companies' leased premises where squatters were living. Considerable animosity developed between the squatters and the railroad, animosity that only intensified when the railroad directed the Bouton Water Company to cut off the water supply to the squatters. Thomas Gibbon, known to many as T.E. Gibbon, was instrumental in the deal—he served on the boards of both the railroad *and* the water company, not to mention the Chamber of Commerce.

While the residents of Terminal Island who had purchased their lots from the Terminal Land Company may have been somewhat ambivalent about the jurisdictional battles between the two cities, island businesses were confused because multiple annexation elections had been held. With both San Pedro and Long Beach claiming jurisdiction, businesses had to pay taxes to both cities and hold business licenses from each. Some refused to pay Long Beach, and four merchants wound up in jail. Island residents objected to Long Beach swooping in and taking over the Terminal Island school. They showed their displeasure by converging on the school and posting a threatening notice on the school door objecting to the takeover. By the time the superintendent of Long Beach schools arrived on the island, the crowd had dispersed.

On September 19, 1906, fire destroyed about a thousand feet of squatter homes along the jetty and threatened the railroad's shipping wharf. Attributed to a gasoline cooking stove, the fire was a disaster for the squatters and a godsend to the railroad, which immediately fenced off its land. But the squatters raised American flags from the burned timbers and guarded their plots, often with shotguns. Following a September 22, 1906, meeting in San Pedro, two hundred men marched onto Salt Lake Railroad property and tore down the railroad company fence. Long Beach sent police, who retreated when outnumbered, and Los Angeles County sent a force of special police to keep the peace.

As the battle between the railroad and the squatters continued, the railroad sued to evict the squatters. The railroad also proposed moving squatters farther out onto the filled land, agreeing to issue them a lease if they gave up their claim. But the squatters knew the land the railroad was trying to lease to them belonged to the federal government. A longtime resident and squatter named Lillian Barnes Long wrote an article published in the *Los Angeles Herald* on October 28, 1906. Her words sum up the feeling of most of the squatters:

> I am an East San Pedro squatter. I live between the devil and the deep sea. The tides of the blue Pacific creep nearer and retreat on the one side, and the tentacles of the octopus creep nearer—but never retreat—on the other. . . . Among us in East San Pedro the octopus bears the names Salt Lake Railroad, Pacific Wharf and Warehouse company and a few other less materially important cognomens. . . . Various waterfront franchises on the east side of San Pedro were the proverbial chestnuts. . . .
>
> East San Pedro did not "know it." Still less did we desire it—when the morning after the election found the mantle of Long Beach flung over our "squatter-shacks." Nobody could be discovered among us who had voted for annexation (by Long Beach) but there was an odd rumor afloat that two East San Pedro lumber companies each of which shortly afterward received wharf franchises from Long Beach, had thoroughly bestowed a half holiday on their employees and that the Salt Lake road had considerately furthered their outing by a free trip to Terminal Island and the polling booths. Besides

The wharf of the San Pedro, Los Angeles and Salt Lake Railroad (formerly the Terminal Railroad) was constructed right near the squatters' homes. Many squatters regarded the open water between the new wharf and the pier as a free marina and tied their boats to the railroad pilings.

This photograph, originally labeled "after 1909 storm," demonstrates how winter storms wreaked havoc on the precariously constructed squatter homes.

that we had been juggled into a lump vote with Terminal Island whose interests are not ours. . . . As the whole vagary of the election is now working its devious passage for the supreme court, the attorney general will soon have his opportunity.

Meanwhile regardless of the legal pitfalls, Long Beach continued to cluck around us like a mother hen.

Referring to the fire, Long continues:

We enjoyed a notorious fire on the 19th of September, supposed by outsiders to have been caused by a gasoline stove. Long Beach sent us a fire engine, which reached us when the fire was out. She demands robber toll—I mean business licenses—when we try to rebuild our burned out shacks and hales [sic] us to jail when the eye of our conscious does not see its way clear to pay it. . . . She hints she will have to be very strict about our sanitation and plumbing and—worst and most of it—she dubs us West Long Beach. . . . The day after the fire she sends around deputies to help drive us altogether out of our burned out holdings. . . . The octopus showed his tentacles. While these helpless men and women still bent above the smoldering embers, a gang of men from the neighboring Salt Lake station suddenly descended among them and corralled the whole burned district in a barbed-wire fence. . . . That was on a Thursday. The octopus kept its grip until somewhere about 11 o'clock on the following Saturday night. That night an aroused San Pedro swore in half a hundred special police—our

Terminal Island: Lost Communities on America's Edge

men not unwillingly among them—sent this delegation in grim squads across Duffy's ferry, and for some minutes the air of the captured district resounded only with the click of arms. Those arms were our wirecutters.

She concluded with:

Most of us, burned out and otherwise, are hard-working people, mechanics, longshoremen, boat builders, shop keepers, machinists, artists, clamdiggers, fishermen, and a stray scientist or two. . . .

The nucleus of our settlement was made before the Salt Lake came, when the trestlework of the old breakwater was new, a quarter of a century ago.

Our children have been born here, and old folk have died. The old breakwater is the place where we earn our livelihood. Many of us would be hard-pressed to have to establish ourselves anywhere else. We have an odd liking for the place. It is our home. We feel that we have a right to be ousted at least fairly, when our time comes to go.

We are well aware that Uncle Sam is not making a great deep-sea harbor for our tide-washed cabins, our fishing boats, our engine shops, and our little children playing in the sand.

But neither is Uncle Sam making a great deep-sea harbor especially for the octopus.

If we are private individuals, whose welfare must give way before the public good, so also is the octopus a private corporation, whose welfare must give way before the public good.

In the eyes of the law of equity we have equal rights.

So long as Uncle Sam leaves us our breakwater—for, after all, I imagine that we are still his squatters—we will stand upon those rights. And although, like the conies, we are a "little folk," and make our homes "among the rocks," yet just now: our fate seems to be mixed up with the fate of large Issues. For instance, the open harbor; the validity of law; the question of sheer justice of man to man.

Lillian Barnes Long clearly knew the squatters' days were numbered, and alluded to that in the conclusion of her letter. Remarkably, Charles Lummis barely commented in his diary pages on the political shenanigans that had taken place. He only occasionally referenced the aggravations—such as shutting off the water—caused by railroad personnel. Instead, Lummis's diary is filled with commentary on Los Angeles matters, City of Los Angeles library business, and his efforts for the Southwest Museum. Yet his personal files (available for study in the Brand Library) show that he followed the story, because he saved clippings about the litigation over squatter property rights and between the two cities fighting over the island.

Naturally, the annexation by the City of Long Beach put the squatters in a precarious position. The linking of the San Pedro, Los Angeles, and Salt Lake Railroad to a transcontinental line, the desire of Long Beach to have its own harbor with prime waterfront, the recognition by the City of Los Angeles and the U.S. Army Corps of Engineers that the main channel needed to be widened, and the law all conspired against the squatters' desire to preserve their way of life.

The Squatters Lose Their Homes

The battle between the squatters and the railroad lasted four years, from 1905 to 1909, coinciding with Long Beach jurisdiction over East San Pedro. The California Supreme Court ruled on June 11, 1909, that several votes cast by nonqualified voters from Los Angeles, who were connected to either the Salt Lake Railroad or the Pacific Wharf and Storage Company, were not valid. That meant the Long Beach annexation of Terminal Island was invalid. Two days later, the Long Beach police withdrew, and San Pedro took control of East San Pedro.

The squatters were jubilant. They believed that since Long Beach's annexation of the island was determined to be invalid, then the leases issued by Long Beach to the Salt Lake Railroad and the Pacific Wharf and Storage Company also would be invalid. In July of 1909, one month after the state's highest court nullified Long Beach's annexation of Terminal Island, the San Pedro Board of Trustees authorized the city clerk to lease to each squatter their parcel of land for fifty years for the sum of one dollar per year. By now, the local sentiment was to favor an annexation by Los Angeles, so the San Pedro Board of Trustees wanted to be sure that the squatters were happy, to ensure that their votes would support annexation to Los Angeles.

Unfortunately for the squatters, the leases to the Salt Lake Railroad and Pacific Wharf and Storage Company were ruled to be valid, confirming that the squatters had no valid claim to any real estate.

Within four years, the squatters had lived under four different jurisdictions: Los Angeles County, Long Beach, San Pedro, and finally Los Angeles. These governing jurisdictions largely ignored the squatters until their votes proved valuable. Many had lived in East San Pedro on the East Jetty for decades. Living for the most part in shacks built of driftwood, they became self-sufficient, built their own roadway, and created the amenities they needed to survive. But their way of life was now coming to an end. They clung to their homes like barnacles to a piling, hanging on until outside forces tore them asunder.

Besides their legal losses, the squatters also lost out to development occurring at the harbor. The Army Corps of Engineers was widening the channel, thus destabilizing the squatters' homes and businesses facing the channel. In June of 1911, Al Larson, a Swedish boatbuilder who had moved to East San Pedro from San Francisco in 1903, lost his boat-building plant when it was undermined by the channel widening and collapsed into the bay, causing several hundred dollars of damage. After that devastation, he moved farther north in the harbor, across the Wilmington slough to Mormon Island, and did not return to Terminal Island until 1924 (where the operation still exists today). Within a few weeks, a few more buildings followed Larson's into the water. The most pretentious house in squatter town, owned by F.D. Griffith of Los Angeles and operated as a boarding house by Mrs. Jennie Sessions, was also in danger of collapse; residents scrambled to remove their goods. The harbor department had prepared a plan identifying the squatters' lots and locations, a plan that read as if the department had already been planning to remove the squatters.

Lummis and others received eviction notices from the City of Los Angeles. Lummis's was dated April 9, 1912. He was given fifteen days to vacate.

It must have been difficult for many families to

adjust. Unlike Lummis, many of the squatters had no other homes to retreat to. Lummis's neighbors the Jorgensen family didn't survive the change. After having been evicted from their squatter home the previous year, the Jorgensens moved across the main channel to San Pedro. On January 29, 1913, following what neighbors called "a season of bickering among the family," Carl Jorgensen shot and killed his fifteen-year-old son after attempting to kill his eighteen-year-old son, and then took his own life. One of the boys had already prevented Jorgensen from killing his wife. Just a few weeks before the tragedy, Jorgensen had been to Los Angeles to take Lummis a bundle of lobsters. But like many of the squatters, he lived between "the devil and the deep blue sea"—and this time the devil won.

Sarah Monks remained in San Pedro after losing her laboratory, Phataria, and lived in a large house at 223 Fifteenth Street. She became the curator of the Museum of Zoology and Botany at the University of California at Los Angeles. She died July 10, 1926. The Smithsonian Institution named a shell after Martha Burton Williamson, *Vitrinella williamsoni*. When naming the shell, William Dall of the

NOTICE TO VACATE.

To _C. F. Lummis_

and to all other persons occupying the tract of land described in this notice, or any portion thereof, or occupying or maintaining any building or other structure thereon:

You and each of you will please take notice that the City of Los Angeles hereby demands that you and each of you, within fifteen days from date hereof, vacate and deliver up possession to the said City of Los Angeles, each and every portion occupied by you of that certain tract of land, situate in the City of Los Angeles, County of Los Angeles, State of California, more particularly described as follows:

Beginning at U.S.Pierhead Station 301 of Los Angeles Harbor as established by the Secretary of War on July 29, 1908; thence north 64 deg. 14 min. 15 sec. east a distance of 500 feet to a point; thence southeasterly in a direct line to U.S. Station Q of said Los Angeles Harbor; thence southwesterly in a direct line to U.S.Pierhead Station 296 of said Los Angeles Harbor; thence northwesterly in a direct line to the point of beginning.

And you and each of you are further notified to remove from said tract of land, and from each and every portion thereof, within said time, any and all buildings occupied or maintained thereon by you, or each or any of you.

By order of the Council of the City of Los Angeles.
Dated, Los Angeles, Cal. April _9th_ 1912.

CITY OF LOS ANGELES,
By _Louis A Handley_
City Clerk of the City of Los Angeles.

In 1912, Charles Lummis received an eviction notice from the City of Los Angeles telling him to vacate the Jib-O-Jib, a result of the channel-widening project. He did not fully comply with the demands since he left the Jib structure in place.

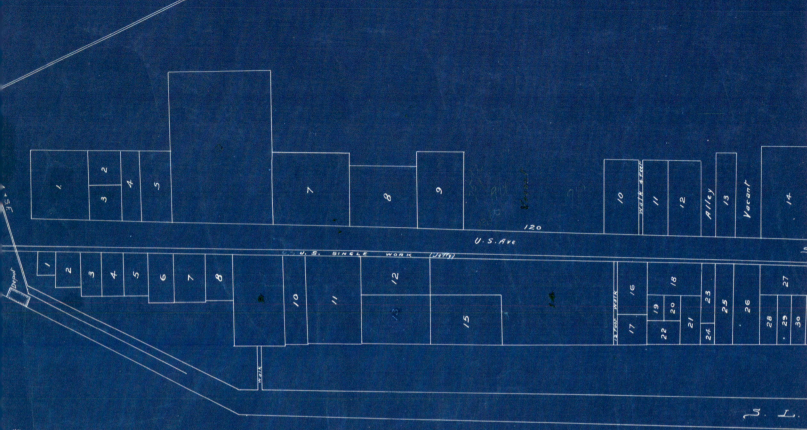

This drawing, discovered in the Port of Los Angeles Archives, was likely made in preparation for removal of the squatters in 1912. United States Avenue, the street constructed by the squatters and the residents on both sides of the jetty, is shown at center. This faithful transcription of the original document includes several misspelled names.

"Names on West Side of Single Works"

1. Donald McKay, 10 ft. x 10 ft.
2. James Johns, 26" x 40"
3. Ed. Rive, 20" x 50"
4. C.L. Radcliffe, 12" x 50"
5. ___ Starks, 25" x 50"
6. Gertie Nelsen, 23" x 40"
7. Lena Sheppard, 34" x 45"
8. Peter Craig, 20" x 45"
9. [crossed out]
10. Thomas Merrifield, 17" x 90"
11. E.T. Scholler, 45" x 90"
12. W.W. Christensen, 46" x 40"
13. Paul La Mar [crossed out], 55" x 45"
14. [crossed out],
15. Mrs. Ella Van Trees, 50" x 50"
16. Robert Miller, 30" x 60"
17. G. Terkins, 30" x 30"
18. James McGowan, 57" x 40"
19. May Selzer, 20" x 30"
20. Chas. Christensen, 14" x 16"
21. Peter Larsen, 22" x 60"
22. ___ Luke, 45" x 24"
23. John Demateis, 15" x 70"
24. Charles Ericksen, 15" x 20"
25. Frank Brown, 23" x 80"
26. Laura White, 40" x 80"
27. Annie Wilson, 38 x 30"
28. Victor Steffensen, 24" x 46"
29. Peter Larsen, 19" x 46"
30. Annie Wilson, 16" x 46"
31. Sophie Selzer, 48" x 40"
32. Al. Pears, 35" x 45"
33. John Carver, 24" x 24"
34. Harry Snyder, 24 x 20"
35. E.T. Setsaller, 55" x 86"
36. H. Hipple, 25" x 86"
37. Al. Larsen, 94" x 86"
38. J.E. Wright, 46" x 50"
39. J.S. Merver, 46" x 24"
40. Harry Barker, 36" x 85"
41. Charles Farr, 15" x 20"
42. Seamens Bethel, 16" x 70"
43. John Gable, 19" x 70"
44. Virginia Johansen, 14" x 72"
45. Frank Givens, 34" x 72"
46. Swan Lee, 60" x 72"
47. Frank Haskell, 66" x 72"
48. E.D. Lucas, 16" x 70"
49. Andrew Andersen, 24" x 70"
50. Tom Olsen, 72" x 72"
51. John Demateis, 22" x 72"
52. Daniel Becker, 25" x 70"
53. Laura Nadau, 19" x 71"
54. [crossed out],
55. Donald McKay, 38" x 71"
56. A. Emerton, 104" x 31"

Within the map image:

18

23

25 26 27

28 30

33 34 35 36 37

20 21 22 24

29 32

Pacific Wharf Storage Co.

East Jetty

15 16 17

15 feet 15 feet

U.S. Ave.

U.S. Single Work [Jetty]

31

32 33 35 36 37

34

38 39 40 41 42 43 44 45 46 47 48 48 50 51 52 53 55 56 57 58 59 61 62 63 64 65 66 67 68 69

12 Foot Walk

MAP of SQUATTERS

East San Pedro

By

E.T.S.

R. R. Dock, or Wharf

NER HARBOR

---

57. Salvador Cares, 20" x 24"
58. Ida Strohbrigde, 59" x 58"
59. F. Bent, 22" x 38"
60. [crossed out],
61. R. Bishoph, 31" x 58"
62. John Falconer, 31" x 58"
63. William Hotzke, 22" x 58"
64. Peter Hill, 22" x 58"
65. Robt. Trunau, 43" x 58"
66. Chas. Ballrige, 29" x 58"
67. John Gustaphsen, 13" x 58"
68. Frank Williams, 24" x 58"
69. Luis Mascola, 125" x 58"

"Names on East Side Single Work"
1. James McNeal, 95 ft. x 125 ft.
2. Jose Riva, 33" x 70"
3. John Evitch, 33" x 40"
4. James McNeal, 24" x 125"
5. Lina Sheppard, 30" x 80"
6. [crossed out], 80" x 300"
7. Cal. Brass Co., 42" x 80"
8. W.W. Christensen, 58" x 60"
9. Emil Christensen, 35" x 60"
10. John Demateis, 26" x 50"
11. Gabriel Miranda, , 40" x 60"
12. Antonio Avandez, 65" x 60"
13. Frank Brown, 24" x 50"

14. Charlie Ericksen, 40" x 100"
15. Sophie Selzer, 45" x 100"
16. E.T. Scholler, 50" x 100"
17. Annie Jinkens, 60" x 100"
18. Charlie Petersen, 63" x 100"
19. [crossed out], , 57" x ??"
20. Charles Bradford, 14" x 75"
21. Mrs. E. Striff, 29" x 90"
22. Andrew Anderson, 35" x 34"
23. Lee Albert, 62" x 58"
24. Pratt Tillon, 35" x 75"
25. Laura Nadau, 43" x 107"
26. Frank Haskell, 100" x 104"
27. T.E. Wright, 78" x 104"

28. Luise Perkins, 43" x 75"
29. Laura Nadau, 43" x 37"
30. Donald McKay, 140" x 144"
31. [crossed out],
32. Laura Nadau, 35" x 52"
33. Sam Wilhite, 25" x 140"
34. Dr. J. Chamberlin, 37" x 140"
35. Wm. Kotehle, 50" x 147"
36. T.P. Phillips, 50" x 150"
37. R. Bishoph, 50" x 150"

The Smithsonian Institution's William Healey Dall, Alaskan explorer and one of the founders of the National Geographic Society, named a shell after Martha Burton Williamson, who discovered the fossil shell on Deadman's Island.

Left: Martha Burton Williamson, naturalist and squatter on the East Jetty, was one of the earliest female naturalists to undertake biological research in San Pedro Bay.

Smithsonian took the unusual step of using the masculine genitive ending, *i*, rather than *ae* that would normally be used to name a species for a woman. Dall said that her name was "inherently masculine." Ida Oldroyd became curator of the Geological Museum at Stanford University in 1916 and contributed ten thousand species to its shell collection that she and her husband, Thomas S. Oldroyd, collected. Her gift to Stanford made the university's shell collection the second largest in the world after the Smithsonian Institution's. She died July 9, 1940.

According to his diary entry dated Saturday, June 19, 1919, Charles Lummis returned to Terminal Island to see what had become of the Jib-O-Jib. He had not visited the island for almost five years, and the change was dramatic:

> Almost all the little fisherman shacks from the [Salt Lake] wharf down to [Sarah] Monks's have disappeared—mostly burned down by the Salt Lake Railroad, which planned to Hog all this land. But three houses to the north of us and those to seawall are intact; and the dear old Jib-O-Jib fine as ever—except that the outer twenty feet of the wharf has perished.

For many years afterward, pilings protruded from the sand at low tide, haphazardly angled in a line where the squatters' homes once stood.

Olive Percival captured East San Pedro in a cyanotype, and the print created the illusion of a painting. 1906.

Fishermen check their catch in a beach seine, a weighted net that is dragged along the ocean floor to the shore, capturing marine life in its path.

The Heyday of Terminal Island Resorts

Bathers enjoy the beach at Terminal in front of the bathhouse. Visitors who arrived with street clothes could rent a bathing suit or just wade in.

In its heyday, Terminal Island was considered one of the safest and most popular beaches, second only to Coronado Beach in San Diego. Because the beach receded gradually, the water was quite shallow and bathers could walk into the sea a far distance before the water got too deep. Unlike most other Southern California beaches, which faced west, the beaches on Terminal Island faced south or southeast, eliminating the glare of the afternoon sun that plagued beach goers at other resorts.

The Terminal Land Company began promoting Terminal Island as a resort destination immediately after purchasing it in 1891. The development company constructed a bathhouse and pavilion and then subdivided the land along the ocean into private lots. By February 1892, George H. Peck, the company's general land agent, was placing advertisements showcasing oceanfront properties with fine bathing, fishing, and boating, all made highly accessible by frequent rail service to the island. In 1893, the Los Angeles Terminal

Railroad Company ramped up its efforts for the summer season. The idea of having to "push" the island as a resort was described by the *Los Angeles Herald* as a "picnic" because of the delightful surf, music, dancing, and clambakes, as well as the yachting and boating opportunities, including steamers to San Diego, Catalina Island, and San Clemente Island. By July of that year, a large toboggan slide that would propel its rider into the ocean was erected near one of the new bathhouses. The press touted the beach as a place that trumped other seaside resorts because there was no undertow and the water was so warm that no one came out of it "with teeth chattering and shivering all over with cold."

Lots started selling, and by 1895, new homes were already being built. The first five lots to change hands were actually traded to Mrs. Martha Boschke for her land on Smith Island. In 1891, Boschke's Smith Island home was destroyed by fire, killing her mother. The opportunity to trade her land for a new location on Terminal Island must have been a relief to Boschke, who

could leave behind the painful memories of her former home. Hers was one of the first houses on the island in 1895, she planted and nurtured some of the first trees on the island, and later she sold

the other four lots to the Pacific Electric Railway. The second and third houses on the new island resort were built by Mrs. Sara Urquhart and Mrs. Maria Christie, who would later combine their properties to create the Glenburnie Hotel.

By 1897, a number of well-known Los Angeles citizens had purchased lots on Terminal Island, including: J.D. Foster; S.B. Hynes, general manager of the Los Angeles Terminal Railroad; E.T. Wright; E.K. Benchley; Joseph Satori, founder and president of Security Trust and Savings Bank (which became Security Pacific) and his vice president, Maurice Hellman; T.E. Gibbon; Sumner P. Hunt, architect; E.D. Silent; Horace G. Miller; Fred Wood; W.B. Nicholson; Gervaise Parcell; Dr. Kirkland; A.B. Cass; Judge Waldo York of the Los Angeles Superior Court; A.R. Kellam; C.A. Sumner; Major E.W. Jones; and Mrs. M.S. Lindley. Nearly all were businesspeople who were members of the Los Angeles Chamber of Commerce. T.E. Gibbon, vice president and attorney for the Terminal Railway, had already spent time on the island, having rented a house for the

summer of 1895.

Why so many were prompted to purchase lots for summer homes concurrently was likely linked to many of them being part of the Sunset Club. In May of 1895, Charles Dwight Willard suggested that he and his associates create a club that would bring men together for dinner and discussion. Willard was the secretary of the Los Angeles Chamber of Commerce, and he had just passed off the editorial responsibilities of *Land of Sunshine* magazine to Charles Lummis. The club would be modeled after the Chicago Sunset Club, a fellowship

A notice in the *Los Angeles Herald* newspaper alerted Los Angeles citizens to the Sunday concert and bathing conditions. June 29, 1902.

Opposite: Edward Hodgson, right, surf fishing on Terminal Island. Circa 1908. Hodgson worked for the Borden family (who owned the Borden Condensed Milk Company) and was granted permission to use their home on Brighton Beach.

TERMINAL ISLANDS, CALIFORNIA.

This early postcard refers to Terminal Islands (as the harbor contained several islands) and shows oceanfront homes in the communities of Terminal Beach and Brighton Beach.

organization, with few rules, that brought men together to debate topics of the day. Willard's idea took hold. The closest friends came together by invitation only. With no dues, no bylaws, and no dress suits allowed, the Sunset Club met monthly for a hearty meal around a U-shaped table, followed by cigars and a short, sometimes-heated, discussion. Many of these men—the "power elite of Los Angeles"—would soon become embroiled in the "Free Harbor Fight," an effort to ensure the appropriation of federal funding for harbor improvements in San Pedro Bay instead of Santa Monica Bay. Many were already members of the Free Harbor League that Willard had created the same year.

In addition to the monthly meetings, the Sunset Club held an annual summer outing, an event they called "back to boyhood" where they might "travel half a day to reach a location, but cover a distance of a half century." These were usually overnight events with their families. In 1897, the Sunsetters, as the club members called themselves, traveled to Terminal Island. After the 1897 summer outing, Willard explained in a letter to his father on August 13, 1897, why he had purchased a lot:

A wealthy friend of ours who had rented a pleasant furnished house there, right on the water's edge, loaned it to us, servant and all, during the month of June. A movement started, largely among the Sunset Club men to buy up most of the good beach space, and all build there together. So I bought a lot and gave it to May. 50 feet by 140 feet with rights to the water's edge. It's a beautiful bay with excellent bathing right in front of the house. 15 cottages were then

Top: The Dudley family stands on the porch of their home, Las Olas, on Terminal Island. Circa 1900.

Bottom: The Jackson Graves home was built in 1899. Graves sold the home to Mr. and Mrs. Frank Kiff after the walk to the beach became too long. During World War I, the sunroom on the right side was used by the Red Cross to make supplies for the soldiers.

erected. . . . Ours is one of the best. Most of them are occupied by our most intimate friends and they are the most desirable people in this section. Of course a lot of nice people going in together that way pumped up the values of the property and May could sell tomorrow if she wanted to clear up to two hundred dollars.

Most of the power elite purchased lots on Ocean Avenue between Ninth and Eleventh Streets in Brighton Beach. That put them just far enough away from the bustle of the Terminal Tavern and the pavilion at Terminal Beach, but only two short blocks to the Brighton Beach Hotel at Thirteenth Street.

Unfortunately, Willard was not wealthy, so he could not afford two homes. He moved his family permanently to Terminal Island. A hand-drawn floorplan he included in the letter to his father shows a two-story cottage with four bedrooms, three for the family and one for a servant. But it was difficult to find a servant to live on the island, so the family had their meals at the Brighton Beach Hotel.

Every morning, Willard took the train to Los Angeles, arriving at 8:00 a.m. and leaving at 5:00 p.m. to catch the last train down to the island. In 1897, he left the employ of the chamber to become the managing editor at the *Los Angeles Express* newspaper. Beset with health problems, he only worked there for two years,

A view along Brighton Beach shows the summer homes built directly facing the water. Circa 1900. They are named, from left to right, the "EEEE" (four E's or "For Ease"), Nelwil, Summer Sea, Bonnie Blue (only the white porch pillars are visible), the Cotton House, (a vacant lot), McKenzie's, Armstrong's, (Kirkpatrick's home not visible), Sandhurst (with the cupola on top), Mission, and the Pinkhams' Wailili.

then left to focus on writing and civil reform. In 1898, the Sunsetters took their summer outing to Redondo Beach, but in 1899, they were back at Terminal Island. At that event, the Sunsetters elected Willard the "Mayor of Terminal Island." Willard was active in and founded so many organizations that, in 1898, the *Los Angeles Times* poked fun at him in an imaginary interview, theorizing he would say that the key to happiness in Los Angeles was to buy a cottage on Terminal Island; to join the Chamber of Commerce, the Sunset Club, the League for Better Government, and La Fiesta Association; and to read his editorials.

In the year 1900, Willard considered going to work for the Terminal Railroad. He had worked with T.E. Gibbon helping him make a presentation to the Los Angeles Chamber about connecting the Terminal Railroad to Salt Lake City. But Willard worried about his lack of railroad experience. It was a job others could do. The call to usher in a new era of municipal reform in Los Angeles was too strong. Willard wanted to devote his energy to that cause.

Willard enjoyed living on the island in the winter more than in the summer, despite his worry about winter storms carrying the house away. At one point, he considered moving the structure to a different lot, but weighed the cost of the move (three hundred to four hundred dollars) against the chance (one in twenty) that the house would be damaged in a storm. He decided to stay put, and built himself a woodworking shop at the back of the house. Willard's wife, May, was less enamored with living on the island and was lonely in the winter. As time went on, they often rented out the house for the summer (the going rate in 1902 was $225) and rented a place to live in Los Angeles.

Because of Willard's tie to the Chamber of Commerce and the Sunset Club, his wealthy cronies in both groups were among his Terminal Island neighbors, though most of them used the island as a vacation retreat rather than a permanent residence. J.S. Slauson, for whom Slauson Boulevard in Los Angeles is named, owned a home on Terminal Island. Other island homeowners included: Jackson A. Graves, banker and attorney with Henry O'Melveny; Judge Russ Avery; Harry R. Callender; Ferdinand K. Rule; Lyman Stewart, who started the company that became Union Oil Company; William F. Bosbyshell, an investment broker; Dr. Kirkpatrick W. Nordhoff; Lynn Helm; Miss D. Lankershshim; W.D. Woolwine; W.C. Patterson, who was a president of the Los Angeles Chamber of Commerce; and Gail Borden, of the Borden Condensed Milk Company.

Charles Sumner and Edward Silent worked selling real estate on the island, primarily in the summer when the business was brisk. In 1899, Graves purchased a seventy-five-by-two-hundred-foot lot facing the ocean, where he built a large home to take advantage of the beach free from the fog and cold winds of west-facing Redondo Beach. In his book, *My Seventy Years in California*, Graves recalls summer evenings watching the huge threatening waves roll in, reduced by the shallowness of the beach. He commissioned Joe Fellows, who had a boat-building business on the island, to build a thirty-foot gasoline launch, which Graves and his family used for trips to Catalina. Graves was one of the first to build his home on pilings. A storm in 1900 destroyed many homes not supported on pilings by washing out the sands underneath them. Before the next winter, many followed Grave's example, and a wooden bulkhead was built to protect the homes.

The word about the desirability of the resort spread widely. A description of the homes appeared in the *Missouri School Journal* in June of 1899:

> Terminal Island is strictly a seaside resort of elegant homes which are occupied by their owners throughout the year. These homes bespeak refinement, culture, substantiality, and wealth, and surpass in their architectural beauty and substantial character any resort in Southern California. The grounds are beautified by trees and shrubbery and the older places show with what prodigal lavishness Dame Nature responds to the care bestowed upon her offering.

More than two hundred homes were built along the beach in the communities of Terminal and Brighton Beach, either on Ocean Avenue or on one of the numbered cross streets (later, portions of Ocean Avenue became Seaside Avenue). Railroad Avenue, which ran parallel to Ocean Avenue, was where many of the businesses were located. Unlike the homes in East San Pedro, the homes in the resorts were substantial homes, rich in architectural details. People who lived in the homes facing the beach only had to open their front door and walk about twenty-five feet to reach the water's edge. Historian Anna Marie Hager described these seaside homes, creating a picture of Victoriana quite like the interiors

Few photos remain of the interior of the Terminal Island homes. This photo is a view just inside the front door of the Pinkham home that was called Wailili. Circa 1915.

Visitors rest in front of the Terminal Tavern, which was a combined hotel and restaurant constructed by the Terminal Railroad to attract visitors to the island. Martin Wood was the proprietor of the tavern. Mrs. Martha Boschke's house is seen to the rear on the right side. Circa 1900.

of summer retreats known as "camps" and popularized by Theodore Roosevelt in the Adirondack Mountains of New York State:

> They were decorated in the elegance which prevailed, ornamental mantels adorned with plush runners from which dangled little furry-balls: snapshot albums piled high on marble-topped tables, portieres [curtains hung in doorways] made of hundreds of tiny shells, carefully and lovingly sewn together, and the inevitable cluster of the fringe-edged pillows embroidered with words and pictures and such mottos as "Daisies won't tell."

Having a home on the island brought out the whimsy and carefree spirit of many of the people who chose to live there. They named their homes rather than having address numbers, so creativity took over. Judge Avery's home was called Nelwil, a word made from his two sons' names. Ellen P. Rhone called her house the Ark. Harry Callender, who was in the real estate business, built a home with W.C. Patterson that they named the Kilkare House. C.B. Boothe called his home Sandhurst. The Bosbyshells' home was dubbed EEEE ("four E's" or "For Ease"). The names of other homes celebrated the beauty and calm of the island: the Bonnie Blue, Summer Sea, and Sleepy Hollow, owned by the Dudley family. Creativity surfaced other ways, too. For instance, some

The Merwins celebrate the Fourth of July at their home. Circa 1908. They had four daughters: Margaret, born in 1896; Kathryn, born in 1898; Myrtle, born in 1901; and Mildred born in 1904.

Mrs. Hazel Pinkham and her daughter Anne (later known as Anne Drasdo). Hazel's husband, James Pinkham, was manager of a fruit farm. The house in the center of the three homes belonged to Morgan Adams, Sr. 1917.

Opposite: Margaret Bushnell stands on the beach along Ocean Avenue. The bulkhead behind her was built after a 1900 winter storm damaged those beachfront homes that weren't built on pilings. Circa 1902.

islanders used huge whale bones as part of their landscapes and other industrious crafters would make chairs out of whale vertebrae.

There were three major hotels on the island and a number of boarding houses. The Terminal Tavern and Hotel was one of the original hotels on the island, located on Ocean at First Street. The Terminal Tavern also had a café, or visitors could eat at Mrs. Sample's boarding house on Ocean between First and Third Streets. The Glenburnie Hotel, located on Ocean between Third and Fifth Streets, not far from Mrs. Sample's place, consisted of small cottages. In 1899, Frank S. Gordon built the Gordon Arms Hotel at the corner of Ocean Avenue and Thirteenth Street. The Gordon Arms was designed so all hundred rooms faced outside; twenty of its suites were complete with bathrooms. The hotel retained its own rules of decorum: ladies, for instance, were not welcome to play cards with gentlemen; women played in a separate room. On May 5, 1901, the Gordon Arms Hotel was reopened as the Brighton Beach Hotel. A rambling structure operated by Harry Fryman, Brighton Beach Hotel was equipped with bowling alleys, a billiard and pool room, tennis courts, and croquet grounds. On Saturday evenings, guests might have an opportunity to go to an island ball in the hotel.

For the more mundane needs, residents and tourists could purchase general merchandise and groceries at one of the Beal, Fawcett, and Sandstrom stores at First or Fifth Streets or at Philip Real's Grocer on First. In 1908, Bunker and Dudley established a grocery store on Third Street. A Community Church later affiliated with the First Methodist Church also opened on Ocean and Fourth Street to support the growing community.

Terminal Island: Lost Communities on America's Edge

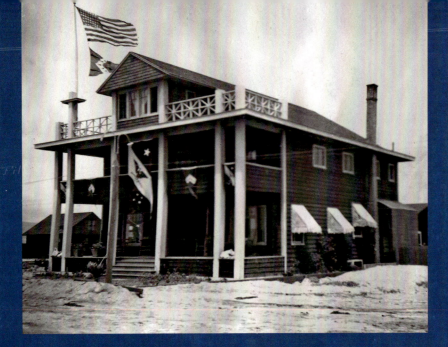

Above: Gail Borden had one of the more imposing houses along the ocean. He was the grandson of the Borden Condensed Milk Company founder, Gail Borden. Originally known as the New York Milk Company, Borden's marketed sweetened condensed milk for babies in the early twentieth century. Borden would often let his favored employees use his beach home; this photograph was taken by one of them, Edward Hodgson.

Right: Mrs. Eva Samples and her husband John operated a boarding house on Ocean Avenue between First and Third Streets, pictured here in 1906 or 1907. Mrs. Samples is on the lower right, holding the hand of her granddaughter Eve, whom she adopted as her daughter. John Samples holds Hugh Reed, son of Annie Samples Reed. Family members operated the boarding house until they were evacuated in February of 1942. The 1910 census indicates that the Samples had one cook, Mary Loring, two waitresses, and two hired hands, as well as eighty-two boarders and lodgers. Most were lumbermen.

Below: This rather modest-looking home, which had a home in the rear for servants, was owned by Lyman Stewart, oil millionaire and philanthropist. He founded Union Oil Company, which many years later became Unocal. He also founded the Union Rescue Mission in Los Angeles and the Bible Institute of Los Angeles, which was later known as Biola College.

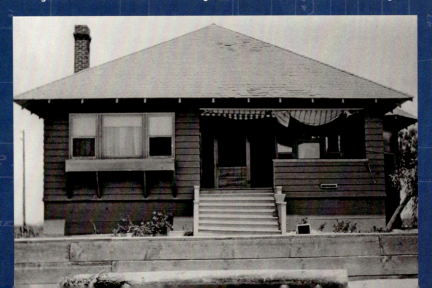

Eva and John Samples lived in a house next to their boarding house in Terminal. Left to right are John Samples, his daughter Annie Samples Reed, Eva Samples, and John and Eva's daughter Louise Samples Dorsey. The children in front, left to right, are Eve Dorsey, a granddaughter of Eva who was later adopted as her daughter; an unidentified girl; and grandson Hugh Reed.

Frank and Jennie Merwin lived on Terminal Island with their children. Jennie Merwin is on the right, and the house visible on the right is Cotton House named for the family who occupied it at that time. The Merwins' house called Summer Sea is at the extreme left. Frank Merwin was employed on the government dredge. Circa 1900.

Above: The Hotel Glenburnie, which was located near the Terminal Tavern, consisted of cottages that were available for rent. The land for the hotel was purchased in 1895, and the first record of visitors that has been located was dated 1897.

Left: A note on this photograph states that the Community Church, at Ocean Avenue and Fourth Street, was built by "Mr. Wolsey, Mr. Carnahan and Mr. Powell." Circa 1920. Begun as a community church, it later affiliated with the First Methodist Church in San Pedro. The building was later enlarged to include a social hall at the rear.

Opposite: This is one of several general stores and grocery stores that were established on the island.

George Luke, a boatman and squatter, lived on the west side of the East Jetty with his wife, Mabel, a curio dealer, and his son Wayne. This 1909 postcard shows his power launch *Emiline*, which was used for fishing and island excursions.

Los Angeles's Playground

People flocked to Terminal Island for the summer. The pages of the *Los Angeles Times* society pages were filled with the comings and goings of Los Angeles visitors to the island. The *Times* extolled the "virtues" of the island: the best French chef, everything was clean and fresh, and as the paper (now shockingly) pointed out, no Chinese were employed. On holidays like July the Fourth, there was such a demand for bathing suits that it was hard to rent a dry one. This little ditty was used to characterize Terminal Island by the *Times* in the year 1900:

Watch the kids down at the beach;
Far beyond their parents' reach.

See them dive and swim about;
Hear them kick when ordered out.

Festive maiden, full of glee,
Plunges in quite recklessly.

Fat man rolls in like a log;
Puffs and paddles, à la dog.

Everybody full of vim,
Everybody in the swim!

The Brighton Beach pier was built for the convenience of guests at the Brighton Beach Hotel. Circa 1900.

Mr. and Mrs. John Peck are photographed with John Bushnell, right. In the summer of 1904, the Pecks leased the home at 504 Ocean Avenue, known as the Ark, from Clara Ellen Rhone.

George Bushnell paddles a skiff in 1904. The home directly behind him was owned by Burton McKenzie, principal of the Terminal School, and later sold to the Hammond family. Next to the McKenzie home, and left to right, are the Armstrong home, the Kirkpatrick home, and a home called Sandhurst, owned by the Boothe family.

Terminal Island

Construction began in 1897 on a pleasure wharf that extended 610 feet into water that was 12 feet deep at the end. The California Yacht Club also began building its clubhouse. Behind the pavilion was a picnic ground with swing sets for the children. A boardwalk extended from Brighton Beach Hotel to the beach at Terminal. Electric lights were strung along the boardwalk, giving visitors an opportunity to stroll in the evenings, or they could listen to music from the bandstand or dance at the pavilion.

Terminal Island was paradise for children—they roamed freely. In a 1927 *Los Angeles Times* column, Mellen Chamberlain recalled turn-of-the-century days at the beach. He observed what he called "the island experience"—children roaming freely on the beach, racing to see what the fishermen had drawn in with their nets, delighting over live fish flopping and strange creatures wriggling. Little ones were squealing and shrieking as they spotted baby sharks, and he watched grown women coming to the beach with their frypans to carry home fresh fish for dinner. It was all part of the

Opposite: The Terminal Boating Club, on the bay side of Terminal Island. Circa 1906. Standing second from right is Elizabeth Helm Rosecrans with a group of unidentified people. Helm married William S. Rosecrans III, the son of oil magnate Carl Rosecrans. William III was also the grandson of the celebrated Major General William Starke Rosecrans, who owned what came to be known as Rosecrans Rancho (a large portion of the original Rancho San Pedro), served as a U.S. congressman from California from 1881–1885, and was U.S. Ambassador to Mexico. William III took over the family oil business and railroad interests when Carl died in 1926.

Boating around the islands in Los Angeles Harbor, especially Deadman's Island, was a popular pastime for visitors.

island experience. After a fifteen-minute walk across the island to the mudflats toward Wilmington, children could row around in a small skiff or dig for clams. After a storm, it was time for collecting. The beach was littered with kelp, sand dollars, and deepwater shells. Chamberlain noted in his column that the children paid special attention to an old lady who lived by the rail station. One little island girl, Anita Thomas, called her "Gammy" or "Gam Bocky," not the woman's actual appellation, but because the little girl just couldn't say "Grandma Boschke" like the other kids did.

Her own children grown, Grandma Boschke lived alone, having separated from her engineer husband, Alfred A. Boschke, who came to the harbor in 1874 to dredge the sandbar at the harbor entrance for the Army Corps. But her house was always full of visitors and she was always ready to dish out ice cream and cake to the barefooted hoard who gathered on her veranda. She was one of the old-timers, and her home became a gathering place for young and old. Even after the children grew up, they would come back and visit her. Lucy Banning, daughter of Phineas Banning, was seen driving her big blue car down Ocean Avenue to visit Grandma Boschke. Although Lucy Banning never lived on Terminal Island, she could have formed an attachment to Mrs. Boschke when Boschke lived on Smith Island, closer to the Banning home in Wilmington. Boschke lived on the islands of Los Angeles Harbor for forty-three years until her death in 1928. Even after the resorts shut down,

many continued to make a pilgrimage to her house on the island.

Besides the bathers, there were the beach "sitters," those who wouldn't think of sticking a big toe into the salty ocean or baring an inch of skin to the dreaded sun, preferring to sit fully clothed in proper Victorian fashion in a pillowed chair that looked as if it had come off the deck of a transatlantic steamship. These beach sitters were probably shocked by the "Naughty Nineties." Consider that Florence Silent, daughter of prominent Los Angeles Judge and Mrs. Charles Silent, donned a black taffeta bathing suit. Flaunting the fact that she had limbs, she covered her lower legs only with black stockings, and her arms below the puffy sleeves of her suit were actually bare. Newspapers weren't above making corny jokes about the swimwear, calling them "way above see level." That streak of independence that prompted Florence Silent to flaunt the latest in risqué bathing-suit fashion led her to join the artist community in Carmel, California.

Fishing and boating attracted people to the island.

Martha Boschke was married to Albert Boschke, who was awarded a contract in 1874 by the Army Corps of Engineers to dredge a channel across the sandbar obstructing access to the harbor. When Albert decided to move to Northern California in 1890, Martha settled on Terminal Island and lived there until her death in 1928. Their sons, Albert and George, followed their father into engineering careers.

The Heyday of Terminal Island Resorts

Brighton Beach Hotel...

Opening Ball--Saturday Evening, July 5th

Bowling Alleys, Billiard and Pool Room, two new Tennis Courts, Croquet Grounds, and 30 New Rooms added.

For rates, etc., address H. C. FRYMAN, Proprietor, P. O. Terminal Island, Cal., or call at 354 South Broadway—237 South Spring.

Left: Los Angeles Herald advertisement about the July 5 opening ball at the Brighton Hotel and the expanded facilities for the summer season of 1902.

This hotel, built by Frank Gordon of Pasadena, was originally called the Gordon Arms and later the Brighton Beach Hotel. In addition to accommodating one hundred guests, it had several small cottages in the rear. It was later leased to Harry Fryman who also owned the Hayward Hotel in Los Angeles.

One could fish from the end of the two piers at either Brighton Beach or Terminal Beach for surf fish, rock bass, smelt, or whiting. From a boat, one could catch barracuda and yellowtail tuna. Both Terminal Beach and Brighton Beach were rallying points for yachters. Two yacht clubs were listed in the Terminal Island directory in 1899, the Terminal Boat Club and the Catalina Yacht Club. The Catalina Yacht Club disbanded and sold its land to the Southern Pacific, giving a second railroad a long-desired spot for a ferry landing on the island. The South Coast Yacht Club also purchased a lot in 1897, along with many of the other citizens, and erected a large clubhouse. The club changed its name to the Los Angeles Yacht Club and merged with the Los Angeles Motor Boat Club. George Davis established a boatyard in the year 1900 and, along with the Joe Fellows boatyard, catered to the needs of the wealthy who needed yachts and sailboats for fishing or excursions to Catalina.

Recreational opportunities weren't limited to the water, however. There were tennis courts on the island, and three-day tennis tournaments would conclude with trophy presentations and dancing at the Brighton Beach Hotel. The Terminal Island Golf Club had its own golf course, laid out by Q.W. Grindley, the professional at the Los Angeles County Golf Club.

From Terminal Island, visitors could take side trips to the Hot Sulphur Springs at White Point or the lighthouse at Point Fermin. They could explore the Palos Verdes hills and the ruins of the hide house that Richard Henry Dana referred to in *Two Years Before the Mast*. The brave would venture to Deadman's Island, especially after a heavy rain exposed a coffin or two. Some adults recall being too scared to ever visit Deadman's Island as a child.

A fun day at the beach could be concluded with a cool, refreshing Coca-Cola, now available in a glass bottle. It became the most popular drink at the beach within five weeks of its introduction. In the evenings, residents and visitors alike could enjoy the view of the ocean from the veranda of the Brighton Beach Hotel or their own porches.

A 1911 photograph of Mrs. Harry Schultz at the Zinc railroad station looks like an inspiration for the 1914 silent film serial *The Perils of Pauline*. Harry Schultz was the superintendent of the San Pedro, Los Angeles and Salt Lake Railroad's wood-preserving plant located on Terminal Island. Because railroad ties were preserved with zinc chloride there, Schultz named the railroad stop Zinc Station. The Schultzes lived in the house in the center of the photo, with Brighton Beach behind it. The zinc treating plant was across the tracks to the left. A kelp- processing plant known as Pacific Products Company established a fertilizer plant at Zinc Station and became known as "Stink" Station.

The Transcontinental Railroad Comes to the Island

In August of 1902, the *Los Angeles Times* carried a small note that T.E. Gibbon and his wife had entertained Mr. and Mrs. J. Ross Clark at an elegant luncheon at the Brighton Beach Hotel. But there was more on the table than just lunch. They were celebrating. These two men had been instrumental in assuring that another transcontinental railroad had access to the harbor at Los Angeles. The Terminal Railway had been created to reserve access for another transcontinental railroad to link to Los Angeles Harbor; its primary raison d'être was not tourist travel. Promoting tourism and local business interests was merely a way to bide time as this little railroad with an "attractive dowry" looked for the perfect marriage.

Gibbon had been especially anxious for this rail line connection. Not only would the route to Salt Lake City have the lowest grades and largest curvatures, it would be less expensive to construct since the alignment required fewer bridges and trestles, and could avoid heavy snow. But its construction was still too much for the Terminal Railway to finance, and many capitalists were reluctant to invest in another transcontinental line that could potentially devalue their stock in the Southern Pacific and Santa Fe Railroads. Gibbon had been looking for a financier to undertake the project and found him in an office adjoining to his in Los Angeles: J. Ross Clark, a fellow Los Angeles Chamber member.

Clark had moved to Los Angeles for his health in 1892 and invested in banks, oil wells, and sugar beets. His older brother, Senator William Andrews Clark, was a mining speculator, newspaper publisher, banker, politician, and one of the wealthiest men in the United States. Senator Clark was ranked among the robber barons of the day, with a fortune and a desire for power comparable to William K. Vanderbilt, Andrew Carnegie, and John D. Rockefeller.

Gibbon's true goal in wooing J. Ross Clark early on was to get to his brother, the senator. His plan worked. Gibbon convinced J. Ross to take the opportunity for the new rail connection to his older brother William. J. Ross had a vested interest since he operated the Los Alamitos Sugar Company, serving as vice president, and saw the benefit of the new direct line to Salt Lake City from the harbor; brother William immediately recognized the opportunity to save time in shipping copper to the West Coast.

On August 21, 1900, the Los Angeles Terminal Railway announced that William A. Clark of Montana had acquired an interest in the Terminal Railroad Company and that a line to Salt Lake City would be constructed. In March 1901, the San Pedro, Los Angeles, and Salt Lake Railroad was officially created, incorporating the Los Angeles Terminal Railroad in the new company. Gibbon continued on as attorney for the Clark interests. The new railroad became known as the Salt Lake Railroad or Salt Lake Road. The announcement was met with hostility, and interference came from both the Union Pacific and the Southern Pacific. The Union Pacific had always considered it would one day take over the Terminal Railroad. Edward Henry Harriman, who had controlling interest in the Union Pacific and was intent on increasing his holdings in the Southern Pacific, offered the senator five million for the newly created company. Clark refused. Physical blockages along the construction route and legal maneuvers, along with the announcement of a competing line, were the result. Cooler heads recognized the folly of two rail lines from Los Angeles to Salt Lake City. Gibbon and J. Ross Clark sat down and negotiated on behalf of Clark with the representatives for Harriman. Negotiations began in January 1902 in New York and a deal was inked on July 9, shortly after a court ruling favorable to Clark in Los Angeles Superior Court by Gibbon's fellow chamber member and Terminal Island neighbor, Judge Waldo York.

When the two men sat down for their lunch with their wives at the Brighton Beach Hotel that summer, the three-week-old agreement they celebrated was not yet public. When it was made public in October, it was hailed by citizens of both Los Angeles and Salt Lake City along with industries that would benefit by using the line. Clark gave Harriman half-interest in the San Pedro, Los Angeles and Salt Lake Railroad Company in exchange for Harriman ensuring that land and rights

to share trackage were made available by the other railroads. Clark was to operate the railroad for a period of years, after which control would shift to the Union Pacific Railroad. The rail line to Salt Lake City from Los Angeles Harbor opened in 1905.

A transcontinental railroad connection to Salt Lake City would have profound consequences on Terminal Island. Although the railroad began to market the resorts to tourists from Salt Lake City, the new railroad accelerated the industrialization of the island. The inevitable increase in commercial port activity doomed the resorts. Gibbon would continue to promote port expansion, and would go on to become president of the Los Angeles Chamber of Commerce's Harbor Committee and then a member of the first Board of Harbor Commissioners in 1907. In 1912, Gibbon resigned as attorney for the railroad to lend his support and that of the newspaper he owned, the *Los Angeles Herald*, to the creation of a municipally owned railroad.

An advertisement for Terminal Island appeared in a local newspaper in 1902. A ticket from Los Angeles to the island was fifty cents. The Salt Lake Route was the name often used for the San Pedro, Los Angeles and Salt Lake Railroad, the successor to the Terminal Railroad.

The Industrialization of Terminal Island

The harbor's destiny as a world commercial harbor, which was envisioned by many in the early part of the twentieth century, trumped the desires and concerns of the Terminal Island residents, including those who were wealthy and influential. The citizenry of Los Angeles had been sold on the idea of rapid harbor development during the Free Harbor Contest, the battle over where the Army Corps of Engineers would recommend investment of federal dollars for harbor improvements. The growth of Los Angeles during the first decade of the twentieth century proved that the town might someday have more people than San Francisco. Between 1900 and 1910, the population of Los Angeles more than doubled while the population of San Francisco grew only 21 percent. Ever since construction of the new federal breakwater began in 1899, expectations were high that the harbor would expand to reach its destiny as a world-class port.

But the breakwater alone did not provide what was needed to improve the commercial status of the harbor —wharves and terminals were needed. Beginning in the early 1890s, waterfrontage on the Terminal Island side of the main channel was leased to private enterprises, including many lumber companies, a cannery, and the Terminal Railway. As early as 1894, large gangs of workers took the ferry to the island to work in the industrial facilities. Now, Terminal Island was not only a resort but a place that supported a working-class population, especially as jobs were available for both men and women. Locals now took the ferry from San Pedro or Wilmington to the island every day to work, not vacation. They were waitresses, cooks, hotel workers, and employees in the stores or other establishments that catered to the wealthy. As the availability of jobs increased, many people moved to the island rather than take the ferry. They lived in smaller, more modest homes or rented rooms in boarding houses.

Little Mildred Maxson Onsolen and her family first lived in San Pedro when her parents moved her and her five older siblings to the San Pedro vicinity from Ohio in 1911. According to an essay she later wrote for the *San Pedro News-Pilot*, Mildred was a year old. Her uncle, Paul Eachus, had opened a fish market in San Pedro and believed that California would be a better place to improve Mildred's mother's failing health. Mildred's father engaged in work at the San Pedro–based fish market, then in the military, and then the shipyard. The California climate apparently had a positive impact on Mildred's mother, because she was able to work at a cannery on Terminal Island. After her mother secured that position, the whole family moved to a Terminal Island residence around the corner from the Brighton Beach Hotel, where little Mildred took great delight in wandering through its hallways and playing amid its hundred rooms. The war years were also when the influenza pandemic first hit the United States, however, and, unfortunately, Mildred herself was touched by illness. "We had to use our own cups and masks," she wrote. "The school closed. I got very sick with the flu and fell into a coma. When I woke up, Mama was by my bed. She had to carry me to the bathroom." Mildred made a full recovery, and when the Great War was officially over, the family moved back to San Pedro.

The island became a less-desirable place to live for

In the early twentieth century, the East San Pedro train station, in the foreground, was surrounded with commercial structures as port facilities expanded into East San Pedro.

some and a real opportunity for others when industry started to boom there. Before the end of the first decade of the new century, wealthy Angelenos began to leave; the grand old homes with lots of bedrooms became boarding houses for ethnic minorities who worked in the canneries. Local families purchased larger homes that had once been on oceanfront property—dredging had changed the coastline, so the homes were far from the beach and suddenly more affordable for the working class.

The County of Los Angeles and the City of San Pedro both supported granting property rights to businesses that would build wharves and engage in harbor commerce. During its brief period of control over the entire island from 1905 through 1909, the City of Long Beach issued major leases to the San Pedro, Los Angeles and Salt Lake Railroad and the Pacific Wharf and Storage Company. So by 1906, nearly all the water frontage on the Terminal Island side of the harbor's main channel was leased to private companies, including a lease to the first cannery on the island, the California Fish Company. These companies helped drive the creation of industrial jobs on the island. The locals and newer residents of the island worked at the lumber-planing mill, loaded lumber or coal onto ships, and helped board passengers and cargo onto the steamers *Hermosa* and *Cabrillo* bound for Catalina Island. And still others worked in the cannery.

The Army Corps of Engineers continued dredging the inner harbor turning basin, depositing the dredged material on the seaward side of Terminal

Island, just as the San Pedro, Los Angeles and Salt Lake Railroad Company and Pacific Wharf and Storage Company had done. When the City of Los Angeles annexed San Pedro and Wilmington in 1909, the city engineers' concern centered on the width as well as the depth of the channel; the main channel was still only five hundred feet wide, the entrance near Deadman's Island only four hundred feet. The Board of Harbor

Commissioners made an application to the Army Corps of Engineers to widen the channel to one thousand feet with a depth of thirty feet. Lieutenant Colonel McKinstry from the engineers' Los Angeles office did not approve of the project; he did not anticipate that the channel would need to be that wide for the future and recommended a channel width of seven hundred fifty feet in 1914. No appropriations for the work came because of concerns about an impending world war. The Harbor Commission took advantage of the opportunity to press for the one-thousand-foot width and was successful in the Army Corps approving the one-thousand-foot width in 1915. The additional two hundred fifty feet sealed the fate of Deadman's Island—it would be in the way of a one-thousand-foot wide channel. It would have to go.

The Heyday of Terminal Island Resorts

The Creation of Fish Harbor

The development of the fishing industry and fish canneries on the island would have the most profound effect on the island demographics. As stated earlier, the first company to construct a cannery on the island was California Fish Company, which filed its articles of incorporation on February 25, 1893. The two-story factory had its own steamer and salting house; five to ten tons of sardines were caught each day by its one fishing boat, the *Alpha*, and other smaller vessels in the harbor.

Andrew F. Smith in his comprehensive book, *American Tuna: The Rise and Fall of an Improbable Food*, has written extensively about one of the cannery founders, Albert P. Halfhill, who had been involved in the

The California Fish Company in East San Pedro used advertising on postcards to promote their "genuine" sardines.

wholesale grocery business in both Ohio and Minnesota before relocating to California for his wife's health. A talented salesman, Halfhill first promoted canned sardines, but when the sardine catch suddenly became negligible, he turned to canned tuna, an oily, long-finned fish that ranged from twenty to forty pounds and was popular in places like Italy, but not the United States.

American Tuna amply documents the changing attitudes toward albacore, which also was commonly spelled "albicore" in the 1900s. Described as unpalatable and valueless as food by various trade magazines and leading ichthyologists, albacore went through an image transformation when cooking and canning techniques were able to isolate its delicious white meat. The decline of the sardine catch, which continued to fluctuate over the years, also forced the canneries to seriously consider albacore as a viable alternative.

The California Fish Company extends out over the water in East San Pedro. Circa 1895.

Cutting and cleaning took place inside the California Fish Company. At the far left in the photograph is Raymond B. Bentley, the cannery superintendent. Wilbur F. Wood, who went on to become the founder of Chicken of the Sea, stands in the rear (an arrow points to him). Young boys often worked in the cannery. 1907.

Women pack sardines inside California Fish Company's cannery on Terminal Island. 1907.

In 1897, Wilbur Wood, a native of Nova Scotia, joined California Fish Company as a can maker. He served as plant superintendent for two years, pioneering the round sardine can, as well as experimenting with precooking tuna. The National Bureau of Fisheries recognized Wood as the "Father of the Tuna Industry" for perfecting tuna processing, while other observers felt that Halfhill should also be credited in successfully marketing the concept of canned tuna.

In addition to developing a slow-steaming method to remove the oil in albacore, Halfhill and Wood needed to find an answer to another challenge: catching the fish in the first place. According to a report published in 1928 by the University of Chicago, *Resident Orientals on the American Pacific Coast*, albacore had never been caught commercially in California prior to the introduction of the hook-and-line method the Japanese fishermen used around 1912 and 1913. Other ethnic fishermen, especially the Italians, experimented with catching albacore with nets, which was fine for smaller fish like sardines and mackerel. The sturdy and strong albacore, however, would put up a fight and leave blood spots in their flesh, which proved unappetizing for the consumer.

The Japanese, on the other hand, practiced an intricate fishing technique using a stout bamboo pole, strong line, and barbless hook. In a process called "chumming," live bait was dumped into the water, luring schools of tuna to the boat. During this eating frenzy, the Japanese fishermen used the barbless hooks on the short bamboo poles to catch the tuna. After snagging a bite, the men quickly snapped their wrists back, and soon there was a pile of fish in back of them on the deck. Heavier tuna required the efforts of two to three men, who combined poles on a single line. Soon the Japanese fishermen were dominating albacore fishing.

Wood was one cannery leader who cultivated good relations with the Japanese. The canneries went through times of great consolidation and mergers during lean years, and as a result, many of the people like Wood were connected to multiple canneries. For instance, Wood left the California Fish Company in 1912 to start a new cannery in San Pedro with Paul Eachus, the uncle of Mildred Maxson Onsolen. Their enterprise, California Tunny Canning Company, was later bought by Van Camp Sea Food Company, which was founded by pork-and-beans canner Frank Van Camp. Wood stayed on as manager for a couple of years before becoming involved with another cannery. There were enough Japanese fishermen and cannery workers to form a "Japanese camp" on Timm's Point by 1912. Eventually these workers, the equipment, and even the housing—all now under Van Camp—were relocated to the new operation in Fish Harbor.

The creation of Terminal Island's Fish Harbor marked a dynamic intersection of city government, commerce, transnational ethnic community, and world politics. Its designers, the harbor commissioners, could not have predicted the complex manifestations of their early decisions. In March 1912, the commissioners engaged the services of E.P. Goodrich, an eminent engineer who had laid out the terminals in Brooklyn, New York, to develop a plan for harbor development. The Harbor Department had no engineering staff of its own and relied on the Board of Public Works and the City Engineer for engineering services, a situation that often resulted in conflicts. The Board of Public Works supported the hiring of Goodrich, who arrived in April and spent time touring the harbor, promising a plan for

The landscape of Fish Harbor evolved as landfill was added to create space for canneries. October 2, 1917.

a great harbor. A month later, Goodrich had approved plans for the construction of a fishing harbor to the east of the main channel.

Construction of Goodrich's plan for Fish Harbor began in 1915. His harbor plan proposed to segregate the fishing industry from the shipping industry so that the "maloderant [sic] residue of the packing end of the industry will thereby be carried seaward on the prevalent breezes." The first stage of the project was the building of a 1630-by-30-foot wharf. With a rock jetty, and dredging and landfilling to follow, sixty-five acres of land would be reclaimed, as well as forty acres of

Terminal Island: Lost Communities on America's Edge

anchorage to accommodate boats. "There is every indication that there will be considerable demand for sites on this area," the Harbor Department's annual report stated in 1915.

In his doctoral dissertation, Kanshi Stanley Yamashita, a native of Terminal Island, artfully describes the physical change that his boyhood home would undergo before a large number of Japanese would move in. "Along the ocean side of Terminal Island, a one-half mile square harbor was built. Small breakwaters at the southern entrance provided the necessary protection from storm waves. Along the northern side of the main wharf were eight canneries, each with their own finger piers alongside of which the fishing vessels tied up to unload their catch." Other than these fishing vessels, the other ways to access Fish Harbor before World War II

The construction of San Pedro Packing Company in November of 1917; today, Berth 262.

were by ferries (first privately owned and later a municipal ferry), rail, a drawbridge for cars near the Ford plant in Wilmington, and the bridge from Long Beach.

California Fish Company, the original Terminal Island cannery, was the first one to relocate to Fish Harbor in 1917 under the name of Southern California Fish Company. Its new site was on the far east side of the wharf along Ocean Avenue. Wilbur Wood and a group of canners opened the second cannery at Fish Harbor, the International Packing Company. Others followed, including Neilson and Kittle, Seacoast Cannery, American Tuna Company, French Sardine Company (which

An interior shot of a tuna cannery on Terminal Island. The long dorsal fins of these tuna indicate they are albacore (*Thunnus alalunga*). The average length of the albacore tuna is about 3.5 feet, and the fish can weigh as much as 130 pounds.

later became Starkist), Franco-Italian Cannery, and California Seafood Company. Another early cannery was White Star Canning Company, operated by the two brothers Warren J. and Walter King, which had taken over the California Fish Company's original site when it was destroyed in a fire in 1915. White Star had coined and even trademarked the phrase "Chicken of the Sea," which continues to appear on cans, even as various canneries went bankrupt and merged in the tumultuous tuna market.

Generations of San Pedro residents will attest to the fact that Goodrich's prediction about the odor being carried seaward was decidedly incorrect. But to many, the smell of fish was the smell of money.

A January 23, 1918, report by the harbor's traffic manager Clarence H. Matson to Los Angeles Mayor Frederick T. Woodman verified the immediate success of Fish Harbor. In an area that once supported only one cannery, six canneries had taken residence, with possibly more on their way. "These canneries will give employment to thousands of persons, and since the development of sardine canning, they operate practically the entire year," wrote Matson. "They will also augment the food supply, which is an important item in the present war emergency." More than one hundred bungalows were being built for fishermen, with an area reserved for cannery worker housing.

"All this has been done on an area which two years ago was under water," he continued. "This area is yielding the city an annual [rental] income of more than twenty-seven thousand dollars, exclusive of wharfage on fish."

Requests for permits to create new fishermen's barracks at Fish Harbor came in fast and furiously. Van Camp Sea Food came in for an order first. Then White Star Canning Company wanted 2,784 square feet, followed by another request for 4,408 square feet, and then 1,276 square feet. Not to be outdone, Van Camp Sea Food asked for 4,000 additional square feet of barracks, and then 10,000 and 15,000. More canneries followed, including North American Tuna Canning Company with its request for 5,270.

As Van Camp already had a reputation for hiring Japanese fishermen and cannery workers, it was not a surprise that other Japanese decided to take a chance on this newly created community. Soon Japanese from the same villages in Japan told their friends and extended family about Fish Harbor. The immigrants began to move in by the hundreds.

The development and construction of Fish Harbor apparently had its ups and downs. Southern California Fish Company filed a complaint on December 26, 1916. "We wish to offer a vigorous protest against the way Fish Harbor is being taken care of," wrote the cannery's representative, W.I. Turck. "The entrance to the harbor is very unsafe whenever there is a heavy southeast wind. Outside of that, the rock jetty which was supposed to be finished a month ago, has not been taken care of, and in front of our cannery, the sand has filled in so that it is getting too shallow for boats to come up close to the dock at the lower end."

In addition to the canneries, a wholesale fish market building and wharf were completed across the main channel from Terminal Island in San Pedro on land that was also under the Harbor Department. The City of Los Angeles Wholesale Fish Market was 305 feet long and 60 feet wide, costing thirty-five thousand dollars. It was getting heavy use from the beginning, prompting a warning from the county health commissioner, Dr. Luther M. Powers, who was particularly concerned about the drainage and protection of the structure. "The offal and blood and the washings of the floor will by absorption create offensive conditions with wood as it is now constructed," Powers wrote on December 29, 1916.

A number of Japanese-owned fresh fish markets moved into this new building in San Pedro. Among these were Central Fish Company, represented by K.B. Masmoto, involved in the California Tuna Supply Company, and Pacific Coast Fish Company, established by Seiichi Nakahara, described as a "fish merchant entrepreneur" and the father of Mary Nakahara, later known as civil rights activist Yuri Kochiyama.

Central Fish Company soon joined forces with the Pacific Coast Fish Company in requesting the harbor commissioners make changes to the north end of the harbor to ease access for their fishermen. In their letter, they explained that "when . . . plentiful," the two companies pulled in 150 tons of fish a month.

The issue of race and ethnicity surfaced in subtle ways. For example, in November 1917, the secretary of White Star Canning Company, unhappy with a delay in a permit to produce chicken meal from fish, wrote a letter to harbor commissioners: "We are American born and we cannot understand how a Japanese cannery within a short distance of us received their permit, as well as another cannery in San Pedro (or Los Angeles) and other canneries within a few hundred feet of us, when we do not."

Despite the underlying tension from competing

California Fish Company, the first cannery on Terminal Island, in its original location in East San Pedro. 1907.

An early Japanese business on Fish Harbor, Yamamoto boat landing. A man with laundry hanging from a clothesline is photographed next to a boatbuilding-and-repair shop established by S. Yamamoto in 1917 on leased tidelands next to the wharf. 1918.

enterprises, the Harbor Commission nonetheless continued to issue permits to Japanese businessmen and representatives. By December 1917, paying monthly rent on harbor-related property included three fisherman's supply stores, Y. Hama (1,060 square feet), U. Tanaka (5,000), and T. Teniji/Taniji (2,083). Also leasing land were S. Yamamoto for a 3,100-square-foot boat building and repair shop and K. Nakamura for a 4,000-square-foot "fishermen's house," or more officially, the Southern California Japanese Fishermen's Association. From month to month, the names changed slightly, reflecting the unstable and unpredictable nature of the fishing business.

The Decline of Resort Living on Terminal Island

The heyday of Terminal Island as a resort began in the 1890s and peaked shortly after the year 1900. Beginning about 1906, a slow but steady decline ensued. Ocean Park and Venice Beach started to gain popularity about 1904. These areas, along with Long Beach, became increasingly popular as Terminal Island faced the end of its resort era. By 1910, many of the homes built by the original owners from Los Angeles had been resold, as the wealthy patrons looked to other resorts for recreation and relaxation.

A fire in June of 1911 destroyed four buildings in the community of Terminal, including two boarding houses that were run by Mrs. Samples, one in the old Yacht Club building and the other called the Caledonia. The grocery store and the post office were also lost, including its cash, stamps, and all the mail. In 1915, vandals attempting to steal the chandelier from the empty Brighton Beach Hotel started another fire, and the hotel burned to the ground.

Many summer residents abandoned Terminal Island, selling their homes as the dredged material from the inner harbor was being discharged onto the beach. In the words of Jackson Graves, whose home was on Ocean between Ninth and Eleventh Streets, the City of Los Angeles "absolutely ruined it as a pleasure resort." Graves watched the value of his oceanfront property decline:

> The water used to come within twenty-five feet of the house; now it was at least a mile to the water. When Terminal Island was laid out, a twenty-five-foot strip was left in front of the lots as a street and so marked on the map. If this street had not been there, the accretion formed by the sand pumped from the inner harbor would have belonged to the lot owners, but as the city owned the street, the accretion went to it.

Pacific Wharf and Storage Company secured a lease in 1906 at the time that the City of Long Beach had annexed East San Pedro. It was the first multipurpose cargo operation on Terminal Island that could handle any type of cargo that could pass over a wharf, including lumber. 1915.

Left: Fishermen hang their nets on racks while they mend them. This type of image impressed a young Scott O'Dell, who used similar imagery in his 1960 children's book, *Island of the Blue Dolphins.*

Long after the majority of the squatters had left East San Pedro, some open areas remained with houseboats. San Pedro historian William Olesen called this area Slaraffenland meaning the "land of milk and honey" or more appropriately in this case, the "land of idle living."

Graves sold his house to Mae and Frank Kiff for 25 percent of what it originally cost him. Some of the Terminal Island homeowners were not going to go without a fight, however. Judge Waldo York, Frank J. Thomas, C.A. Sumner, Sumner P. Hunt, C.B. Boothe, and Mrs. J.R. Pinkham converged at a Board of Public Works meeting to protest the beach filling on June 25, 1911. The homeowners suggested that the board consider alternative locations for dumping the material from the Army Corps of Engineers' dredging of the inner harbor turning basin.

The board puzzled for a moment, then directed their contractor to consider alternatives. Two days later, at a subsequent Board of Public Works meeting, Thomas threatened to seek an injunction to stop the deposit of material on the beach. Meanwhile, Board President General Adna Romanza Chaffee stood firm on his refusal to revoke the city's permission for the disposal of dredged material on the beach. Public works board members commented that with industry growing very fast in the harbor area, it was only a matter of time before the cottages would disappear.

One month later, however, the ongoing dredging operation was moved to another location in the harbor due to a softening of the board's position. The reprieve was short-lived. While there was some effort to find a permanent alternative in the inner harbor to dispose of the dredged material rather than the Terminal Island beaches, the Harbor Commission informed the army that it was not prepared to build a retaining wall and provide such a location. Therefore, on July 31, 1912, Lieutenant Colonel McKinstry notified the harbor commissioners that he would continue to pump dredged material across Terminal Island to the ocean side.

Not only did the residents of Terminal Island have to deal with losing their beach, the railroad also made it more difficult for people who lived on the island by changing its passenger train schedule. This was a subtle way to make living on the island inconvenient. Charles Dwight Willard described it as the railroad playing a purposeful game of "freeze out," treating the residents "as shabbily as they can." In 1907, Willard made plans to leave the island and move to Pasadena.

The only "ocean" that remained for the wealthy homeowners was their street address, Ocean Avenue. Only a world war could slow the further assaults on the recreational communities on Terminal Island. Federal appropriations for the channel-widening work were not available during wartime. And World War I gave Deadman's Island a few more years of productive existence in the harbor.

The bohemian artist colony of East San Pedro was gone, but the picturesque environment of Fish Harbor attracted the next generation of artists. Loren Barton, the grandniece of Clara Barton, founder of the Red Cross, became well-known for her etchings of Fish Harbor, and the *Los Angeles Times* covered her success and art showing beginning in 1919. Bennett Scott, who was station master for the San Pedro, Los Angeles and Salt Lake Railroad moved his family to the island. In 1898, his son O'Dell Gabriel Scott was born on the island and, like most children, spent his youth at the beach watching the fishermen work their nets and erect racks on the beach to dry abalone. Decades later in 1960, under the name Scott O'Dell, he incorporated images from his youthful days on the island into a children's book called *Island of the Blue Dolphins*.

Loren Barton became known for her etchings done of the Fish Harbor area in the late 1920s and 1930s. Barton started her artistic career designing book plates for the Red Cross. The plates were sent to famous people to sign and then sold in the Los Angeles Red Cross shop. Barton was a grandniece of artist and nurse Clara Barton, who founded the American Red Cross.

An early souvenir of Los Angeles Harbor, commemorating the new breakwater, which was completed in 1911. This sterling teaspoon was made by Mrs. E.C. Fleming, who had a jewelry business in Los Angeles on West Sixth Street in 1914 and relocated to 315 West Third Street in 1920.

A Last Gasp for Brighton

In 1917, Dr. H.H. Stone, an Arizona mining man, formed a corporation with Venice Pier promoter Ernest Pickering and leased a strip of land two thousand feet long and nine hundred feet wide from the Los Angeles Harbor Department. By this time, however, the bulkhead built to protect the homes had been partially washed away, and the edge of the water was no longer near. The plan was to develop a tent city and have two large buildings for amusements along with a large bathhouse and dancing pavilion.

But Brighton Beach would never return to its halcyon days.

Locals would make longer treks across the new land created by the city to reach what remained of the beach, a sandy shore that was managed by the city's playground and recreation committee. Once the construction of the middle breakwater was finished in 1937, Terminal Island and most of Long Beach Harbor were cut off from the ocean waves. There was no turning back to the resort days of surf and sun.

Yet many of the original summer homes were still inhabited by people employed on the island until World War II, often still carrying the original house names. Most of the East San Pedro squatters were removed when the city evicted them to widen the channel in 1912, but some managed to remain, mostly old-timers who liked the simple life, tucked away in any nook and cranny that escaped development. Houseboats began to

Terminal Island resident Arnold Esparza recalls that in the 1930s, one could buy a hamburger for five cents at the remaining concessions.

L.A.H.D.
PHOTO

Salt Lake R.

Houseboats with squatters could still be found on the north side of Terminal Island in the 1930s. This image, from the Port of Los Angeles Archives, was referenced as a "Legal Photograph" and was dated August 8, 1935. When squatter removal was under consideration, documentation photos of properties were carefully labeled.

Opposite: Aerial photograph of Terminal Island homes on Seaside Avenue, between Harris Street and Genoa Street, at Brighton Beach. The south-facing homes were formerly beachfront sites, but lost their ocean access in the late 1910s when fill from dredging increased the size of the island, relocating the beach about a mile south. Borden House is visible on the far right, and the Brighton Beach Hotel, destroyed in 1915, would have occupied the block to the left of it. October 25, 1929.

appear, and a "subdivision" known as "Tin Can Alley" sprang up near the ferry landing on the island.

Another eviction proceeding by the Harbor Department in May 1935 removed the forty-eight residents of a houseboat colony on the island, most occupied by elderly men who sailed "when men were iron and boats were wood." One of these elderly men, Captain Charles Christensen, had sailed into the harbor in 1897 on a three-masted schooner named *Malancton*. He had been evicted in 1912 from East San Pedro along with Charles Lummis and the other squatters. Christensen had been a squatter nearly all his life, but with no place on the mainland to go, he probably made his boat as seaworthy as possible, and set out to find another tucked-away place where he could tie up. His name did not appear in the 1940 census records.

This photograph, looking south on Deadman's Island from the northeast corner of the island, is the last taken by the U.S. Army Corps of Engineers, prior to the demolition of the island. March 21, 1927.

Opposite: The San Francisco Bridge Company undertook the demolition of Deadman's Island under contract to the U.S. Army Corps of Engineers. The work took eighteen months and was completed on May 28, 1929, at a cost of $1,187,000.

Terminal Island: Lost Communities of Los Angeles Harbor

The Fate of Deadman's Island

From a mariner's marker to a burial ground to a scientific and geological wonder that yielded more than three hundred species of fossils, Deadman's Island evolved and eroded. By the time Martha Burton Williamson visited there in 1896, the island's summit was close to a hundred feet by fifty feet, although she said it had been twice that size in an unspecified earlier time. Only five of the graves were visible then. As far back as 1891, there were efforts to save the island. Frequent exploring by the resort visitors hastened the erosion. Treasure seekers looking for Spanish gold left holes over its entire surface. They found nothing, only the bones of the souls buried there. The *San Pedro Times* suggested a monument be placed on top of the island in memory of those in random graves, urging the preservation of what remained of the island.

In June of 1901, the *Los Angeles Times* reported several instances of the ground caving in, exposing coffins and skeletons that slid down the side of the island. By then, the remains of marines who had been buried there had already been disinterred and relocated to Los Angeles. At the start of World War I, the navy set mines at the entrance to the harbor, and Deadman's Island became a Harbor Defense Post of Fort MacArthur. A gun emplacement called Battery Lodor, consisting of four three-inch guns mounted along with several searchlights, was constructed on the island to provide support to the minefield. The battery was deactivated in 1927.

It was during these war years that the island served as a film location. Harold Lloyd, an actor and producer

The demolition of Deadman's Island was completed eight months ahead of schedule and entailed the removal of 2,075,000 cubic yards of earth, blasting 300,000 cubic yards of rock, widening the channel from 545 to 1,000 feet, and deepening the channel to thirty-seven feet. The contract also entailed building 7,000 linear feet of rock dike to enclose a sixty-two-acre piece of land known as Reservation Point.

Opposite: Deadman's Island was considered of such historical importance that the Southwest Museum received permission to station scientist Charles Amsden on site throughout the demolition period. Amsden sifted through tons of material seeking bones, fossils and other treasures.

of silent comedies, filmed *Lonesome Luke's Wild Women* on the island. In that 1916 movie, Lloyd was shipwrecked on Deadman's Island, and he encountered a sheik and his harem. The island also served as backdrop for Lloyd's *All Aboard* (1917), and Charlie Chaplin's two films, *Shanghaied* (1915) and *A Day's Pleasure* (1919).

Legend has it that after World War I, rumrunners used the island as a convenient hideout for contraband liquor. Eventually, portions of the island were removed by dynamite, exposing more remains of the long dead. The last blast, on June 1, 1929, removed all visible traces of the island above the waterline. What remained below was incorporated into the ninety-two-acre peninsula that became Reservation Point, which was used for a quarantine station and a U.S. Immigration Station. The Federal Correctional Institution at Terminal Island and the U.S. Coast Guard Station have been located at Reservation Point since 1938 and 1939, respectively.

The *Los Angeles Times* provided a fitting epitaph for Deadman's and Rattlesnake Islands on May 27, 1928:

Aye, a sad fate mates, is that of the Lost Isles of San Pedro, but the soul of modern mariners will perchance be saved the sin of sundry deep-sea oaths emitted when the spectral shape of Deadman's Island would loom up in fog on the starboard quarter so suddenly that shipwreck on its ghastly rocks was averted only by a hair's breath. Yet the lover of California will pensively sigh over the Lost Islands, La Isla del Muerto, La Isla de La Culebra de Cascabel and mournful Mormon Island. But even ancient isles must give precedence to the sea-paths of progress, in this age of fierce competition between rival harbors leaving behind these vanished relics naught but romantic or dramatic memories of their former glory and possibly a bronze tablet bearing the pathetic and plaintive epitaph so suitable for all earthly things or persons: Gone but not forgotten.

Terminal Island, circa 1900

SAN PEDRO

LONG BEACH

TOWN of TERMINAL

BRIGHTON BEACH

Pavilion
Bathhouse
Terminal Pier

School on Terminal Island

Brighton Beach Pier

Town of East San Pedro

Single Works

Squatter Shacks

Sea Pansy Bay

Bathhouse

Double Works

East Jetty

Deadman's Island

These maps were compiled from historic documents in the Los Angeles Harbor Department Historical Archives and show the development of Terminal Island over four decades. Sediment from dredging the harbor channels dramatically transformed the geography of the island. As the island's acreage increased, beaches, pleasure piers, and rugged coastlines were replaced by harbors, canneries, and airfields. Community and industry existed side by side for more than forty years. But World War II brought an end to the island's community. The federal prison, which still stands, would be the last stop on Terminal Island for many residents on their way to relocation and internment.

Terminal Island, circa 1940

SAN PEDRO

LONG BEACH

BADGER

DOCK STREET

MORMON ST.

FERRY ST.

OCEAN AVENUE

SEASIDE AVENUE

BRIGHTON BEACH

TOWN of TERMINAL

Reeves Field Airport

SO. SEASIDE AVENUE

Ferry Landing

Ferry Landing

TERMINAL WAY

CANNERY STREET

BARRACUDA STREET

Fish Canneries

Municipal Fish Market

SO. SEASIDE AVENUE

Fish Harbor

Federal Prison

N

During the week of the full moon, fishermen stayed away from their boats and instead repaired their nets. Terminal Way, where the fishermen often spread their nets to dry, was one of the first paved streets in Fish Harbor.

The Rise of the Japanese Fishing Village

From weekend retreat and bohemian playground, the newly created Fish Harbor would grow to be a thriving community of more than two thousand residents with an expanded grammar school dedicated to the education of the second-generation children, the Nisei. Circa 1925.

The Japanese came to what would later be called Terminal Island, or Taminaru, from various parts of the American West. They were mostly men who had crossed the Pacific Ocean at the turn of the twentieth century, landing in the territory of Hawaii and on the western coasts of Canada, Mexico, California, and Washington State. Those who arrived legally needed to prove that they had at least fifty dollars in their pockets. Some had been called over (*yobiyose*) by relatives who had already arrived. A few were intellectuals enamored with the West and the concept of democracy. Many were *dekasegi*, sojourners who did not intend to stay but return to Japan with their fortune in hand.

At the end of the 1800s, Japan was in the height of a modernization campaign under the new Meiji government, which had stripped power from the samurai as well as enforced high land taxes and used artificial measures to keep agricultural prices low. Families in the countryside suffered economically and looked overseas for work. Labor contractors established themselves in the territory of Hawaii and throughout the Pacific West Coast, including Latin America. Chinese laborers had

worked the railroads and mines during the California Gold Rush and segued into domestic work and farming, but were now pariahs to xenophobic leaders. The 1882 Chinese Exclusion Act and other legislation that followed effectively shut down the flow of these men from overseas and prevented the growth of the Chinese American population. But grapes, strawberries, and peaches still needed to be harvested, lettuce and tomatoes planted. The Japanese replaced the Chinese as low-wage workers on farms and railroads.

A history book published in 1937, *San Pidoro Doho Hattenroku* (*Record of the Development of the Japanese in San Pedro*), named three Japanese houseboys working and living on the island in 1899, but none were listed in early East San Pedro or Terminal Island directories, or even the U.S. Census in the 1910s or 1920s. They probably did not stay and establish families on the island. Rather than the wealthy households on the beach, other elements brought more long-term Japanese immigrant settlers, known as *Issei*, to East San Pedro. One was the namesake of Terminal Island, the railway. The other, the sea.

Huntington's Port Los Angeles

As recorded in the prodigious body of historic research and writing by Ernest Marquez, railroad magnate Collis P. Huntington had fought for a seaport to be established in Santa Monica, thirty miles northwest of San Pedro, and had even spearheaded the construction of the 4,720-foot wooden Long Wharf in anticipation of success. Eventually Congress defied the Southern Pacific's strong-arm tactics, and San Pedro became the official deepwater port of Los Angeles in 1897.

A vibrant Japanese fishing village remained just north of the Long Wharf. According to a Japanese-language biographical listing unearthed by Marquez, Hatsuji Sano was the first Japanese immigrant to settle there. A native of Chiba Prefecture, Sano first tried his hand at abalone harvesting in Mendocino in Northern California before moving south to attempt fishing in Santa Monica in 1899. He and other Japanese leased land from Southern Pacific Railroad, and over the next ten years, the village attracted three hundred permanent residents despite the "persecution by white fishermen" noted in his biographical profile in *Zaibei Nihonjinshi* (*The History of Japanese in America*). Sano went on to establish a beach inn for Japanese vacationers; silent-film heartthrob Sessue Hayakawa even filmed in the location, which was so reminiscent of Japan that it could stand in for the archipelago. Unfortunately, in 1916 a fire destroyed the village, and the city prohibited any rebuilding plans because sewers that accommodated the residents were polluting the ocean. As a result, the fishermen sought another seaside home. For some, that place was Terminal Island.

Postcard featuring Japanese immigrants using wooden racks to dry abalone at White Point. These pioneers eventually made their way to Terminal Island. Circa 1900.

Pioneers

Written accounts, both in English and Japanese, based on interviews conducted in the 1930s, tell of either twelve or fifteen pioneering men who had reportedly worked for Southern Pacific Railroad in San Pedro at the turn of the twentieth century before turning their attention to abalone in White Point, a coastal area west of Point Fermin. These men had surnames such as Hatashita, Tatsumi, Tani, Uragami, Koji, Hanamura, Ryono, Higashi, Kobata, Seko, Kitsu, and Mori. Although many of these families have long-standing ties to Terminal Island, a search of immigration records and the *Rafu Shimpo* 1917 directory failed to support a consistent time period to make generalizations about all of these men.

However, information about at least two of them seems to verify their early presence on Terminal Island. One pioneer was Kobei Tatsumi. According to *San Pidoro Doho Hattenroku*, San Pedro was his actual destination when he arrived in the United States in 1899. His intention was to go to school in America, but he soon became involved in the dried abalone business with several other Japanese men on White Point. However, in 1905, California state laws, targeting Chinese and Japanese, limited abalone harvesting to certain seasons before completely barring their collection five years later.

Animosity toward Japanese fishermen actually was even more fervent in other Pacific Coast states and even in Canada. "Now Is Time to Oust Japs" was a message included in the Seattle-based trade magazine *Pacific Fisherman*'s November 1, 1911, article, "Japanese Said to Control British Columbia Fisheries," which accused Japanese immigrants of colluding with each other to advance the interests of their ethnic community at the expense of "the white men in this industry." Other immigrant groups historically involved in fishing on the Pacific West Coast were Italians, Portuguese, and Yugoslavians. Those who had come from island fishing villages off the Dalmatian coast of Croatia were also referred to as Austrian, Slovenian, Yugoslav, Slav, or Jugo-Slav.

According to the 1910 Census, only about 880 Chinese and Japanese were working in the continental United States as fishermen and oystermen. By this time, America's national Japanese population had grown to 72,157, with an additional 79,675 just in the territory of Hawaii. More than 40,000 lived in California.

While certain California politicians definitely attempted to realize their anti-Japanese agendas, their complete success was thwarted by commercial interests. By 1915, both Oregon and the state of Washington had virtually banned "aliens ineligible for citizenship," namely the Chinese and Japanese, from fishing, but California had not. Businessmen saw that there was money to be made with the help of Japanese expertise—they had no time for debates over racial purity or separatism.

Fishing in the state was concentrated in three areas—San Pedro, San Diego, and Monterey. Sardines were the primary catch, but everything changed with the canners' demand for albacore. As discussed earlier in chapter 3, the Japanese fishermen's skill with their bamboo poles and barbless hooks gave them an extraordinary advantage. By 1914, 150 Japanese immigrants, or Issei, were fishing in San Pedro, manning fifty out of 131 tuna boats.

The former abalone diver Kobei Tatsumi was one of the Japanese immigrants who rode the wave of sardine and albacore fishing. After engaging in a dried abalone business in White Point, he moved to East San Pedro and became involved in two fish-related enterprises, North American and Los Angeles Sea Food Packing, the latter being managed by J. Nishiha [sic]. According to Standard Corporation Service, seven men were directors of California Tuna Supply Company, which was incorporated in November 1914 with $100,000 of capital. The directors included K.B. Masmoto, V. Suzuki, O. Yamamoto, K. Uyemura, R. Tatsumi [sic], K. Egawa, and T. Kojima. (On many legal documents of the early 1900s, misspellings of Japanese names were relatively common. On the other hand, Masmoto is the correct spelling of a name that has often been changed to Masumoto.)

Despite this great infusion of capital, the enterprises experienced a great setback during World War I, as the U.S. government temporarily confiscated Japanese-operated boats for so-called security reasons. Remnants of Tatsumi's entrepreneurial efforts apparently survived, as former Fish Harbor residents recalled a pioneering *"Nihonjin,"* or Japanese cannery, believed to be the same Los Angeles Sea Food mentioned above, which was later absorbed by Sea Pride Packing Corporation. Tatsumi eventually shifted gears and, while raising a family in Fish Harbor, worked at White Point Sulphur Springs, a hot springs resort with a two-story, fifty-room hotel operated by the Tagami family.

Another pioneer was Jinshiro Tani. Like Tatsumi, he was from the seaside town of Shimosato in Wakayama Prefecture. According to *San Pidoro Doho Hattenroku*, he came to America in 1897 and worked for the railroad in Seattle before doing farm work in the California agricultural towns of Watsonville in the Salinas Valley and Fresno in the San Joaquin. He then was employed by the Santa Fe Railway in Los Angeles County for a decade. Apparently known as "Jumbo" among non-Japanese fishermen, Tani committed the rest of his life to the sea—first in abalone harvesting at White Point, presumably alongside Tatsumi, and then manning his own fishing boats (*Western, Standard,* and *Standard II*) in East San Pedro.

Fish Harbor had yet to be created during these Japanese settlers' first appearance, so it's not known exactly where they lived initially, although some anecdotal reports say that early pioneers created shelters out of old canvases and overturned abandoned boats. Writing one of the first English-language academic papers on Terminal Island, Kanichi Kawasaki claimed that the Japanese settlers drove lumber piles on the shore of a sandy beach one hundred yards in width and built twenty houses on stilts with room for boats to be tied underneath the structures. He identified the area as East San Pedro, but it was most likely across the main channel in *San Pidoro/Sankou* (San Pedro). Early Issei settled in other places such as *Nagahama* (Long Beach) and *Wiruminton* (Wilmington).

The prejudice that Tatsumi and other men experienced in the fishing industry reflected the pulse of the

Looking north from Deadman's Island to the area that would be filled in to create Fish Harbor. 1909.

nation regarding the expanding Japanese population in the United States. Anti-Asian legislators were constantly at work devising bills that would restrict Chinese and Japanese economic development, yet that would not be challenged in courts for being unconstitutional.

As a result, instead of a specific ethnicity, the term "aliens ineligible for citizenship" was used in anti-Asian land laws from 1913. In 1790, Congress had established that only a "free white person" was eligible for naturalization; thus, a foreigner of Asian descent would, in most cases, fall under this category of "aliens ineligible for citizenship." Remarkably, this general ban on Asian immigrants becoming citizens remained in effect until the McCarran-Walter Act passed in 1952.

In addition to these barriers to citizenship, it was increasingly difficult for Japanese to enter the country. First, labor migration from Japan to the U.S. territory of Hawaii was closed in 1907, immediately followed by a face-saving Gentlemen's Agreement in which Japan tacitly agreed not to issue passports to laborers who wanted to go to the continental United States. There were, however, exceptions—specifically parents, wives, and children. As the geography of Terminal Island would literally change over the next decade, so would the Japanese community—from bachelor fishermen to families.

Women Come to Fish Harbor

As businesses grew, so did the families of Issei. Women from Japan were making their way to Hawaii and the Pacific West Coast as picture brides, a continuation of the traditional Japanese marital practice in which a *baishakunin* or *nakodo*, a matchmaker or go-between, recommended couplings to families. Its name derived from the exchange of photographs across the ocean, the concept of picture-bride marriages is often thought of as a union between complete strangers, but more often than not, family friends were involved in the matchmaking.

At age seventeen, one Wakayama woman was approached by a *nakodo* to marry an Issei fisherman on Terminal Island. He was first described as being twenty-five years of age, but prior to the wedding she discovered he was actually ten years older. Yet, the young woman, excited about coming to America, agreed to the nuptials and married him the following year.

In most transnational marriages of that era, the picture bride would not meet her husband until she arrived in a foreign port. Fumi Yoshida traveled to San Francisco with her married name, Fumi Izumi, on her passport even though she had not been formally married in a ceremony. After going through Angel Island immigration station, she was picked up by her husband, Kuichi Izumi, who made sure that they were officially married in the United States the same day.

The women who came to Terminal Island would discover a culturally comforting yet physically taxing life. When Orie Mio first came to the island with her fisherman husband as an eighteen-year-old, she spent seven years washing and mending clothes for him and his crew members. Then, upon entering the restaurant business, Orie, who would have four children, found herself working until midnight and then washing diapers on a washboard at one o'clock in the morning. During sardine season, she slept only a couple of hours to prepare for a six o'clock opening.

"Many times, my legs were so swollen that I could barely climb the stairs to our living quarters situated above the restaurant," Orie stated in an oral history

Newlyweds Kuichi, seated, and Fumi Izumi, in their wedding photo. 1915.

Orie Mio, second from left, after arriving on Terminal Island at age eighteen, became a mother to four children and helped her husband open two cafés. Her family and friends stand in front of the first Mio Café, located at 777 Tuna Street. Circa 1928.

Orie Mio, in apron, with her friend, Tamae Yamamoto. Circa 1940. Many immigrant women described Fish Harbor as "home away from home."

Southern California Japanese Fishermen's Association

While Japanese-operated businesses multiplied on Fish Harbor, three early structures—a grammar school, a Baptist mission, and finally a fishermen's hall, the latter actually spearheaded by the Japanese community—signified that this ethnic population was actually establishing roots here.

Previously published accounts have characterized the Southern California Japanese Fishermen's Association (or *Nanka Nihonjin Gyogyo Kumiai*) as a social club or a resurrection of an informal group based specifically in the San Pedro area. However, recently discovered primary documents suggest that the association, at least in its more official genesis, was intended to play more of a political role.

According to an article written by August Felando and Harold Medina, "The Origins of California's High-Seas Tuna Fleet," the Fishermen's Association included active chapters in both San Pedro and San Diego. While other ethnic fishermen could not replicate the hook-and-line method of fishing that the Japanese excelled in, the canneries began to explore developing more effective nets. The Japanese fishermen went on the offensive, even attempting to negotiate exclusive contracts to supply albacore and ban the use of expensive nets. The association failed in its attempt, but looked to establish a permanent home for its operations.

Cognizant that the organization needed help and influence from the outside mainstream world, the Issei leaders hired a San Pedro man, H.A. Linkletter, to apply for a permit to erect an assembly hall in Fish Harbor. The estimated cost of construction? An impressive five

with the Japanese American National Museum. "I literally pulled one leg up at a time with my hands to climb up the stairs." Despite her schedule, "I did not feel very lonesome because at Terminal Island there were many, many Japanese immigrants and they all spoke my language. So quite frequently, I felt I had not left Japan at all," said Orie Mio.

thousand dollars in 1917.

The hall, located near canneries and 150 fishermen's houses, was completed by the end of January and ready for its grand opening. The association even requested that its members take a loss of their daily income and suspend fishing for three days to prepare for a special event on January 26, 1918. Both the *Rafu Shimpo Japanese Daily News* and the *San Pedro Daily News* covered the dedication. According to the *Rafu*, approximately 1,200 people—both Japanese and "whites," crowded the hall, some even arriving hours before its opening. Notables who made speeches included a Japanese representative from one of the leading canneries, Van Camp, and Japanese Consul General Oyama. A *dohyo*, or sumo mound, was created and featured competing local wrestlers, providing "the most interesting portion of the program," according to an account in the *San Pedro News-Pilot*. Music, plays, and races completed the entertainment, which lasted throughout the evening.

One of the speakers from the Fishermen's Association was its secretary, Kihei Nasu, who spoke about the importance of the relationship between the fishermen and canneries, all in the English language. That day, everything seemed harmonious and celebratory. Within a couple of years, however, the Issei fishermen were fighting for their survival.

Southern California Japanese Fishermen's Association. Circa 1930. Located at 241 Terminal Way, the hall was the largest indoor meeting place in Fish Harbor.

FINEST QUALITY

SEA Glory TUNA

YOUR *BEST* TUNA BUY

SOUTH COAST FISHERIES, INC.
TERMINAL ISLAND, CALIF.

Because Japanese fishermen were masters at catching albacore, the canneries were able to rely on the albacore business to save them when the sardine supply dwindled.

Left: A matchbook featuring a brand of South Coast Fisheries, a Terminal Island cannery located at 821 Ways Street.

Opposite: The Japanese were famous for their hook-and-line fishing technique, in which albacore, caught on a barbless hook, were tossed behind the line of fishermen onto a pile on the deck.

第五章

Fish Harbor was in full operation by 1929, thriving just a decade after it was established. The tall wooden structures, called fish elevators, transported catch from the boats below to canneries like Van Camp. The small, anchored jig boats, seen at left, could be manned by one person, while the purse seiners accommodated as many as a dozen crew members.

Kihei Nasu
Writes to
Congress

"The Pacific fisherman harbors no enmity toward the Japanese. They are a wonderful, bright people, frugal and industrious. But—they are orientals. We are Caucasians. Oil and water will not mix. We do not want them to continue pouring in here any more than they would allow our people to emigrate in large numbers to their country." —MILLER FREEMAN, publisher of the *Pacific Fisherman*, in an August 1908 article he quoted when testifying before the House Committee on Immigration and Naturalization hearings in 1919

"The drudgery and squalor of a fisherman's life has not appealed greatly to the American citizen, and probably never will, hence the ranks must be recruited from our foreign population." —KIHEI NASU, secretary of the Southern California Japanese Fishermen's Association, Terminal Island

On Friday, June 20, 1919, a year before voters would decide whether he would serve another term, Senator James Phelan of San Francisco testified before the House Committee on Immigration and Naturalization in Washington, D.C. The topic was the Japanese in California, and Phelan had much to say. He argued that the Gentlemen's Agreement of 1907–1908 failed to achieve what the Chinese Exclusion Act had effectively done—significantly reduce the population of an unwanted ethnic group.

"We are willing to receive diplomats, scholars, and travelers from Japan on terms of equality, but we do not want her laborers. We admire their industry and cleverness, but for that very reason, being a masterful people, they are more dangerous," he stated. He was most concerned about agriculture—how he felt the Japanese, rather than just being laborers, were seeking to control their farms and crops despite California's 1913 Alien Land Law, which barred land ownership and limited property leases to three years.

He railed against the practice of picture brides and the birth of children on American soil, a new generation referred to as *Nisei*. In an interview he submitted to the committee, he maintained:

The State, therefore, is obliged as a simple matter of self-preservation to prevent the Japanese from absorbing the soil, because the future of the white race, American institutions, and western civilization are put in peril. The Japanese do not assimilate with our people and make a

Kihei Nasu, one of the secretaries of the Southern California Japanese Fishermen's Association, holds his daughter Ikuyo, who was born on Terminal Island. He and his wife, Kiyo, center, had four other children in the United States: from left, Kazuko, Noriko, Mieko, and Kiyoshi. Circa 1922.

homogeneous population, and hence they cannot be naturalized and admitted to citizenship.

Phelan also was concerned about the Japanese access to the sea. He maintained that with the Japan Consul's complicity, boats traveling to San Diego and Los Angeles Harbors were bringing in Japanese stowaways via Mexico. He also made accusations that Japanese fishing boats were participating in these smuggling crimes.

Back on Terminal Island, these attacks did not fall on deaf ears. From its inception, the Southern California Japanese Fishermen's Association seemed to have sharp insight into what kind of political and diplomatic conflicts they would face. They employed savvy, well-educated staff people. One was a Stanford graduate in economics, Hirosaburo Yokozeki, who ably worked with non-Japanese commercial fishing interests.

The other was Kihei Nasu, who came to the United States in 1902 to study at Cornell College, a private liberal arts college in Iowa. According to Yuji Ichioka in his seminal work, *The Issei: The World of the First*

Kihei Nasu's children and their friends pose in the sand of Fish Harbor. Circa 1920. Politicians who successfully introduced anti-Asian legislation specifically mentioned feeling threatened by the growing number of Nisei children who had U.S. citizenship, unlike their parents.

Generation Japanese Immigrants, 1885–1924, the first Japanese immigrants to come to the United States were indigent students or student-laborers. It is not known whether Nasu received financial assistance from his parents or a patron in Japan, but it took him nine years to finally graduate, suggesting that he most likely worked his way through school. Soon after, Nasu relocated to California, married, established a school for Japanese, and served as secretary for the Japanese Agricultural Association of California.

From there, he worked as manager of the Watsonville office for the *Nichibei Shimbun* (Japanese American News), published by Kyutaro Abiko, who advocated for Japanese Americans to settle permanently rather than be temporary "birds of passage."

It is not known why Nasu was recruited to work for the Southern California Japanese Fishermen's Association. He did not seem to have any kind of maritime background or fishing experience. However, his bilingual ability and his association with one of the most powerful Japanese American newspapers, as well as an agricultural group, certainly indicated that he understood how to wield political power in the larger world.

As the Committee on Immigration and Naturalization was holding hearings in California regarding specifically the issue of "Japanese Immigration," Nasu produced a multipage report, which was delivered to Congressman Albert Johnson through a couple of attorneys, H.A. Massey of Los Angeles and E.P. Morey of Washington, D.C.

The report, point by point, refuted Senator Phelan's allegations that Japanese fishermen were attempting to monopolize the American fishing industry.

Nasu alleged that because of the "drudgery" of fishing, only 1 percent engaged in the industry were American born. The remaining 99 percent, however, were not only Japanese, but also Italians, Austrians, and other nationalities. (These figures also included fishermen in other areas of California, including San Diego.) "Of this ninety-nine percent, probably one-third are Japanese," he wrote.

[If] it be true that the American fishermen are being driven from the industry, why blame the thousand Japanese exclusively and omit the other foreigners who constitute two-thirds of the whole industry? If the Japanese, who are one-third of the fishermen, are driving out American fishermen, but do not only not drive out the other foreign fishermen but are actually outnumbered two to one by them? The statement of Senator Phelan seems so illogical that it should fall of its own weight.

There is a very valid reason why the Japanese choose fishing as a means of livelihood, and that is that only agriculture and fishing are open to the Japanese, for the other trades are dominated by trades unions, and no Japanese is eligible to membership in a trade union.

Nasu also made mention of two early types of vessels that were popular for fishing: the purse seiner and hook-and-line boat. The purse seiner enabled fishermen to catch valuable bluefin and yellowfin tuna using expensive nets that encircled fish on the water's surface and then closed around them like a drawstring purse. According to Nasu, the Japanese only owned one of the many purse seiners in the area. Their domain remained the smaller hook-and-line boat, which was used

Canneries and fishing boats along Fish Harbor Wharf. Circa 1925.

Opposite: To be used successfully, expensive nets required the coordination of the crew.

for albacore, sardines, and mackerel. Out of 300 in San Pedro, 195 were owned by Japanese.

With a lack of purse seiners, the Issei fishermen provided catch primarily for canneries. "If the Japanese were trying to monopolize the fresh fish market," Nasu asserted, "would it not be reasonable to suppose they would have more purse seiner boats?"

Both Nasu and the association's legal representative, most likely H.A. Massey, seemed open to appear before the committee in person, but apparently were never called to testify.

Phelan ironically lost his bid for reelection in 1920, yet he still remained active in Democratic Party politics in California. In 1924, his efforts to close the doors to the Japanese were rewarded—the Immigration Act of 1924 was passed, effectively banning any more permanent Japanese residents.

In his lobbying work in California, Nasu apparently saw the writing on the wall. He and his wife, Kiyo, had five children in California, including a daughter who was born on Terminal Island. In the interest of their children, the couple decided to move their large brood to Japan. The entire family boarded S.S. *Anyo Maru*, a cargo ship, to Honolulu, Hawaii, and then transferred to the S.S. *Siberia Maru* bound for Tokyo. Kihei Nasu would never see Fish Harbor again.

Boys in the interethnic Terminal neighborhood enjoy playing harmonica at the local playground. Circa 1940.

Community on the Island

An aerial view of Fish Harbor, June 27, 1935. Leasing land from the Harbor Department, canneries rented housing to their fishermen and line workers. The Japanese fishing village was sandwiched between those canneries, the oil refineries, shipbuilding yards, and train station.

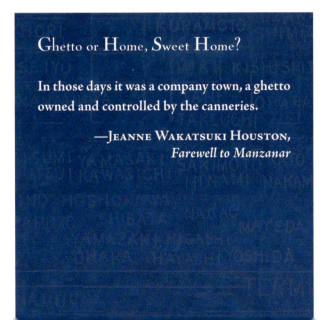

Ghetto or Home, Sweet Home?

In those days it was a company town, a ghetto owned and controlled by the canneries.

—JEANNE WAKATSUKI HOUSTON,
Farewell to Manzanar

Whether Fish Harbor was a ghetto, with lines of nondescript housing with negligible yards and a pungent scent of fish and salt, depended on an individual's point of view. Certainly, short-term visitors from "mainland" cities of Long Beach and Los Angeles sometimes characterized the ethnic enclave in that way.

On the other hand, for nearly three thousand Japanese Americans who lived on Terminal Island at one time—Fish Harbor and Terminal combined—this sand-infested place was certainly "home, sweet home," a

Connecting to the ferry landing, the paved thoroughfare, Terminal Way, was wide enough for fishermen to lay out and repair their nets during their full-moon fishing hiatus.

magical and nostalgic place for some young residents who frolicked in the sea at Brighton Beach in the summers.

"To me, Terminal Island was a fascinating, fantastic dreamland. I call it, 'Enchanted Island,' " explained Charlie Hamasaki, who came to the area when he was a few months old and continued to live there until he was eighteen.

All land in manmade Fish Harbor was owned by the City of Los Angeles under the jurisdiction of the harbor commissioners and thereby needed to be under a lease agreement. Many Issei and their families lived

Community on the Island

Our Next Door *Obasan* (Lady)

Wearing a white apron
She says good morning
She wipes the floor, she wipes the table
She puts on a white hat
Our next door *Obasan* goes outside
Bow-wow, she cleans his home, too
She also gives him a lot of food

—Chizuko Ishii, first grader at
Seisho Gakko Japanese-language school,
in an essay originally written in Japanese

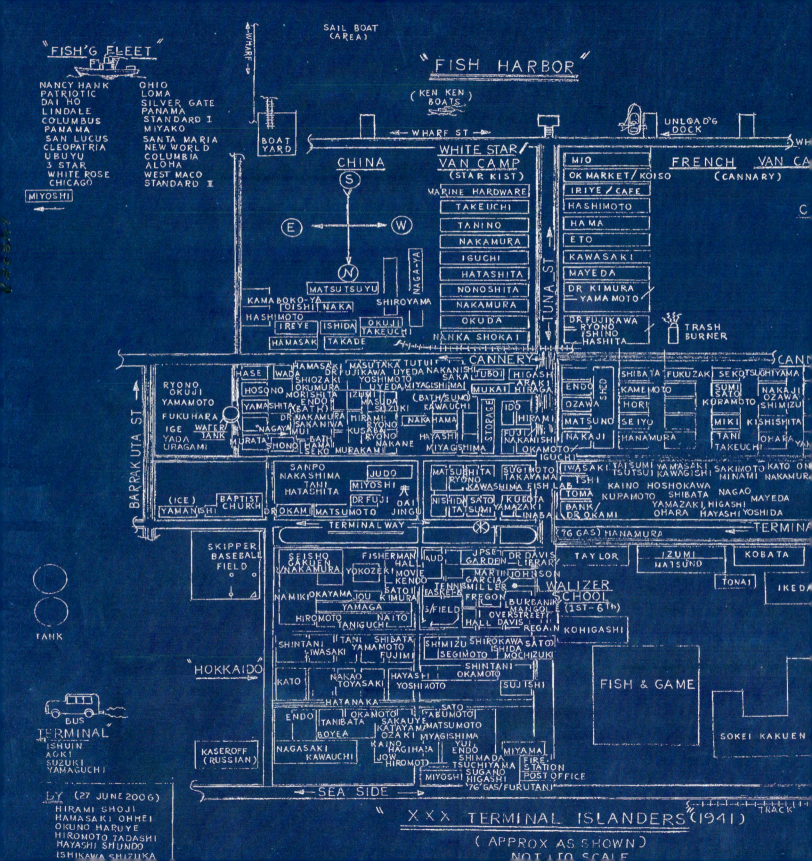

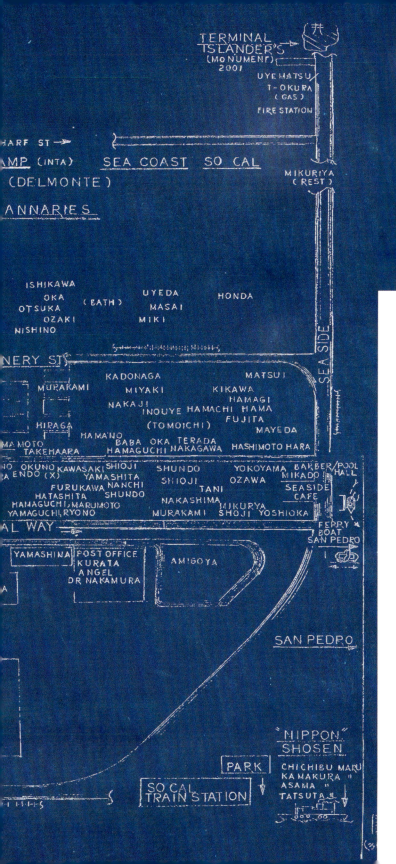

This detailed map of 1941 Fish Harbor was recreated by six former Terminal Islanders in 2006.

Above: **Close quarters were a fact of life in cannery housing. At one time, more than two thousand people lived in a five-square-block area.**

in the housing built by their employers, the canneries, which held the leases. Issei businesses went directly to the harbor department regarding lease approval, changes, and payment.

According to Yamashita, the island's approximately 330 houses were almost identical in size and appearance aside from the *nagaya*, "long houses," designed for multiple occupants. Differences in class—for instance, the family of a large vessel's skipper versus a bachelor crew member or jig-boat operator—were reflected not by house exteriors, but by the interior furnishings.

Rented for six dollars a month, the wood-framed houses typically had a porch, a very small fenced-in yard, and two bedrooms—very tight quarters, especially for large families with more than three children. There was little space between each house. "In fact," stated Mas Tanibata in an oral history interview, "lots of times, we knew what our neighbors were having for dinner. That's how close we were. Whenever they had a family feud,

From left, Iku, Kanshi, and Kei Yamashita were all born on Terminal Island. Circa 1926.

we'd hear the worst of it. We didn't want to be caught dating a girl . . . because it would be the talk of the town."

Bathrooms were usually shared by neighboring families. The *furo*, Japanese bath, was an important feature, big enough to hold at least three people. Children sometimes bathed with their siblings or grandparents. In some households, women were responsible for stoking the fire; in others, teenagers filled the firebox outside the house with hardwood planks discarded by steamships. Lucky families who lived in Del Monte Company housing, which had constructed new housing in 1921 to entice fishermen, had access to an indoor water heater.

As was practiced in Japan and in many Japanese American rural households, bathers first soaped and scrubbed outside of the tub and, once clean, then soaked in the hot water, which was then saved for the next bather that evening.

Fish Harbor was divided by streets named after

Wealthier families had upright pianos in their cannery homes. One storekeeper even had a grand piano in his upstairs apartment.

either fish (Tuna, Albicore [sic], Sardine, Barracuda, Pilchard), the fishing industry (Cannery, Wharf), or the place (Terminal, Seaside). The northern side of Fish Harbor was referred to by the locals as Hokkaido, the most northern prefecture of Japan.

Roy Hideo Yamamoto's family lived in a *nagaya*, "long house," in Hokkaido. Constructed by Yamamoto's carpenter father, Eisaku, this large building was comprised of approximately twelve rooms that housed Roy, his parents, and multiple fishermen. In this multifamily dwelling, Eisaku also had built a three-car garage with an attached carpentry workshop.

"I could look out our kitchen window and see the ships from all over the world dock at the berths on the other side of the railroad tracks," remembered Roy, who foraged through trash barrels in search of postage stamps on envelopes from foreign countries. Also on

Although many Japanese fishermen and cannery workers did not own vehicles, outsiders came to Tuna Street to do business and socialize. 1929.

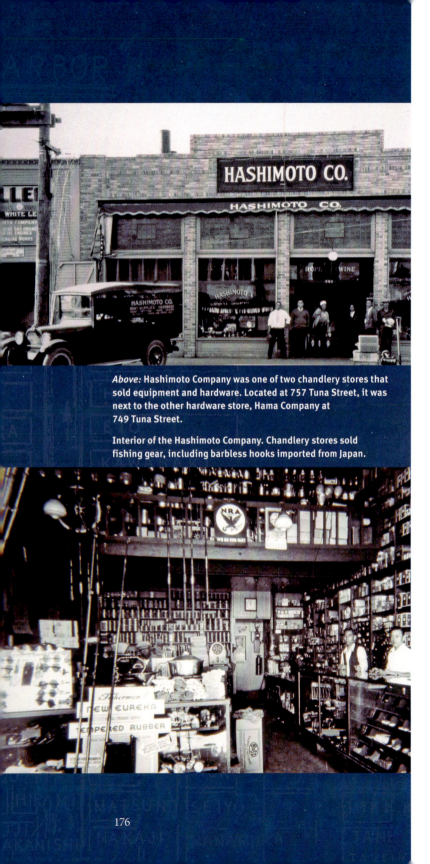

Above: Hashimoto Company was one of two chandlery stores that sold equipment and hardware. Located at 757 Tuna Street, it was next to the other hardware store, Hama Company at 749 Tuna Street.

Interior of the Hashimoto Company. Chandlery stores sold fishing gear, including barbless hooks imported from Japan.

the northern side of Fish Harbor was the Union Pacific train station, the post office, the Fish and Game office, and the Buddhist Japanese school and church, built in the 1930s. Non-Japanese residents tended to live on this side of Fish Harbor.

Sand was ubiquitous. Minoru "Min" Tonai remembered Terminal Island being sandy without many sidewalks. "There were cement roads on Terminal Way and Cannery, [but] I used to walk in that sand all the time." There was so much sand, in fact, that some children went barefoot, saving their parents the cost of buying new shoes.

On the island, there was little need for vehicles. Everything was in walking distance. For instance, at the heart of Fish Harbor was Tuna Street, the main drag that intersected Wharf, Cannery, Terminal Way, Albicore, and Seaside. While the canneries were lined up along Wharf, facing the sea to receive incoming boats full of fish, Tuna was home to a majority of the eateries that served fishermen and cannery workers, including Mio Café (both No. 1 and No. 2) and Butterfly Café, which advertised beer on its storefront window. For local residents, there were two chop suey houses, Showa Low and Tokiwa Low, and Ben Sweet, an ice cream parlor. Jimmy Pool Hall and Tuna Pool Hall provided recreation for men. A grocery store and various other establishments ranging from a photography studio to a beauty shop were scattered on a half dozen streets. Although there was no police station, Fish Harbor supported two fire stations, including one that patrolled the waters. Terminal Island also had its own post office, which was located next to one of the fire stations near Seaside Avenue. News that Terminal Island post office might be consolidated into the San Pedro station in 1933 prompted a successful petition drive among the Terminal Islanders to keep the two separate.

There was not much competition between businesses offering the same products and services. Hama Company and Hashimoto Hardware—both chandlery shops that specialized in items for boats—were adjacent to each other and even connected by a doorway. This open access way made it easy for a fisherman to go next door to the other chandlery shop if he could not find the exact piece of equipment he was looking for.

The grocers often dispensed credit to the families, invaluable when the fishing catch was poor, as it was at certain times. "Terminal Island was like one large friendly family," stated Fumi Marumoto in an oral history interview with Los Angeles's Japanese American National Museum. "The giving and receiving was not on the basis of 'you gave me something, I've got to return a like item.' When we got vegetables from farmer friends, it was distributed to all our neighbors. And likewise, if a neighbor came into some goodies, this was also shared by all."

The iceman and the milkman made their regular rounds. For a short period of time, the milkman was Fred Wada, who later would become a noted community philanthropist instrumental in securing Tokyo as the site of the 1964 Olympics.

Perhaps it was this sense of community, rather than the physical environs, that brought a "sweetness" of home to its residents. Ill mothers received help from neighboring women who assumed cooking duties and childcare. A father, hearing of another fisherman's debilitating stroke, made the rounds through the neighborhood to collect funds to aid the family.

Among the boys, there was a friendly rivalry between

The second generation of Tuna Street proprietors. Circa 1939. Yoshio Takeuchi, far left, and his twin brother, Takao, were part of the family who owned Takeuchi Pool Hall. Misuko Nakamura, second from left, was the daughter of the owners of a popular noodle house. The father of Yosh Hashimoto, second from right, was a fisherman with his own boat.

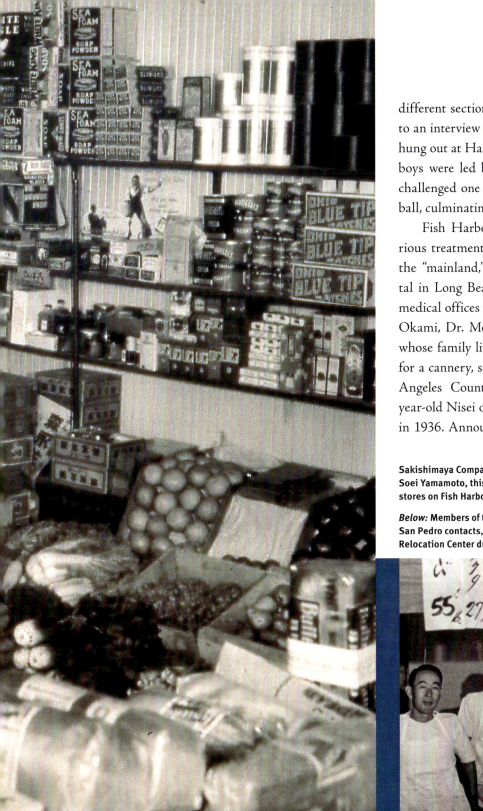

different sections of this concentrated area. According to an interview with George Mio, the Tuna Street boys hung out at Hashimoto Company. The Cannery Street boys were led by Soup Nakanishi. Each tiny district challenged one another to games of football and baseball, culminating in the island's own mini-Olympics.

Fish Harbor had no hospital. Those seeking serious treatment had to travel either by ferry or car to the "mainland," which usually meant Seaside Hospital in Long Beach. However, there were doctors with medical offices in Fish Harbor, including Dr. Shigeichi Okami, Dr. Morton Kimura, and Dr. Fred Fujikawa, whose family lived on the island. Fred's father worked for a cannery, so after completing an internship at Los Angeles County General Hospital, the twenty-six-year-old Nisei opened his own practice on Tuna Street in 1936. Announcing his presence with a banquet at a

Sakishimaya Company at 232 Terminal Way. Circa 1935. Operated by Soei Yamamoto, this establishment was among a number of grocery stores on Fish Harbor.

Below: **Members of the Terminal Island community, using their San Pedro contacts, operated a fish cooperative in Manzanar War Relocation Center during the World War II incarceration.**

The office of Nisei physician, Dr. Y. Fred Fujikawa, was above Ryono Café, 701 Tuna Street, operated by D. Ryono.

Opposite: Hiroshi "Chuck" Furutani, who was turning twelve, had a special birthday cake, the *S.S. Hiroshi.* June 1938.

Terminal Island: Lost Communities on America's Edge

China-*meshi*, or Chinese chop suey house, Fred began seeing ten to thirty drop-in patients a day. Circumcisions, tonsillectomies, and drainage of abscesses were all conducted in the office, while more complicated procedures were done at Seaside Hospital in Long Beach. In the beginning, most of his patients were Japanese, but as time went on, half his patients were non-Japanese living in Wilmington, Long Beach, and San Pedro. He made house calls as far as Orange County.

Fujikawa usually charged his patients at the end of the year. But if a family was experiencing a hardship, the doctor told them not to worry about payment. With the sense of obligation and honor so typical in the community, however, patients insisted on paying, even if, as it was in the case of one family, they paid just a dollar to show their good faith.

The doctor also handled home births, but there were also midwives, both in Fish Harbor and San Pedro. Min Tonai, for example, was delivered by a midwife in San Pedro in her home. The more local option in the 1930s was Hayashi Midwife, located at 234 Terminal Way.

The island had two drugstores and two Nisei USC-educated pharmacists, Frank Takeuchi, who was raised on Terminal Island, and Misako Ishii Shigekawa, who came to the island with her husband.

There were a number of dentists. One of them, Dr. Tooroku Fujii, was also an instructor of kendo, the Japanese martial art of fencing. He reportedly roused his young charges out of their beds at four o'clock in the morning in the midwinter, telling them to shout at the top of their lungs to fully awaken themselves. One of the young kendoists, Roy Yamamoto, recalled going to an out-of-town bout and then returning home. "The instant we came on the island, the smell from the canneries was awful." Fish fertilizer was apparently being produced from tuna scraps. "Living there, we were used to it and didn't notice," he stated in an oral history. But after going away for a few days, their sense of smell had to go through a "readjustment."

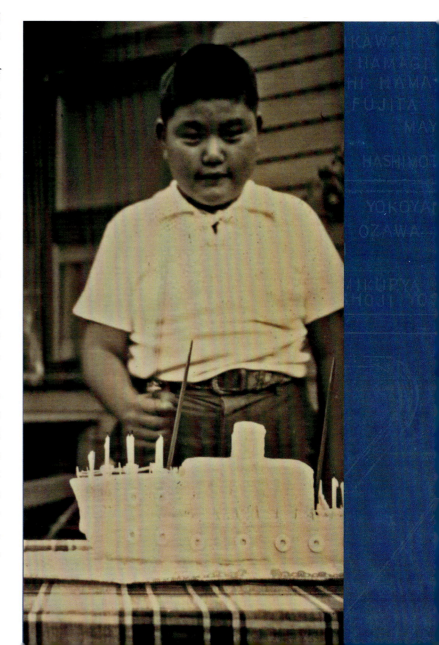

Bringing Japan to Terminal Island

Where the Issei residents of Fish Harbor came from in Japan differentiated the island from other agricultural communities in Southern California. According to Kanshi Yamashita's dissertation for the University of California at Irvine, 65 to 69 percent of Issei on Terminal Island in the 1930s were from a southern coastal prefecture, or state, called Wakayama. Located on the expansive Kii Peninsula, Wakayama was, and continues to be, sparsely populated compared to its neighbors, Osaka Prefecture to the north and Nara and Mie prefectures to the east. Other Terminal Islanders were from the neighboring prefecture of Shizuoka.

Many Japanese emigrants did, in fact, come to California from Wakayama. In 1892, a leading labor contractor from the prefecture, Yoshimatsu Kataura, contributed to the flow of people from his home prefecture to the Americas. Two others, Daigoro Hashimoto and Umetaro Minabe, also recruited railway workers. The Nanka Wakayama Kenjinkai, a prefectural organization in Southern California established in 1911, reported that 30 percent of the Japanese in Southern California were from Wakayama in 1914. The group had five hundred members at that time.

Despite those numbers, more Japanese sojourners left the prefectures of Hiroshima, Okinawa, Fukuoka, and Kumamoto than left Wakayama. The fact that so many of the Fish Harbor residents had ties to the same prefecture and, in some cases, even the same village, confirms the power of transnational networking as well as the attraction of a shared fishing tradition.

Known for its agricultural production of the *ume*, a small Japanese plum, and the *mikan*, a mandarin orange, Wakayama had a thriving fishing industry and remains involved in tuna production in the twenty-first century. The coastal city of Taiji was an early whaling town, and many Terminal Islanders could trace their roots back to Taiji or adjacent areas. In her dissertation chapter, "Home: A Trans-Pacific Community," scholar Yuko Konno explores how former residents of Terminal Island remained connected to their parents' home villages even decades after the end of World War II. According to her research, the decline in whaling caused Taiji villagers to seek overseas opportunities. Australia, with its pearl industry, was a popular destination. When Australia adopted a policy to limit immigrants from countries such as Japan in 1902, the people of Taiji looked toward the United States of America.

Yukizo Ryono was one of these natives from Taiji. Despite "eight years of schooling, there was no work of significance at that time." Ryono had to resort to collecting shellfish in the summer, while winters were just days empty of work. Ryono eventually became a carpenter. When he saw that his older brother was making money in America, Ryono decided it was time to cross the Pacific.

In a directory published by the Nanka Wakayama Kenjinkai in 1927, thirty-five out of fifty-five Taiji households in Southern California lived on Terminal Island. Konno, in her dissertation, explains that rather than getting involved with the larger and perhaps

Sardine harvesting peaked on the West Coast in 1936.

more prestigious prefectural organization, Terminal Islanders opted to form *sonjinkai*, village associations. That way, the islanders could be involved in homeland organizations without traveling to downtown Los Angeles's Little Tokyo, where Nanka Wakayama Kenjinkai meetings were held. In fact, in the *Rafu Shimpo* directory of 1939–40, a number of these village associations are listed with Terminal Island addresses. They include Taiji Association, located in the Toma Company retail store; Tanami Kyoyu Club in the Murakami Market; Tahara Sonjinkai in the Iwasaki barbershop; and Hidaka Shinyu Kai in the Tokiwa Low chop suey house.

At least one of the *sonjinkai*—Katada Association, housed in the *Southern Coast Herald* newspaper offices —was linked to a village in Mie Prefecture, which neighbors Wakayama. As was the case for the Wakayama groups, special Mie prefectural gatherings took place on Brighton Beach.

In addition to keeping in touch with villagers back in Japan, the Terminal Islanders sent remittances to relatives and sometimes donated money for projects, such as the building of schools. In some cases they even returned, as Min Hara's parents did in 1938. After being a captain of a midsized fishing vessel, Hara's father retired. As he could not become a U.S. citizen, he felt his best option was to return to his native town of Tahara. One of the last things he said to his son was, "Your country's in big trouble if they keep up this discrimination business."

Terminal Island Lingo

With this concentration of fishermen from Wakayama, formerly known as the Kii Peninsula, Terminal Island life was infused with colorful language. While some have identified the lingo as stemming from the Wakayama-based *Kii-shu* dialect, the language more likely evolved because Fish Harbor was a closed island community focused on the fishing industry.

For example, Haruye Okuno Sakamoto recalled the way her father, Daikichi Okuno, spoke while on his boats like the *Aloha*. "When you fish, you can't be nicey-nicey," she said in an oral history interview with the Port of Los Angeles. "Right now, the fish is gonna run. 'Get it—go get it.' It's like real, real fast. Don't be slow kind of thing. So language was rough."

John Katsuyuki Marumoto, the son of a lifelong Terminal Island fisherman who became a skipper for Van Camp, made the same observation. "The fishermen, when they're fishing, they're out at sea. When they have the fish in the net, they have to get it on board as soon as possible; otherwise the net breaks. So everything is doubletime. You can't dilly-dally, so you can't speak nicely. Language is really rough."

English was mixed in with Japanese. For instance, common phrases were "you-*ra*" and "me-*ra*," stand-ins for "you all" and "we." (*Ra* is a pluralizing suffix in Japanese.)

The Terminal Island lingo, also referred to as *Taminaru-ben* (Terminal Island dialect or pidgin), was an amalgam of this type of fishermen's talk, Japanese, and English. Because it was an island community, Terminal Island Nisei spoke more Japanese than Nisei in other Southern California communities.

For instance, Iwao Hara was nicknamed Belly; his last name really meant "field," but with a different Japanese intonation and a completely different *kanji* (Chinese character used in written Japanese), it could be interpreted as stomach. Tadao Ikari's nickname became Anchor, the meaning of his surname.

Further intensifying this "transnational" or bicultural environment was the common practice of sending Nisei children to Japan, usually Wakayama, for at least a portion of their education. Charlie Hamasaki did not go to school in Wakayama, but embraced *Taminaru-ben*. "The thing is, the school was 99 percent Japanese and 1 percent Caucasian, so we all talk Japanese until the sixth grade. We talk nothing but Japanese," he said.

Indeed, the young Nisei in Fish Harbor did lead linguistically schizophrenic lives. Attending Japanese-language school after public school multiple times a week, they moved back and forth between the two languages. One student observed that they would often speak Japanese during recess at public school and

Charlie Hamasaki, who learned boxing from a Filipino cannery foreman, embraced Terminal Island lingo. Circa 1939.

English during breaks at Japanese school. Apparently the use of Japanese at East San Pedro School became so pervasive that the teachers created a rule that only English could be used on a certain day of the week, either Wednesdays or Thursdays.

No matter how unsophisticated the fishermen seemed to be on the outside, the business of fishing required a high level of capitalization, investment, and legal know-how.

Chikao Robert Ryono in his booklet, *Although Patriotic, We Were Drydocked*, explained that jig boats were small boats with five- to ten-horsepower gasoline engines. Jigs, or *ken-ken*, referred to lures with hooks made out of bone, metal, or abalone shells. Five hundred hooks were threaded on a single setline with lures and then baited. Lures were fastened to lines attached to poles that functioned as makeshift outriggers mounted on the sides of the boat.

Haruye Shimada Matsumoto remembered that after her father, a *ken-ken* boat operator, delivered his catch to Van Camp cannery, her and her sisters' work began. They sat and untangled all the hooks and lines for the next day's voyage. Mas Tanibata and his three siblings and mother did the same.

After one-man *ken-ken* boats, the next level of vessels were *lampara*, which traveled faster than six to eight knots and could be manned by seven to twelve crew members. *Lampara* were known for their ring nets in which crew members, usually singing in unison on deck, pulled in both sides of the nets full of fish.

After the *lampara* came the purse seiner, which used a net that was "heavier, harder to manipulate and

From *Ken-Ken* Boats to Tuna Clipper

Poppo, poppo, ken-ken boat
From the blue sky, rings appear
This morning again, he left early.

Poppo, poppo, ken-ken boat
In the blue sea, waves form
He went to catch some fish.

—YOSHIO FUJITA, first grade at
Seisho Gakko Japanese-language school,
in an essay originally written in Japanese

required speed and hard work on the part of the crew." Cork was attached to one side of the rectangular net to serve as buoys, while lead weights were on the bottom. A skiff operator helped to encircle the net over a school of fish before the net was "pursed." These various nets cost a small fortune: an estimated twelve thousand dollars for a sardine net and as much as twenty-five thousand dollars for a tuna net in 1929.

When tuna began to be depleted in local waters, large vessels like tuna clippers were equipped with bait boxes and refrigeration. Carrying a crew of as many as twenty men, a tuna clipper could travel hundreds and even thousands of miles to Mexico, the Galapagos, and Central and South America. Since these boats were very expensive, skilled Issei fishermen with some capital usually had to partner with a cannery to build these vessels. Such agreements would require legal documents, and from 1924 to 1933, a bilingual Issei journalist,

Circles of cork helped buoy nets on the sea to catch large schools of fish.

Masaru Ben Akahori, had a legal office on Terminal Island to help draw contracts, sue for unpaid labor, and even handle divorces. Since Issei could not be attorneys in California, Akahori was not officially a lawyer, yet essentially worked as one.

Under these agreements, the cannery usually maintained a majority share of 51 percent of the tuna clipper. Kiyoo Yamashita, a relative of pioneer Jinshiro Tani, and four partners teamed with Van Camp to build a 200-ton, 125-foot vessel, which was later named *Columbus*, a suggestion by Yamashita's eldest daughter, Iku, who was studying world explorers in school.

Usually the completion of a new boat was cause for a celebratory trial run. Catalina Island, about twenty-five miles from Terminal Island, was a favorite destination. Permits were obtained from the Wrigley Company, owner of the island at the time; picnic lunches were prepared; and family members, friends, and children climbed aboard with their bathing suits in hand. As the new boat, decorated with flags, embarked on its maiden journey, fishermen on their boats offered their congratulations by cheering and tooting their horns.

In contrast to these joyful moments, there was definitely a dark side to fishing, one of the world's most dangerous occupations. Monterey-born Kisaye Nakasaki Sato remembered all the wives, including her mother, getting worried as storms hit the coast of California. Sometimes even one-man *ken-ken* boats would be gone for days as fishermen took shelter in coves on their way home from islands near Santa Barbara. One fisherman never made it back; his body was never recovered. Decades later, his clothing was finally buried in a cemetery plot. The same family would experience another death at sea, and the man's wife vowed not to look at the ocean

for the rest of her life.

A more publicized ill-fated voyage was one related to the *Belle Isle*, a purse seiner under the leadership of Captain John Ivan Gabelich, a cofounder of the Jugoslav Club of San Pedro. The *Belle Isle* had been last seen leaving Terminal Island in June 1934 on its way for a forty-day fishing expedition to Galapagos Island. Two months later, it was reported missing, and even the navy was contacted to look for the vessel in Central American waters to no avail. One of the twelve men on board was Terminal Islander Takeshi Morizawa, thirty-five.

Charlie Hamasaki actually witnessed his friend's boat, *Cleopatra*, sinking after crashing into a reef in heavy fog. In 1924, Harumatsu Yamasaki and his crew, while coming home with a boatload of sardines, hit a reef on a foggy night in 1924. All were killed. Even Kiyoo Yamashita's celebrated *Columbus* only lasted three years, as it sank after a mishap in Baja California. In the case of the *Columbus*, however, the shipwrecked men were able to survive on ship provisions and were fortunately spotted by another tuna clipper and saved.

Fishing was also extremely strenuous, and the days long. Sardine fishing season was usually five months, from September to January. Sardines were usually caught at night, as their movement and phosphorescence made the little fish easy to spot. The best time to catch mackerel, on the other hand, was early in the morning. Tuna was fished during the summer months.

Despite its danger and physical demands, fishing was an occupation that paid handsomely when the catch was good. In fact, Hamasaki remembered that as an apprentice fisherman in 1941, he made five hundred dollars during his first month, which happened to be at the height of sardine season. "The money was there compared to these guys working on the land for fifteen dollars a week," stated Hamasaki. Fishermen were paid monthly ("dark moon" to "dark moon"), and each received a share of gross, clearly stated in legal documents. Sometimes the owner of the vessel received as much as 50 percent of the gross, and the remaining, minus daily living expenses, was split among the working crew. More shares went to the captain and more-skilled laborers like the engineer and mast man.

Price and payment was one area of the industry that was highly protected by the Issei fishermen. A number of strikes occurred on Terminal Island over the price of fish offered by canneries. These labor strikes involved a number of associations, some in San Diego, and the most contentious walkouts required the intervention of federal and state agencies.

In January of 1924, the Southern California Japanese Fishermen's Association and the Japanese American Fishermen's Club (Nichibei Fishermen's Club) staged a successful strike against the canneries for a higher price for sardines. It is not exactly clear how the families weathered these financial setbacks during strikes and the Depression, but the community members definitely shared their resources whenever possible.

The names of boats were especially meaningful and often paid homage to either family, homeland, or the fisherman's new home. Iwamatsu Yamamoto's boat was *NKT* after his three sons, Noboru, Kiyoshi, and Takashi. (Noboru was renamed Kenji, or "Healthy," to ward away sickness that had plagued him as a small child.) Wakayama-native Mankichi Nakasaki's

ken-ken boat was called *Kisae* [sic], to honor his daughter, Kisaye. *America*, co-owned by Genichi Kimura and Masaichi Shibata, clearly expressed a connection to their adopted home, and there was also the Chiyomatsu's *Patriotic* and Fujii's *Golden Gate*.

Ubuyu Maru II, owned by Ryokichi Hashimoto, was named after his hometown in Wakayama, Japan.

Experienced crew members worked quickly on the sardine boats.

Opposite: A fishing boat docked in front of a cannery is full of sardines that are ready to be cooked and processed.

Fishing and Family: Lives Ruled by the Tides

Family life on Terminal Island was unique. Depending on what type of fishing they were involved in, fathers could be gone for weeks or even months at a time, leaving their wives with sole-parenting duties. In households in which mothers worked in the canneries, children had to take care of themselves. The village itself served as kind of big family that watched, supported, and sometimes controlled the actions of its people.

Life on the island was ruled not by man-measured time, but by the tides and the moon. For instance, the full moon period—two days before the full moon and two days afterward—was reserved for repairing nets and boats, as well as for recreation. "Because when the moon is out, the fish doesn't come up, so you can't see them, anyway," explained John Marumoto.

The popular recreational treat on the island was going to see Japanese movies, including action-packed samurai films, at Fishermen's Hall. Eager attendees saved their seats early by placing *zabuton* (thin cushions) from home on chairs, while more protective mothers prohibited their children from being exposed to such worldly entertainment. A Japanese couple and projectionist would travel from Los Angeles to take care of all the details. During the silent-movie era, the man acted as the *benshi*, or live narrator, while the woman changed records for appropriate musical interludes.

Drinking took place during this week and sometimes after work. Men congregated at a chandlery store to swap stories on their fishing experiences and drink homemade sake. John Marumoto recalled being sent by his mother, Fumi, to fetch his father at ten or eleven in

> *Ha-a*, if you're going to dance,
>   then waitaminute!
> Big-catch dance, *yoi yoi.*
> Even the moon dances at sea.
> *Yaatona, sore yoi yoi yoi.*
> *Yaatona, sore yoi yoi yoi.* *
>
> —first stanza of "Tairyo Ondo"
> (Fishermen's or Big-Catch Dance)
>
> * italicized words are rhythmic beats with no particular meaning

the evening. Frightened by Japanese *obake* (ghost) stories, he clutched his flashlight in the pitch-black night until he spied a familiar figure staggering in the street.

"Everyone came home tired from work," added Fumi Marumoto, "especially the fishermen. Their work, compared to workers on land, was much more hazardous, cold, and taxing both physically and mentally. Their release from this tension was cups of sake that flowed despite the law. The womenfolk all made home brew, and the thirsty crew members always stopped at our place before going home. Often the sake wasn't ready, but that didn't make any difference. The dipper would scoop up milk-colored home brew until everyone was satisfied."

People described as "lawmen" would make surprise visits to the island to conduct their inspections during Prohibition. Once they were spotted, news traveled through the cannery housing like wildfire. One Nisei woman remembered her father hiding his sake jug in the sand underneath the bedroom floorboards, where he had cut a hole for access. Before the authorities arrived, the two beds were pushed together, hiding the hole. Wives poured their brew down the toilets. "The remaining lingering odor surely was enough evidence to arrest us all," commented Fumi Marumoto. Immigration authorities reportedly visited the island at the same time, causing those without legal papers to also scramble and hide underneath houses.

Less innocent carousing took place in Little Tokyo

Hiroshi "Chuck" Furutani, kneeling on right, joins out-of-town guests on Brighton Beach. Circa 1938.

in Los Angeles at its notorious gambling house, the To-kyo Club. Men also reportedly frequented red-light districts to visit "women of the night."

Cannery work also did not abide by nine-to-five office hours. In the Japanese community, women and young people, not the male head of household, worked the canneries' packing lines. In terms of tuna canning, Filipino men, many of whom lived in the eastern Terminal neighborhood, were responsible for gutting the raw fish. After the fish were steam-cooked whole, the line workers cleaned, skinned, and deboned the tuna before it was ready to be hand-packed into cans.

Fish needed to be packed immediately, so when the fishermen arrived on Terminal Island with their catch, a whistle, unique to each cannery, sounded through the wooden housing units. No matter the time, even if midnight, the women assigned to that cannery had to drop everything, change clothes, don their white caps, pull on their rubber boots, and report to work. It was physically taxing hard work that sometimes resulted in accidents. Toshiro Izumi remembered his mother, Fumi, and her coworkers being temporarily blinded by saltwater when a full tank of sardines were released during the height of the season. Fortunately, after a few days of cleaning her eyes with boric acid, his mother regained her sight. Shortly thereafter, the workers started wearing goggles as eye protection.

"Looking back to those cannery days, the ladies worked under wet and terrible conditions without complaints," wrote Izumi.

On her first day of work, newly married Fumi

The canneries had a multicultural workforce, which included Filipino men as well as white and Mexican women.

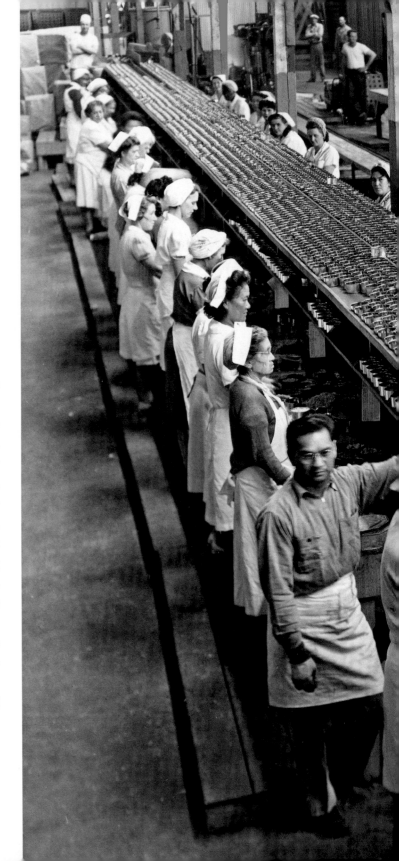

Responding to their cannery's unique whistle, these women, wearing caps and rubber boots, walk to work. Circa 1940.

Women of the neighboring (from left) Yamashita, Hatashita, and Shioji families enjoy a brief respite from their cannery work.

Marumoto faced cleaning a huge tuna that she had to practically embrace to complete the task. It took the novice cannery worker the whole day to do one fish. Haruye Okuno Sakamoto's mother, a former pearl diver for Mikimoto, was obviously more skilled or perhaps more patient, because she was the designated person to train new workers. In addition to cleaning albacore, she also handled sardines and mackerel at other canneries.

The women were constantly at work. Extra income was generated by drying salted fish, usually Spanish mackerels, king fishes, anchovies, and sardines on top of roofs on wire racks and poles. It was precisely these poles that government investigators later claimed were antennas being used to communicate with Japan prior to the bombing of Pearl Harbor.

Prolonged physical separation from their fathers was a reality for the Nisei children. "Oftentimes the only contact we had with our fathers at sea was listening to them on a shortwave radio as they conversed with other fishermen on other boats," said John Marumoto.

As his older brothers and sisters had all been left in Japan to be raised by relatives, Charlie Hamasaki was

Formal portraits didn't reveal the harsh everyday lives of the fishermen and cannery workers. Here, the growing Izumi family. First row, from left: mother, Fumi; son Katsumi; father, Kuichi; and daughter Mary. Second row: daughter Satsuki; son Toshiro; and daughter Kaneko. Circa 1936.

Young teenagers go from household to household to help pound steamed sweet rice for New Year's rice cakes.

essentially an only child for a while on Terminal Island. "[At] night time I was lonely and scared because my father was out fishing; my mother was working at the cannery. . . . I hardly see them. I couldn't go home to sleep after seeing especially a scary movie. I used to go to the cannery where my mother was working and sleep in the empty big boxes which the tin cans used to come in."

More common was to see neighbor women and older Nisei girls helping out with childcare duties. But such responsibilities weren't expected of the boys. In the summertime, while their sisters worked at home, the boys ruled the island. They swam and sailed inside the harbor, playing pirates or samurai warriors on rocks near Deadman's Island. Giant crabs were caught in traps, smelts and sardines with homemade bamboo poles. They camped near the seashore, lighting bonfires with which they cooked potatoes buried in the sand. More adventurous boys surfed; the sun turned their exposed skin dark like their fathers'.

In terms of holidays, New Year's Day was the most anticipated one on the island. Certainly the most important celebration in Japan and Japanese American communities, it was observed with an especially high level of enthusiasm in Fish Harbor. Food preparation, especially *mochitsuki*, or the pounding of rice for rice cakes, was integral to the festivities.

While *mochitsuki* was very common in places where Issei lived, the close proximity of Japanese residents in Fish Harbor literally made it a rotating neighborhood party. Usually half a dozen neighboring families coordinated their efforts. They rented equipment from one of the Japanese markets on the island to steam fifty to seventy-five pounds of sweet rice. Strong teenage boys followed the equipment from house to house to pound the rice in an giant *usu* (mortar) with mallets. After the pounding was finished, the women took the sticky concoction into the house to form into balls—larger ones were used as decoration while smaller ones, each the size of a child's palm, were saved to either put in a traditional soup, to grill, or to make into a confection with sweetened red beans. Cooking continued until New Year's Day, and presentation was key. Steamed lobsters, for example, were displayed on a fresh bed of grated *daikon* and garnished with a *naruten* branch strung with origami cranes. On January 1, friends and families made their rounds from one house to another, and captains could expect to entertain their well-wishing crew members with some home-brewed sake. Children waited with anticipation as guests arrived—not only for the delicious food but also the *otoshidama* (gift envelopes of money) that would come their way.

Raising the Nisei Children: A Bifurcated Life

For the children of Fish Harbor, public school was perhaps the single most important institution that contributed toward their acculturation into their predominantly American world. There were only two grammar schools and no secondary school on the island. Terminal Island School, in the more established neighborhood of Terminal, was the older of the two and more integrated. East San Pedro Grammar School (later renamed, posthumously, after principal Mildred Obarr Walizer) was at least 95 percent Nisei, and was housed in multiple bungalows on Tuna Street and Terminal Way, on the same block as Fishermen's Hall and Seisho Gakko. This block had the oldest community structures on Fish Harbor.

In the fall of 1917, after Fish Harbor first opened, the Los Angeles County Board of Education held classes for its children in a private dwelling. The board of education, seeing the harbor's growing population, asked that one acre of land in Fish Harbor be reserved for classroom bungalows. The Harbor Commission, through correspondence, didn't seem enthused about creating a permanent school building "because of the transient nature of the population," but by law could not deny the educational needs of the children of Fish Harbor. On November 7, 1917, East San Pedro School was officially established by the Board of Education.

The devotion and commitment of the teachers, mostly women and all non-Japanese, left a lasting impact on their students and families. While the educators attempted to enforce English and widen their students' world beyond the island, they also

> I've grown up quite a bit; all of this is due to my father and mother. That is why I want to study very hard and become a person of substance. Some days I want to become an inventor; other days I think about going to Japan to study and become a great businessman. My parents, wanting me to make something of myself, have sent me to school, so I, in turn, want to somehow make my parents proud. That is what I am determined to do.
>
> —IWAO HARA, in his essay, "Our Determination," originally written in Japanese

This class picture from the 1920s includes three Nisei who were interviewed for this book: Chizuru Nakaji Boyea, seated, far left; Kisaye Nakasaki Sato, seated, third from right; and Yukio Tatsumi, former president of the Terminal Islanders, standing, third from right.

Right: From its original single bungalow, the grammar school expanded to seven structures and this playground.

This is the most important time in our lives.

—Kimiko Oka in her Japanese essay,
"What Should We Be Doing in the Future?"

The Fish Harbor school was part of the Los Angeles City School District. Circa 1925.

Opposite top: Mildred Obarr Walizer, dressed in a kimono on Terminal Island, stands with Tsuruko Yokozeki, one of the leaders of the *Fujin-kai*. 1926.

Opposite bottom: The heritage of all children in Fish Harbor was recognized and celebrated, including this special Russian Day event.

embraced the Japanese culture, promoting celebrations like Girls' and Boys' Days. On Terminal Island, these traditional holidays were quaintly reconceived. Girls' Day on March 3, for example, included American dolls among kimono-clad Japanese dolls on display. On Boys' Day on May 5, carp banners hung above homes as was traditional in Japan, but the holiday was expanded to include children dressed up as circus animals and clowns. Like language and religion, tradition could be transformed to reflect the bicultural reality of the islanders.

Also, not all the residents of Fish Harbor were of Japanese ancestry. A notable exception was a "White Russian" family, the Kaseroffs, who lived in the Hokkaido neighborhood on Pilchard Street. The father, Moises, fished on a jig boat, and the children—James, Ann, and Tonya—not only attended school with the Nisei, but also the Baptist church. (There were also two older sons, Russia-born Joseph and California-born Jack, who both lived with the family and fished on Terminal Island.) During the Girls' Day celebrations, the Issei women lent their kimonos to the Kaseroff girls, even going so far as to dress them. The Russian children were known for speaking Japanese, at least the Terminal lingo of their peers. A Latino resident of Terminal, Arthur Terraza, the son of Marina and Blasé Terraza, also apparently picked up the Japanese language at school.

Whether it be the Kaseroffs, the Latinos, or the many Japanese children, the beloved educator Mildred Walizer cared for all. Childless herself, she was like a second mother, accompanying children to get their tonsils removed and buying shoes for barefoot students at warehouse sales. "I doubt if she ever saved any money, because every cent that she earned as a teacher, she always spent it on the kids," said Toshiye Kobata in an oral history interview. Although she had an official place of residence across the channel in San Pedro, she virtually lived at the school, many times sleeping on a cot and ordering takeout soup from Mio Café for dinner. Even after getting married in 1921 and being promoted to school principal shortly thereafter, Walizer managed to keep in touch with her former students who had gone on to high school. Wanting to impart her love for the great outdoors, she created a Senior High Outing Club and took girls to places like Palm Springs and the San Bernardino Mountains. During a weeklong trip to San Francisco and Yosemite in 1931, Walizer not only drove, but pitched tents and cooked for twenty girls.

Her energy and zest for life—hosting Halloween, participating in clog- and tap-dancing lessons—was infectious. Even the most traditionally minded of Terminal Islanders could not help but to respond positively to her. In fact, a group of leaders, including businessman and philanthropist Tsurumatsu Toma, decided that they needed to express their appreciation to the dedicated educator by introducing their homeland to her. The Issei raised a stunning four thousand dollars to send the principal to Japan, specifically to the small villages in Wakayama where they were from.

One evening, Walizer called a special meeting of the Outing Club. She had grim news to share. The beloved educator had terminal cancer and would have to leave Terminal Island. When Walizer eventually died in 1933, her funeral was held in the largest building on the island, Fishermen's Hall. The school was named

Events at the Fish Harbor grammar school blended cultural elements from both Japan and the West; even outside visitors from other parts of Southern California came to observe the festivities. Circa 1925.

Fish Harbor children commemorate Armistice Day, the anniversary of the end of World War I, in 1924.

Opposite: Girls' Day, typically celebrated in Japan as *Hinamatsuri* on March 3, was an all-day affair on the island, with a series of folk dances and doll displays. People traveled from all parts of Southern California to attend the festivities. Back row, from left: Kiyoe Oshima, Kaneko Izumi. Front row: Kisaye Nakasaki, Michiko Nakamura, Satsuki Izumi, and Kikue Yamaguchi. Circa 1925.

Principal Mildred Obarr Walizer visited twenty-one schools in Wakayama Prefecture in 1930 on a trip to encourage goodwill between the United States and Japan.

posthumously after her, and her former students even made regular pilgrimages to her gravesite.

The transition from grammar school to junior high school and later to high school was major, literally requiring crossing over the channel. Ferryboats were necessary to transport students to San Pedro, where they attended Dana Junior High School and either San Pedro or Banning High Schools. The walk to school from the San Pedro ferry landing could be as far as two miles; wealthier students could afford the five-cent bus fare.

In their "mainland" schools, Nisei youth found themselves in the minority—ranging from 4 to 14 percent of the Dana student body—yet many held school leadership positions; for example, boys were active members of sports teams.

There was still a significant population of students, perhaps even half, who were traveling back and forth from the United States to their parents' hometowns in

Under the auspices of the Fukei-Kai, community members helped construct a Japanese garden on the grammar school grounds. 1924.

The famous red-lacquer bridge, the centerpiece of the Japanese garden, was built by Fish Harbor parents and leaders. This photograph was taken two years after the death of Walizer, who was replaced by Principal Burton E. Davis, seen here next to philanthropist Tsurumatsu Toma. October 1936.

Japan. Referred to as *Kibei Nisei* ("returning Nisei"), these young people pursued at least a portion of their education in Japan to give them more future options. These primarily Japanese-speaking students tended to stick together, even speaking Japanese in high school. One Nisei girl even transferred to Banning to avoid such ethnic cliques. A popular Nisei football player was asked by the administration to encourage certain Japanese American students to mix more with their white classmates. He reluctantly did so without such success.

Some, like Min Hara, who accompanied his parents to their hometown Tahara in the 1938, spent only ten months overseas in school. It had been a terrible, "hellish" experience for Min, who complained of the communication gap and the lack of food. "The principal of the local grammar school made fun of us Nisei since we

The *Islander* municipal ferry made its first routine run at Berth 234 on September 2, 1941. Before the debut of the *Islander*, students traveled on private ferryboats, including the *Ace* and *Matt Walsh*, to get to junior high and high school.

couldn't conform to their way of thinking. I resolved never to come back to such a militaristic state, especially when the secret police picked me up for a couple hours of interrogation right before I boarded a ship at Kobe, Japan," stated Min in *Terminal Island: An Island in Time*, a collection of personal histories.

Others had more pleasant experiences, especially the girls. Many of them actually attended college in Japan after graduating from high school in the United States. Nakako Takeuchi spent two years at Keisen Jogakuen, a women's school in Tokyo. With so many Nisei from different parts of the United States attending the school, there was even a special *ryugakusei*, or class for foreigners.

Kisaye Nakasaki Sato actually wanted to go to college in Japan to improve her Japanese and learn proper etiquette. Carrying a dictionary with her at all times, she was able to graduate from Wakayama Jogakko in 1941. Her Nisei friend Chizuru Nakaji Boyea was also in Japan to attend a women's college connected to Doshisha University. While other Nisei women studied certain arts such as flower arrangement and tea, Boyea took more academic classes. She made a point, however to learn *shuji*, the art of Japanese calligraphy. Sitting on the floor, she and her classmates would take turns showing the brush technique to the professor, who sat in front of the class. "After the lesson, I bowed and thanked him and tried to get up to get back to my place," explained Boyea. "Both my feet were fast asleep, and I had to crawl back. He was laughing, 'Ha, ha, ha.' "

As younger Kibei Nisei returned to Terminal Island, their transition was assisted by a Foreign Oppor-

Belying the turmoil that was to come in a month, dedicated teacher Annie Garcia, in coat, shares a light moment with students in her Special Opportunities English-language class. January 1942.

tunities or "Special" English-language program held in Fish Harbor. It was led by Wilmington-born Annie Garcia, the vice-principal of the grammar school. She was one of its early hires, co-teaching kindergarten through third grade with another young single woman, Mildred Obarr, who later became the beloved principal. According to *Red Lacquer Bridge*, which lovingly records the activities at the grammar school in Fish Harbor and its teaching staff, Garcia became involved in the school district's "Americanization" program, which included language courses at night for the Issei parents.

The Parent-Teacher Association of East San Pedro Grammar School was called *Fukei-kai*, and it was responsible for the financing of many beautification projects, aided by the *Fujin-kai*, literally "Wives' Club," which also was established in 1924. The two groups adopted the common practice of using the Japanese-style garden as a symbol of goodwill and interethnic friendship. Not only was a Japanese garden constructed at East San Pedro School with its iconic red-lacquer bridge, but a garden was also built on the campus of San Pedro High School in 1939, according to Yuko Konno's dissertation.

The same year, a federal Works Progress Administration (WPA) mural was planned for a wall on the Fish Harbor grammar school. As described in Karin Higa's *Living in Color* (2001), the highly acclaimed Issei painter Hideo Date was assigned to the project. A lifelong friend of Justus Sato, the proprietor of Sato Cured Marine Products, Date lived with Sato's family in their home above the business at 102 Genoa Place in Terminal.

Date apparently completed initial drawings. "I chose the Japanese legend of the goddess of light: she was hidden from her mischievous brother in a cave, and

One of the photographs in the pre–World War II album of Fish Harbor teacher Annie Garcia.

everything was dark. People started to play music; women danced. She became curious and started to open the cave," he stated in *Living in Color*. He began the mural, but was not able to complete it. Other artists reportedly stepped in, but there are no surviving images, records, or memories of the finished artwork.

The all-American sport of baseball and the traditional martial art of kendo were two beloved sports in Fish Harbor. Both were points of pride among the English- and Japanese-speaking men. The Skippers, the Nisei baseball team, competed against other Japanese American teams across Southern California, capturing multiple championships. Philanthropist Tsurumatsu Toma, who was also the proprietor of Toma market, paid for topsoil to be trucked in for the large baseball diamond across from the Baptist church. Boat owners were solicited for new uniforms and equipment. Toshiro Izumi remembered that on Sundays, when the Skippers played, captains made sure that they didn't set out to sea until the game was over.

Kendo, which incorporates a bamboo stick as an "attacking implement," was practiced at Fishermen's Hall twice a week. Approximately one hundred young fencers, including girls, attended the rigorous training. In the damp and freezing early mornings of winter, drills were conducted on the cold floor with the young kendoists absorbing blows to unprotected parts of their bodies for three hours.

Apparently their discipline paid off, as the Terminal Island kendo team beat a contingent from the prominent Waseda University at a meet held during the 1932 Olympics in Los Angeles. That victory spurred the community to raise money so that a team, including Nisei from other parts of California, would compete overseas not only in Japan, but also in Korea and Manchuria. Despite the worsening international climate in that part of the world, the coed team was dispatched in 1940 with members of Terminal Island participating.

Frank Takeuchi, who later became a pharmacist on the island, didn't take kendo as seriously as some of the others. "They would tie balloons to the top of your

The Skippers, the 1941 California state champion Nisei baseball team, was the pride and joy of the Japanese Americans on Terminal Island. First row from left: Fred Sugiura, Ned Uyematsu, Jim Okura, Ryoji Terada, Cy Yuguchi, Shorty Hashimoto, Tee Okura, Yukio Tatsumi, Tokio Asari, Nori Nakai. Standing: Seiichi Shimizu, Tsurumatsu Toma, Yosh Nakamura, Ich Hashimoto, Sud Kodama, Moto Shimizu, Paul Ryono, Koo Ito, Yosh Hashimoto, Dick Kunishima, Kazuichi Hashimoto, and Henry Murakami. Missing: Pee Wee Tsuda, one of the Skippers' ace pitchers.

Left: Although team members from Japan were trained to never smile during competition, even in practice, the Nisei kendoists couldn't help but laugh as they competed against friends.

Dressed in kendo uniforms from Japan, these young Terminal Island martial artists beat a Japanese college team in a demonstration during the 1932 Summer Olympics in Los Angeles. Points were tallied when the opposition popped the balloons with their kendo sticks.

Nisei high school girls play table tennis.
Circa 1940.

Left: Even girls participated in martial arts when some traveled to Japan with a special exchange team in 1941.

helmet, and we all got the giggles," he remembered in an oral history interview preserved at the Japanese American National Museum. The young athlete, a shortstop for the Skippers, also dabbled in sumo wrestling on Tuna Street before it was paved. "The point in kendo is that you have to look your opponent straight in the eyes, and that was, at least as far as I'm concerned, that just set me to laughing. You let out all your energies, but it was very controlled by the senseis [teachers]."

The islanders' success in sports, not only regionally but internationally, mitigated any feelings of inferiority within the larger Japanese American community. With their rough lingo and raucous Little Tokyo celebrations during the full-moon breaks from fishing, Terminal Islanders did not have the most stellar of reputations. Dave Nakagawa experienced this firsthand when he attempted to date a Nisei woman in Los Angeles during the Nisei Week Japanese Festival. Her parents were less than thrilled when they discovered that he was the son of a fisherman on Terminal Island.

Without even the full support of Japanese Americans on the mainland, there was little chance of being accepted by the majority culture. "In 1941, you graduate from high school. What are you going to do? Your father and mother are so poor; you don't get to go to college anywhere," commented Charlie Hamasaki, who saw even his peers who gained their college degrees struggling to find work. "We can't get no city job, civil service job, firemen job. You can't work any kind of dealership. Discrimination." Even at the nurturing grammar school, there were no Japanese Americans as part of the teaching staff. Only the custodian and junior head custodian were of Japanese descent.

As a result, many Nisei who became adults on the Island turned to what they knew best. Fishing.

San Pedro's champion *shonen* (youth division) judo team in front of the *dojo* adjacent to the Shinto shrine. 1941. From left: Koshi Seko, Chikara Ozawa, Koji Iriye, Kiyoshi Sugimoto, Teiji Ohara, Paul Naito, Katsumi Ryono, Tanino, Masahiro Miki, Shigeru Miyaki, unidentified.

Sumo, the style of wrestling that was popular since Fish Harbor's earliest days, was sometimes practiced with American sensibilities, namely clothing underneath the traditional loincloth.

May Day, or *Tango no Sekku*, went beyond celebrating in a traditional ways. Some children donned kimono; others pretended to be circus animals, clowns, and Indians.

Religion on the Island

Like the language of the Terminal Islanders, religion was adopted in a unique way: in the case of faith, not necessarily by tradition or even belief, but more relationally or superstitiously—reflecting the perils of life on the sea. The biggest example of the latter was the Daijin-Gu, the landmark of the Japanese on the island. Marked by a *torii* gate constructed out of wood, the shrine was located in front of the judo hall. Shinto, a belief system unique to Japan, is tied to a creation story of the archipelago. In terms of continental North America, there were very few *jinja* ("shrines") that enshrined the *kami* ("sacred spirit"); in fact, Daijin-Gu, may have been the first and only in California before and even after World War II. (Konko-kyo churches, which came out of the Shinto tradition, were in existence at that time in the United States, but they remained doctrinally independent and did not typically practice the enshrinement of *kami*.)

The shrine was built in the early 1930s and its usage was not commonly understood, especially by the Nisei children. Some remembered *Obon* dancing, a Buddhist tradition, being held outside the *torii*, but it quite conceivably could have been one of the seasonal Shinto celebrations. One Nisei recollection included a wedding ceremony having taken place there.

The main priest was Shinkichi Miyoshi, an Issei who remained an enigma to many young people. According to *Life Behind Barbed Wire: The World War II Internment Memoirs of a Hawai'i Issei* by Keiho Soga, Miyoshi had lived in Hawaii before moving to San Diego and then to Terminal Island. In Hawaii he was involved in the theater business, and on Terminal Island, as a divorced father of a young daughter, he worked at a restaurant. The history book *San Pidoro Doho Hatten-roku* reported that it had been Miyoshi's idea to establish a Shinto shrine in 1930. He apparently elicited the help and support of various business leaders and fishermen, including Masaru Ben Akahori, who diligently made sure that the legal papers of the shrine were in order.

The lease permit to establish the shrine, then called the North American Shinto Temple, East San Pedro Branch, at 226 Terminal Way, was submitted to the Harbor Commission and accepted in March 1931. A celebration followed, and then in September, Miyoshi went to Daijin-Gu shrine in Honolulu, Hawaii, for religious study. After two months, Miyoshi came back to Terminal Island a Shinto priest. On December 6, 1931, a public ceremony was held to mark the building of the shrine's foundation. In summer of 1933, with the name change to San Pedro Daijin-Gu, the shrine was formally registered as a nonprofit organization in California, with Miyoshi given the power of attorney.

Beside the *torii* gate were two fox statues, often seen at shrines celebrating the *Inari Okami*, the sacred spirit of industry and worldly prosperity. Other than those powerful symbols, the Terminal Island shrine was a simple one-room structure with a traditional Japanese sloped roof. A photograph of the interior revealed a decidedly American representation on the altar: portraits of George Washington and Abraham Lincoln. The Singaporean newspaper, the *Straits Times*, featured a brief article in its June 8, 1935, issue, "Shinto Sainthoods: Names of Two American Presidents Added." The article reported that a Shinto branch in Los Angeles had enshrined pictures of Washington and Lincoln on May 10 and that their respective birthdays had been added to the Shinto calendar as days of worship. The specific

Officially renamed San Pedro Daijin-Gu in 1933, the Shinto shrine on Terminal Island may have been the only one of its kind in the continental United States.

Shinto shrine was not identified, but it is quite possible that the report originally came from Terminal Island.

Nisei children remembered Miyoshi chanting by himself in a loud voice. As no regular services took place at Daijin-Gu, those with limited interaction with the religion wondered how the priest could sustain a full-time living by being tied to the shrine.

However, an interview with Lynn Yoshiko Hori, the daughter of Shizuoka-born Isaburo Hori, revealed that Miyoshi regularly visited the houses of certain fishermen to offer a blessing over an altar, or *kamidana*, that is often placed on a shelf high on a wall. Miyoshi

usually made his house visits just before the head of the household was getting ready to depart on a sea journey. The minister no doubt received some kind of *orei* (monetary thanks) for his efforts. In a community in which lives were commonly lost at sea, this spiritual covering of safety gave the families great comfort. "Fishermen are superstitious," said Hori, a comment echoed by many interviewees. Isaburo Hori had apparently donated an anchor to be placed in front of the shrine, thereby deepening the connection between the Shinto belief and fishing.

Despite this very visual Shinto symbol on the island

The Baptist Mission at 249 Terminal Way operated the island's first Japanese-language school, which most of the Nisei children attended before the establishment of the Buddhist temple's school in the early 1930s.

from the 1930s, the Baptists had the longest and deepest day-to-day relationship with the Japanese residents. In 1918, it became the first religious institution in Fish Harbor and home of the island's first and oldest Japanese language school. The Baptist presence was surprisingly aided by none other than then-mayor of Los Angeles Frederick T. Woodman.

Before being elected in September of 1917 to his post replacing Charles E. Sebastian, who had resigned

for health reasons, Woodman had served as president of the board of the Harbor Commission for five years. Referred to as the "most modest mayor in America" according to *Sunset Magazine* in 1918, Woodman was known for his unpretentious nature. Mayor Woodman forwarded a letter written to him by the Reverend J.F. Watson, corresponding secretary of the Southern California Baptist Convention, to the Harbor Commission in 1917. Watson explained that "The Missionary Work among the Japanese People on Terminal Island has been assigned to the Baptists and we have two missionaries appointed and several volunteer workers devoting their energies to these men and their families."

Indeed, in *Baptists in America*, author Bill J. Leonard writes that the mission "was instituted in 1916 when women from the First Baptist Church of San Pedro went to Terminal Island, California, to instruct women in English and crochet." Now the Baptist Mission wanted to intensify its efforts and erect a building dedicated to "educational, industrial, and social service work" for the Japanese on the island. "It is our plan to do for these people more than the ordinary religions or missionary work," Watson's letter stated.

By 1918, it was decided. A 100-by-120-foot lot would be leased to the Southern California Baptist Convention for a nominal dollar a month at 249 Terminal Way. The most significant program the mission launched was Seisho Gakko, a Japanese-language school, which was held three times a week immediately after regular public school and then a fourth time on Saturday (a half day). As Seisho means The Bible, Christianity played a significant role in the language instruction. Students sang Japanese hymns, prayed, and listened to a short sermon by the ministers (first Minosuke Ito, followed by Kiyoshi Shiraishi and Eric Kichitaro Yamamoto) before being dismissed to their classes.

As the Seisho Gakko was the first initiation of the Nisei to Christianity, young people were also the main recruits to Sunday services at the Baptist church. Students from Biola (Bible Institute of Los Angeles) came to teach Sunday school, while Reverend Ito and his wife taught American customs to the Japanese wives. A few Issei families chose to convert. By 1931, a total of 256 students attended the Seisho Gakko, which ranged from first grade to junior high school, with six instructors, including the principal.

During the 1930s, a new charismatic figure came to the Baptist Mission, which was becoming a full-fledged church. Her name was Virginia Swanson, a young Midwestern woman who had been deeply influenced by a Japanese medical doctor who served as the Sunday school superintendent of her Baptist church in Minneapolis. While doing a high school paper on the plight of immigrants in the United States, Swanson discovered information about anti-Japanese legislation, which fanned her passion to help the Japanese. Later committing to be a Baptist missionary, she accepted an assignment with the Japanese community in Sacramento before coming to the island. "I knew that they were the people with whom I wanted to share part of my life," she stated in an oral history about the Japanese in the United States.

One of her young charges was Charlie Hamasaki, who found the story of Jesus Christ "fascinating." "I volunteered," he stated, " 'cause I feel sorry for Miss Swanson." Most of the other boys refused baptism, saying "I don't want to take a bath."

Despite the early established presence of the Baptist church, Buddhists still practiced their religion on the island, even without a temple. Soto Zen family services were being held at least bimonthly at the home of *The Southern Coast Herald* publisher, Jusho Hiraga, while another household hosted Shingon services. (The other religion actively practiced on the island was Tenrikyo, a monotheistic religion separate from Buddhism; three households had residential shrines.)

Buddhism finally formally came to Terminal Island

Less than two years after the Buddhist temple sponsored Boy Scout Troop 225, these Nisei members achieved Eagle Scout status in the 1930s.

with the arrival of a minister, Bun'en Ikeda, and his family from Los Angeles in 1930. Ikeda, a native of Shizuoka, had come to the United States in 1927. He served at Zenshuji Soto Mission, the first Soto Zen Buddhist temple in North America, in the Little Tokyo section of Los Angeles for three years. His first goal on Terminal Island was to launch Sokei Gakuen, a Buddhist Japanese-language school alternative. It eventually evolved into a Soto Zen temple community called San Pedro Kotaiji, with Ikeda as the head priest, according to Professor Duncan Williams of USC.

As more of the Issei leaned Buddhist, it was not unusual that many of the students switched over from Seisho to Sokei. The enrollment of the students in the Baptist language school decreased by half, while Sokei's grew to three hundred with six teachers. However, it wasn't unusual for families such as the Nakajis and Horis to split up their multiple children between the two schools. "My father had to distribute his kids so [he] wouldn't be seen as favoring one over the other," said Chizuru Nakaji Boyea.

In the 1930s, two new buildings appeared on the island: the Buddhist church at 463 South Seaside Avenue and a dedicated structure for the Baptist church at 306 Terminal Way (Seisho Gakuen remained at the original location). Christian funerals were held at the Baptist

Terminal Island: Lost Communities on America's Edge

church, while Buddhist ones were usually held on the "mainland," as the Buddhist Hall was a nondescript structure with no special architectural adornments. Large funerals were also held in Fishermen's Hall.

Even as the San Pedro Kotaiji began to offer programs like Boy Scouts for youth, the impact of the Baptist church was still strongly felt by some Nisei. While establishing a preschool for working mothers, Swanson recruited her brother, Buddy, to work with the boys. Buddy taught them how to walk on their hands, and for a while all the boys seemed to be walking on their hands in Fish Harbor.

Dave Nakagawa, a Nisei who later became a youth counselor, had been heavily influenced by the young Baptist minister Kichitaro Eric Yamamoto. Yamamoto, who himself had come to Terminal Island at age fifteen, related closely to the young high school boys, who teasingly referred to him as "Jack" instead of Reverend. He took some interested young men to meetings of the Hillbillies, a Palos Verdes Bible study, buying hot dogs for the whole car in Wilmington afterward. Yamamoto was eventually transferred to a Baptist church in Los Angeles, but his ministry time on Terminal Island would prove to change the entire course of his life.

Below left: Virginia Swanson, a Christian missionary originally from Minnesota, was assigned to serve the Baptist church in the 1930s.

Below right: Rev. Bun'en Ikeda, center in dark suit, stands in front of the Buddhist temple at 463 South Seaside Avenue with members of his family and leaders of the Soto Zen religious community.

Interethnic Relationships in Work, Labor, Business, and Play

Life on Terminal Island in the 1920s and 1930s was by no means monoethnic. Fish Harbor residents were predominantly of Japanese ancestry, but the census study by academician Yuko Konno showed that 3 percent, or 56 people, of the total 1,911 residents of East San Pedro in 1930 were white. Five were Mexican. Moreover, there were the canneries and the harbor, where men, women, and young people of various ethnicities congregated during and after work.

The canneries, more than any other entity, provided the most opportunities for adults of different ethnicities to rub elbows with one another. The cannery owners, after the disappearance of the sole *Nihonjin* cannery on Terminal Island, were white.

One of the pioneers, Wilbur F. Wood, originally from Nova Scotia, was well-known for his good relations with Japanese American fishermen. He joined forces with Paul Eachus to create the California Tunny Canning Co., which was sold to Van Camp in 1915. Wood stayed on as production manager for a couple years before co-founding International Packing Company on Terminal Island. After Southern California Fish Company went bankrupt in 1921, Wood took over as president and remained in that position through World War II.

According to the *Commercial Encyclopedia of the Pacific Southwest: California, Nevada, Utah, and Arizona* (1915), "His fair treatment of the Japanese fishermen in years past when there were great quantities of tuna and

W.B. Ware and his family, who had to resort to living in tents during the Great Depression, faced eviction from their makeshift home on the beach in Terminal Island.

sardines has made for Mr. Wood many staunch friends among this sturdy race, and today when there is considerable competition for the fish, the Japanese loyally stand by him. One of the chief factors making for the success of his new enterprise will be his large fleet of fishermen which is undoubtedly the largest and best in the harbor."

Whether it originated from straight altruism or a mixture of business savvy, Wilbur's generosity toward the Japanese did not go unnoticed. According to Richard Chikami, a member of the Fukuzaki extended family, Nisei fisherman George Fukuzaki paid homage to this cannery leader in the highest way possible: he named his son Wilbur after him.

Other white men who were supportive of the Japanese, according to Chikami, included an insurance agent who spoke Japanese, and Archie Ekdale, a San Pedro maritime lawyer. Ekdale apparently had a close and trusted working relationship with Masaru Ben Akahori, evidenced by several pieces of correspondence on various legal cases, ranging from boat purchases, lawsuits against canneries, the incorporation of Daijin-Gu, and even personal problems involving Issei families. When Akahori had to leave the island because of "messy" financial matters and resettled in Seattle, Ekdale was entrusted to do follow-up work on cases.

Although there was a rare case of a captain hiring men of a different race to go on long fishing expeditions, boats tended to be more monoethnic during the pre–World War II period. The cannery line workers, on the other hand, consisted of Japanese, Mexican, and white women laboring side by side cleaning and canning fish. Filipino men were there, too, usually doing more

Fish Harbor attracted fishermen from around the world, including Yugoslavians and Italians. Most of the non-Japanese fishermen lived across the channel in San Pedro.

Founded in 1924 by Joseph M. Mardesich, one of the Yugoslavian cofounders of French Sardine Company (it adopted the StarKist brand in 1942), Franco-Italian Packing Company hired a diverse workforce.

Van Camp Sea Food cannery workers canned tuna that was steamed before it was packed. 1920.

strenuous work like lifting and cutting whole fish.

In 1934, according to the online exhibit of Taran Schindler's academic work, *Between Catch & Can: The Cannery Women of the Los Angeles Harbor, 1930–1960,* the prevailing wage for cannery workers was thirty-five cents an hour. This low pay propelled a mother of six, Andrea Gomez, to successfully organize a Terminal Island Cannery Workers' Union, which first became affiliated with the American Federation of Labor in 1935.

Montana-born Helen Robello served as one of the union's labor organizers. Formerly a punch-card checker and line worker for Del Monte Cannery, she and her father, the cannery foreman, had lived on the island for two years. According to Robello's oral history with California State University at Long Beach, the Japanese women were first timid about getting involved with the union. Upon joining, however, they faithfully attended meetings, which were usually conducted with both Japanese and Spanish language translations. Japanese women rose up the labor leadership and joined Robello in organizing efforts. By 1941, wages had increased to sixty-five cents an hour after contracted negotiations.

Besides being the prime location for canneries, Tuna Street was where people of different ethnicities sat next to each other in eateries and purchased the same imported hooks at the chandlery stores. Orie Mio experienced this firsthand with her family's two cafés. The first Mio Café, which opened in 1925, had a western-style menu of donuts (two for a nickel), hamburgers (ten cents with potato chips) and dinner with soup, salad, and coffee (up to thirty cents). Targeted toward non-Japanese cannery office workers and fishermen, the café served a diverse customer base, requiring Orie, who was waitress, cashier, dishwasher, and janitor, to learn Spanish. Their second café, started ten years later in 1935, was a larger location that attracted more cannery line workers. The restaurant's employees lived upstairs.

The Yamamoto Company serviced fishing boats owned by Italians and Norwegians. After being paid by canneries at the end of a monthly season, the fishermen finally settled their accounts. The proprietor would calculate outstanding balances on account with his abacus. Non-Japanese customers would balk and insist that calculations be made with an adding machine. In the end, the amount always matched.

Outside of the Fish Harbor was the multicultural neighborhood of Terminal, in which almost 60 percent

The Esparza and Machado children pose with friends on Brighton Beach. From left: Albert Hamlin, Arnold Esparza, Richard Machado, Josephine Esparza, Frank "Snuffy" Machado, Sam Esparza, Leonard Esparza, and Rudolph Esparza. Circa 1930.

Mio Café No. 1, which cannery office workers often frequented, was completely renovated in 1941. The family lived upstairs.

The Fish Harbor chandlery stores had a multicultural clientele.

Terminal Island: Lost Communities on America's Edge

of the more than one thousand residents were white in 1930, according to the meticulous research of Yuko Konno. During the same Census year, almost 32 percent were Mexican, while Japanese and Filipinos each comprised only 5 percent of the total. At its height, when combined with neighborhoods under the jurisdiction of the City of Long Beach, the population in Terminal was estimated at two thousand.

Where the wealthy once lived in resort homes, now cannery workers, lumber workers, and oil company personnel became the core of the residential population in Terminal. The family of Arnold Esparza, who was born on the island, was able to rent a two-story, five-bedroom, two-bath home with a fireplace and garage for fifteen dollars a month in the early 1930s during the Great Depression. The home was a mile away from the beach by then, but one could still get a hamburger at Brighton Beach for five cents. Another San Pedro family who took advantage of the low-cost housing stock was John Olguin's. Olguin, who would become a San Pedro icon and founder of the Cabrillo Marine Aquarium, was able to live in a spacious two-story, six-bedroom home with a garden—a real luxury for his large family. Olguin's mother worked in the French Sardine Company in Fish Harbor with a shift beginning at 5:00 a.m. and ending at 2:00 p.m., so she could be home when her children got home from school. Olguin would climb through a hole in the fence in back of the family home and be on the grounds of Seaside Elementary School.

Interethnic interaction also naturally occurred among the schoolchildren who lived next door to each other in Terminal. Esparza had close relationships with a

The archery club at the Terminal Island playground had white, Nisei, and Latino members. Circa 1930.

number of Japanese American boys his age. His mother, Marie Machado Esparza, operated International Market on Ocean Avenue in Terminal, a grocery store that she acquired from the original owner, E. Swartz. Esparza's father, Samuel, was born in Mexico, but came with his parents to live in the United States when he was eleven years old. Samuel met Marie on Terminal Island when his family moved there, and the couple married in 1921.

Samuel eventually worked as a longshoreman and also for the Hammond Lumber Company, whose garage stood across the street from the International Market.

Arnold Esparza attended the Terminal School with many of the local children, and the boys socialized at the Terminal Island playground, a large park of more than three acres. Ray Hodgson, the beloved playground director, organized archery competitions and a harmonica band. Samuel's semi-pro baseball team, the Deltas, also played there.

While most of the Terminal youth went to Banning High School, Arnold was sent to San Pedro High School, his mother's alma mater, and thus continued his friendships with his Japanese American buddies.

Aside from the public library, Terminal did not have the businesses and attractions that Fish Harbor had. As a result, many Fish Harbor residents, all of whom had ties to canneries, did not set foot in Terminal, while Terminal residents lived more open, multicultural lives.

One such family was the Furutanis, who lived on Ocean Avenue alongside Norwegians, Mexicans, and other Japanese Americans. Both born in Hawaii, Kantaro and Kikue Furutani spoke English well, which was unusual among people in their age group. Unlike the other women, Kikue did not work in a cannery; instead she was the Japanese-language teacher at Seisho School as well as an employee at the immigration station.

Their only son, Hiroshi "Chuck" Furutani, attended Terminal School, and his multiethnic friends exemplified the differences of the two communities on the island. Some Nisei boys in Fish Harbor resented Chuck because his mother, as a Japanese school teacher, was an authority figure. When challenged to fistfights by Japanese American boys, Chuck came with his "gang" composed of white neighborhood boys.

Kantaro Furutani did some seasonal cannery work, but he was primarily known for his work casting propellers for fishing boats at a service station, which also served as a garage and foundry. Across the way were "sporting houses," house of prostitution. He was also aware of the marijuana trade among the bohemian community, which apparently still had a presence on the island in the 1930s.

Once the Nisei from Fish Harbor began attending junior high and high school in San Pedro and Wilmington, their exposure to students of other ethnicities increased dramatically. Again, according to the statistical analysis by Yuko Konno, Japanese only comprised a little more than 8 percent of the graduates of Dana Junior High School from 1930 to 1939. The percentage for San Pedro High School from 1920 to 1941 was about the same, with spikes of 20 percent in certain classes in 1940 and 1941. (This may be due to the worsening relationship between the United States and Japan; Issei parents may have curtailed their Nisei children's education in Japan.)

Boys, especially those who were on sports teams, had more opportunities to socialize with those of another race. Toshiro Izumi was too small to play organized sports, yet went to football games with his Filipino friend, Ben Amores, who apparently lived in Terminal.

Before World War II, four hundred Filipino Americans lived in the Los Angeles Harbor district that included San Pedro and Wilmington, according to *Filipinos in Carson and the South Bay* by Florante Peter and Roselyn Estepa Ibanez. One of the centers of the pre–World War II Filipino community was Beacon and Sixth Streets in San Pedro, where hotels, cafés, and barbershops catered to this population. A much smaller group lived in Terminal, but many prominent community leaders, including those of the Filipino Community of the Los Angeles Harbor area, were employed by the Terminal Island canneries.

As of 1940, Filipinos living in Terminal were predominantly bachelors in shared lodging. There were some instances of mixed marriages, including a Filipino man with an Issei woman. According to Bob San Jose, one of the postwar leaders of the Filipino Community Center in Wilmington, there was even one Filipino leader who followed his Japanese American wife into a wartime detention center.

Individuals from different walks of life met along the main thoroughfare of Tuna Street. June 2, 1938.

Fisherman vs. Fisherman

At the turn of the twentieth century, ethnic relations among immigrant fishermen—in particular those involving the Japanese—was not good in Southern California. In fact, in 1902, the *Los Angeles Times* reported a fishermen's strike in San Pedro in reaction to the "Japanese invasion." With a telling subtitle, "Italian, Austrian, and German Catchers of Sea Food Refuse to Compete with Little Brown Men from Land of the Mikado," the article reported that Japanese fishermen were believed to be driving down the price of fish from three dollars a pound to two dollars. It did, however, also state that Japanese newcomers, more adept at deep-sea fishing, were bringing in different kinds of fish, including grouper and rock cod, than the catch of the other more established fishermen.

As both the Italians and Yugoslavians would go on to develop thriving neighborhoods in San Pedro, they did not live in Fish Harbor or even Terminal. But as many canneries were based in Terminal Island, there were still many points of interethnic intersection.

For the most part, after the establishment of Fish Harbor, there seemed to be peaceful coexistence among the three major ethnic groups directly involved in fishing. According to the Bureau of Commercial Fisheries summary (1931–1932), out of a total of 1,582 commercial fishing licenses issued in the San Pedro area, 603 were for Japanese; 363, Yugoslavian; 134, Italian; and 23, Portuguese.

Various fishing practices were shared from one culture to another. For example, in his dissertation, Kanshi Yamashita asserted that the Italian "felluca" hull-type boat was the model for the *ken-ken* boat. The hooks, lures, and bamboo poles, all imported from Japan, were used by all tuna fishermen, no matter their ethnicity. The lampara net, with its origin in the Mediterranean, was apparently introduced to Wakayama by a Terminal Island fisherman after World War II.

The cooperative spirit on the island was almost extinguished in 1938 when a labor schism divided the fishermen across racial lines. Up to this time, the Deep Sea and Purse Seine Fishermen's Union, which represented some of the Japanese seine workers, also called boat hullers, was affiliated with the American Federation of Labor (AFL), one of the oldest federations of unions in the United States. The Deep Sea and Purse Seine Fishermen's Union was a craft union, which encompassed only individuals working a certain level of trade. A newcomer and rival, the Committee for Industrial Organization (CIO), advocated a different approach—the creation of a national industrial union representing all workers from fishing to canning. Toward this end, the fishermen voted to merge the Deep Sea and Purse Seine Fishermen's Union with two other unions to become the United Fishermen's Union of the Pacific (UFU) in December 1937. According to Leo Baunach's essay "The International Fishermen and Allied Workers of America," UFU was still essentially a craft union, but provided "a first step" toward industrial unionism.

Supporting this consolidation were the Yugoslavian fishermen. Family ties even came into play, according to Baunach, as one influential Croatian leader in Washington state, a CIO and UFU supporter, had relatives in San Pedro and was in close contact with them.

In spring of 1938, the UFU made a bold move: it demanded that the canneries sign exclusive agreements to only buy tuna on boats manned by the UFU. The canneries refused, and in April of 1938 a strike was called. After twenty-two days, 250 fishermen from San Pedro left the UFU, creating a new organization, the Seine and Line Fishermen's Union of San Pedro, which received an AFL charter. With Joseph Mandarano as its temporary president, the newly created union now comprised 250 Italian and five hundred Japanese fishermen. By May 20, the union announced that they had reached an agreement with boat owners and that the "group may go to sea in a few days," according to the *Los Angeles Times*.

Essentially, the UFU was on its way to being "busted." The organization would not go down without a fight. The police patrolled the waterfront on June 21, 1938, as the Japanese and Italian fishermen resumed work. Violence broke out at the AFL-affiliated Seine and Line Fishermen's Union meeting at the San Pedro Central Labor Council Hall in June 1938. Two Yugoslavian men were stabbed in a showdown in a near riot occurring outside of the hall on West Ninth Street.

Then on June 23, 1938, *Rafu Shimpo* reported that "terrorism" had visited Fish Harbor. "One Japanese was being treated for severe knife wounds to his face and body, while three officials of the Japanese Fishermen's Association were thrown off the pier and narrowly escaped drowning at the hands of an angry mob of Jugo-Slav fishermen," the report, which was filed via telephone, stated.

Ironically, the victim, only referred to as Nagata, had been incorrectly identified as a member of the AFL affiliate when he was in fact a member of the Yugoslavian-supported UFU. According to the report, he had been surrounded by a mob of five hundred Yugoslavians in front of California Bank on Tuna Street across from Mildred Obarr Walizer Elementary School. In the other incident, a mob of three hundred "unceremoniously dumped" three Fishermen's Association officials into the water from the pier along Seaside Avenue. Fortunately, "a crowd of Americans rescued the victims of a possible watery grave."

The UFU continued its strike throughout the summer, while the Italian and Japanese fishermen continued to fish. Tension remained high as bricks were hurled at the San Pedro homes of Italian men at sea. On the water, Japanese fishermen faced attacks of rocks, potatoes, and epithets.

The conflict ended with the Seine and Line Fishermen's Union prevailing. In 1939, the office was located in Fish Harbor at Fishermen's Hall.

The U.S. Coast Guard stationed armed guards at various docks in Fish Harbor as early as July of 1941. Guardsmen were assigned to defend oil tank farms and refineries in the distance.

Islanders' Response to Hostile Laws, Conflict, and Americanization

The first anti-Japanese fishing legislation was introduced in the California Assembly in 1919, according to Frank Chuman's *The Bamboo People*. AB 135 sought to limit fishing licenses to citizens of the United States and aliens who declared that they planned to become citizens. Of course, again, because of standing naturalization laws, Japanese could not even consider the possibility of naturalization that was open to Yugoslavian, Italian, and Portuguese immigrant fishermen. "If such a law were passed in California, it would mean utter ruin to the Japanese fishermen," declared Eliot Grinnell Mears in his 1928 report.

Due to the efforts of the Central Japanese Association of Los Angeles (the predecessor of today's Japanese

"All that Dalmatian fishermen, for instance, need to do in order to obtain fishing rights, is to take out citizenship papers; but the Japanese have no such recourse, since they cannot become citizens."

—ELIOT GRINNELL MEARS,
Resident Orientals on the American Pacific Coast (1928)

Chamber of Commerce of Southern California), the canneries, and a coalition of both Japanese and non-Japanese fishermen's organizations, that initial piece of legislation did not pass. But this marked the beginning of a regular barrage of bills that the political leaders of Terminal Island had to fight practically every year for more than two decades. From 1919 to 1933, seven bills requiring citizenship in commercial fishing were introduced in California.

Tom Toshihiko Kamei, who grew up on Terminal Island and later became a leader of the Japanese Chamber of Commerce, recalled that the Central Japanese Association, or Chuo Nihonjin Kai, made annual contributions of three thousand dollars to combat passage of legislation that would limit Issei participation in fishing. Chizuru Nakaji Boyea also remembered the many times her father, as the president of the Fishermen's Association, took trips to Sacramento with the secretary, Hirosaburo Yokozeki, to fight legislation.

Postcard of Fish Harbor. Circa 1925.

Opposite: A line of purse seiners docked outside of Van Camp cannery.

The Japanese-language history book *Zaibei Nihonjinshi* placed fishing on par of importance with both truck farming and floriculture, in terms of Japanese American enterprise in Southern California. One of its chapters, "Economic Status of the Japanese in California" reported the San Pedro fish catch in 1918 as the following: tuna, 8,116 tons at $119 per ton; albacore, 6,431 tons at $125; sardines, 151,480 tons at $20; skipjack (*katsuo*), 2,578 tons at $70; and yellowtail, 1,940 tons at $50. Including $100,000 for miscellaneous fish, the total value for that year was $2,377,055. Sixty percent of the albacore catch could be attributed to Japanese fishermen. While the volume of certain kinds of fish fluctuated throughout the years, fishing in the area hit a pre–World War II high in 1933–34 of $22,000,000.

There was no doubt that the achievements of Japanese American fishermen benefited the development of the larger ethnic community. Moreover, their success also contributed to the economic health of the canneries, which were predominantly owned by non-Japanese. So cannery leaders often came to the defense of the Japanese, with both lobbying participation and dollars.

Section 990 of the State Fish and Game code was always vulnerable to being altered to restrict Issei from fishing commercially. In April of 1933, the code was amended to read that only a person who had continuously resided in the United States for a year prior to applying would be eligible for a license. Every individual working on the boat, even the crew, had to hold a commercial fishing license.

Donald H. Estes's meticulously documented article " 'Offensive Stupidity,' and the Struggle of Abe Tokunosuke" follows the case of a San Diego–based Japanese fisherman who was charged with violating the code because he used Japanese crew members who lived in Mexico. Tokunosuke, the proprietor of the Southern Commercial Company, had twenty-five tuna boats that were sent out to Mexico and Central and South America on a regular basis. The Superior Court ruled in Tokunosuke's favor—saying that the amended code was unconstitutional—and both the court of appeals and state supreme court refused to give it another hearing.

Subsequent efforts to change the code were buoyed by anti-Japanese sentiments that were brewing among California politicians. One maintained that Japanese American involvement in fishing may threaten the country's national security, as vessels could potentially be turned into torpedo boats.

The relationship between the Japanese on Terminal Island and the government of Japan, specifically the military, was a complicated one. The arrival of Japanese naval warships in San Pedro Bay every four years was cause for an intergenerational celebration. Issei organized children to assemble and sometimes even perform songs.

The Issei with close ties to the elite in Japan prided themselves on socializing with the naval officers and donated funds to welcome them. The island also had a branch of the Japanese Association (*Nihonjin Kai*), which was established in 1919. This Japanese Association often served as a liaison between the immigrant community and the nation of Japan.

At the same time, the older Nisei of Terminal Island were coming of age and starting to assume leadership positions. According to an essay written by Lucile Regan on June 1, 1936, published in *Red Lacquer Bridge*, the Terminal Island Japanese American Citizens League (JACL) chapter was established on April 24 of the same year with one hundred members. At the installation were various leaders, teachers, and a member of the Board of Education. According to Ryono's *Although Patriotic, We Were Drydocked*, the chapter leaders in 1936 included George Fukuzaki, president, and Misako Ishii, the female pharmacist who served as secretary. An office was eventually established at 615 Tuna Street.

The JACL, a Nisei organization that initially excluded noncitizens from membership, fought for legislation that would promote the Americanization of the Japanese American people. For instance, one of its earliest activities included lobbying Congress so that Nisei women who married Issei would still be able to retain their U.S. citizenship. They also supported a successful movement in which Issei veterans of World War I would be able to attain naturalization. (This would directly benefit Terminal Island fisherman Henry K. Masai, a World War I veteran and naturalized citizen.)

Through the leadership of a young Nisei attorney from Sacramento, Walter Tsukamoto, the national organization played a pivotal role in 1939 to ensure that Issei could continue to fish.

Following on the heels of the contentious labor battle between the Italian and Issei-supported AFL versus the CIO in San Pedro, Assemblyman Sam Yorty, a supporter of the CIO, introduced AB 336 in January 1939. (Yorty would later become mayor of Los Angeles.) AB 336 proposed amending Section 990 so that only U.S. citizens and legal residents of California could obtain commercial fishing licenses. Anyone who fished for a living, whether a jig boat operator or a captain of a tuna clipper, had to have that license. If passed, the amendment would have removed three out of four Japanese fishermen from the fishing industry, according to Estes.

During this same time period, two other related bills, calling for even broader restrictions, were introduced in the state assembly and the senate. The debate deteriorated into accusations questioning the Issei fishermen's patriotism with again the allegation that tuna vessels could be used to shoot torpedoes.

One of the business leaders who definitively supported the Japanese resident fishermen was B. Houssels, vice president of Van Camp Sea Food Company. He wrote to the committee:

> The Japanese government has absolutely nothing to do with these boats, nor did they subsidize them in any way. The owners and captains have been residents for many years (twenty-thirty). I have known them for more than twenty years, or ever since I have been in the fishing business. If they are naval officers, Japan must have had a long vision and started out twenty-five or thirty years ago. In my opinion . . . [it] is a bunch of hooey.

He concluded, "I don't believe that there is a man in California in a position to better know the relative facts than myself."

In the end, due to a lot of political maneuvering by JACL president Tsukamoto, who consulted with San Diego fisherman Tokunosuke and Hirosaburo Yokozeki of the Southern California Japanese Fishermen's Association on Terminal Island, the bill died in committee.

The following year, three new bills were introduced in the state legislature. They, too, did not pass, but within five years, two amendments to Section 990 eventually were approved.

The Last Issues of the *Southern Coast Herald;* Un-American Activities Investigators Send a Telegram

Besides word of mouth, the Terminal Islanders received their news like most others did in Japanese American communities throughout Southern California: mainstream radio broadcasts, the *Los Angeles Times*, the *San Pedro News-Pilot*, and the Japanese American vernaculars, including the Los Angeles–based *Rafu Shimpo* and *Kashu Mainichi*. Nisei paperboys such as Toshiro Izumi and Yukio Tatsumi collected deliveries of *Rafu Shimpo* from the Pacific Electric train station in the afternoon and dispersed them throughout the island. Frank Takeuchi and Iwao Hara delivered the competing *Kashu Mainichi*, while Charlie Hamasaki handled *Sangyo Nippo*, the morning daily.

In addition to these "mainland" vernaculars, which both had Terminal Island branch addresses, there was also one other special source: *Minami Engan Jiho* or *Southern Coast Herald*, published entirely in Japanese by Jusho Hiraga who was described as "a small hunch-backed man," and edited by Shigewaka Ishida. Released on Sunday afternoon, the paper was assembled and apparently typeset on the island and printed in Los Angeles. According to its legal postal report, a total of approximately nineteen thousand copies were distributed via mail or delivery every year.

Comforting neighborhood news—births and marriages arranged by *baishakunin*, or go-betweens (sometimes publisher Hiraga acted as baishakunin)—were mixed in with essays promoting Americanization. Advertisements ranged from promoting Little Tokyo businesses like the historic bean cake confectionery Mikawaya and a children's store, Baby House, to both mainstream and Japanese-specialty mortuaries in Wilmington, Long Beach, and Little Tokyo.

In one of the last issues of the newspaper, two families—the Tanis and the Kobatas—publicly thanked organizations and individuals who helped to officially send off their sons who had been recently drafted into the U.S. Army. From 1940 to 1941, twenty-five men from Terminal Island, including Charlie's older brother, Tamikazu Tom Hamasaki, had been inducted into the military. Some households with sons in the army even proudly donned blue-star service banners within their Fish Harbor homes.

While there was apparent resistance and criticism about the drafting of these young men for fear they might get caught in the middle of conflict with Japan, the *Southern Coast Herald* was firmly on the side of supporting the American troops. In the November 23, 1941, issue, the lead article implored its readers to comply with United States' policy during this "urgent time." In addition to its monthly parties for draftees, the newspaper sponsored drives to collect money for the USO and war bonds, efforts it described as tangible ways to contribute to a "peaceful" diplomatic relationship that was being threatened by Japan's continued expansion into East Asia and the United States' boycott of oil and scrap-iron exports to natural resource–poor Japan.

Unbeknownst to the islanders, they were being carefully watched by outsiders with ties to Washington, D.C., during this time. Texas Congressman Martin Dies, head of the Special Committee on Un-American Activities, had sent two investigators, James Steedman

Kazuye and Toshiko Hatashita in their home at 154-A Terminal Way. The Blue Star banner on the wall was in honor of Kimio "Kim" Hatashita, the Nisei male in the household who enlisted in the U.S. military in 1941. In the corner is a Shinto altar.

and William Dunstan, to Southern California. On May 9, 1941, the investigators sent a Western Union telegram back to D.C. with their findings.

Like the California politicians who advocated the ban on Issei commercial fishermen, Steedman and Dunstan maintained that the Japanese-owned fishing boats—of which they reported there to be 250 in Los Angeles Harbor—could be converted to "naval craft" and become a security menace. The investigators also claimed that "one thousand Japanese are trained pilots and familiar with harbor and coastline." Their telegram continued:

NO EFFORT BEING MADE TO ROUND THEM UP. CAN FURNISH WITNESS ON THESE FACTS.

The three-page telegram revealed the men's exasperation with Van Camp and other local canneries for their support of the Japanese fishermen. Even the army and navy did not escape the investigators' criticism; they viewed the military as being "unconcerned" by Fish Harbor's close vicinity to strategic sites, such as Reeves airfield, Bethlehem shipbuilding, and the oil refineries. The telegram also identified red-flag organizations: the prefectural groups, which they characterized as "pressure groups operated on same basis as other fascist groups"; Shinto cults; and a Japanese military-veterans association.

The noose was being tightened, and unfortunately for the Japanese fishing villagers on Terminal Island, they would soon feel its grip.

The shops and restaurants on the usually vibrant Tuna Street were closed down the day after the bombing of Pearl Harbor, December 8, 1941.

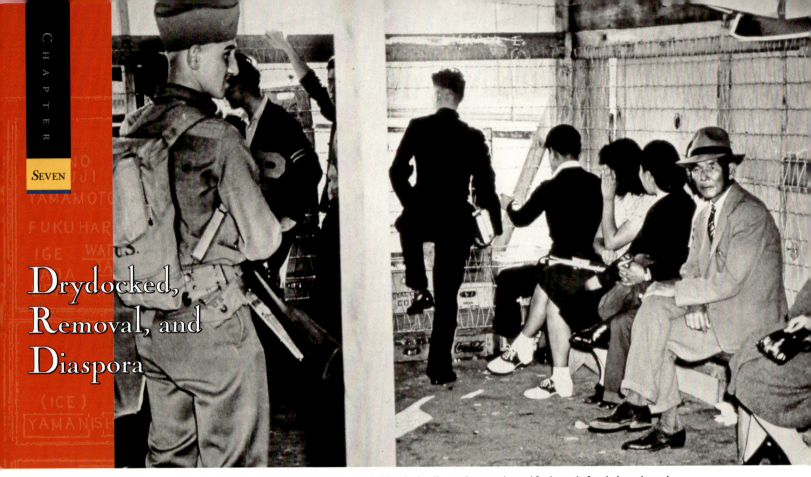

C H A P T E R

SEVEN

Drydocked, Removal, and Diaspora

Passengers waiting for the ferry on December 7, 1941, were held at the landing under armed guard for hours before being released.

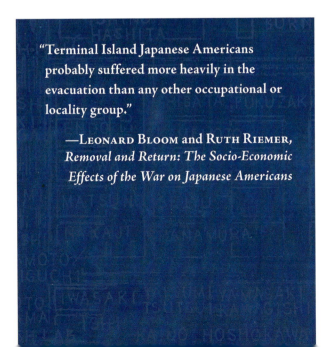

"Terminal Island Japanese Americans probably suffered more heavily in the evacuation than any other occupational or locality group."

—LEONARD BLOOM and RUTH RIEMER, *Removal and Return: The Socio-Economic Effects of the War on Japanese Americans*

December 7, 1941

On Sunday morning, December 7, 1941 (PST), Kimiye Okuno stood on Justus Sato's barge to see if she could see her father's boat, the *Amazon*, on its way home into Fish Harbor. It was a clear, sunny day, but something didn't seem right. It was before noon and all the boats were rushing into the harbor—first come, first unloaded—but this day, the intensity seemed particularly frenetic.

Another young woman, eighteen-year-old Fusaye Mio, was there, too. Earlier she had received a phone call from a friend while she was in the middle of the

Fish Harbor leaders were arrested by police and the FBI without any reasons given.

laundry. "Japan and United States are at war!" the friend exclaimed, but Fusaye thought that she must have been joking. She rushed over to the other Mio restaurant. One look at her father's face, and she knew. Her friend's premonition was right—they would be entering a new era of heightened conflict between the United States and Japan.

Now the "fishing boats were coming home by hundreds," recalled Fusaye. "It was just like a flock of sheep being herded into their pens."

Leading the pack was a small bait boat manned by Thomas Takeshi Okimoto. He operated the boat with his father-in-law, who was ill and stayed home. The boat didn't have a radio, so Okimoto had no clue what was going on. Around Point Fermin, he had been stopped and searched by officials who examined his catch and the boat "from bow to stem." They never explained why.

He docked the boat at California Marine and Canning Company, preparing to unload his catch like he always did. Usually cannery workers helped secure the boat, but today they just watched from a distance. Tying a rope around some pilings, Thomas stepped onto the dock.

"You goddamned Jap," a man cursed and then walked away. The cannery manager then told him that he could not accept any fish that day because Japan had bombed Pearl Harbor. Okimoto was able to unload his catch with some San Pedro–based fresh fish markets. That was the last time this boat would leave Fish Harbor.

Takeo Shintani was working as a radio operator on a fishing vessel when his captain asked him to contact other boats at sea. Getting on the transmitter, he was immediately ordered by the Coast Guard to get off the radio. He was in violation of the military order of radio silence. Perplexed, Shintani turned to a regular radio broadcast station and listened to the report. He wondered, where was this Pearl Harbor that they were talking about?

They immediately set out to return to Terminal Island, but before they entered the harbor, the Coast Guard ordered them to stop and interrogated them: *Who had been the one who had violated the radio silence order?* Shintani stepped forward, showing them his operator's license and seaman's card that proved that he was an American citizen.

The vessel finally was allowed to dock. But the ordeal was not over. Half of the crew were Issei. Without even having an opportunity to see their families, they were taken in by government agents. Shintani, a Nisei, was not detained.

The nightmare continued. Families quickly dug holes in the sand between their houses and buried anything that could be deemed suspicious. In Kanshi Yamashita's home, there were his childhood rifles, his U.S. and Japanese naval magazines, and his pictures of warships.

Tomitaro Marumoto had stopped to help a friend with his boat on December 7 and wasn't able to enter Fish Harbor until two or three o'clock in the afternoon, after the noon order. He was immediately taken to the federal prison on Terminal Island.

Toshiro Izumi, who had to be escorted to the San Pedro ferry landing by a couple of agents so he could return from a football game in Hollywood, came home to discover his father surrounded by four or five government men. Wearing a coat over his suit, his father told him, "I think this is going to be a long war, so take care, and keep healthy." And then he was gone.

FBI agents barged into Japanese American homes throughout Terminal Island from early evening to the middle of the night. Raids were also taking place throughout Los Angeles County, Imperial Valley, and Orange County. Men and women were taken into custody by police and sheriff deputies, and in many cases, were temporarily held in the penitentiary on Terminal Island.

Jenmatsu Mio, the elderly restaurateur, gathered his four children and told them he would probably be picked up because of his work in the community. His hunch was correct; the family was visited by authorities, and he was taken into custody, no matter how much his teenage son George begged for the authorities to take him instead.

Nearby, in the northern neighborhood of Hokkaido, nineteen-year-old Roy Hideo Yamamoto responded to a knock on the door at midnight, only to have a flashlight shone in his face by two G-men. They were looking for the Issei fishermen that lived in the Yamamoto family's expansive, custom-made home. They were taken into cars. Yamamoto never saw the fishermen again.

Some individuals flocked to the Baptist church for comfort. "That week was a dark one," wrote Swanson. "The phone was dead, food was hard to get, lights were blacked out in the evening, and it rained torrents. Wednesday evening we had our prayer meeting in the dark."

Planned Roundup

The individuals who were taken on December 7 and a few days afterward were all Japan-born leaders of an activity or an organization that was considered "very Japanese." That meant the Japanese Association, with its direct ties to Japan, the Japanese-language school, the Buddhist temple, or martial arts groups. Reverend Bun'en Ikeda, founder of the Sokei school, was arrested, while the Issei Christian minister Reverend Jitsuo Morikawa and the Hawaii-born Japanese-school teacher Kikue Furutani remained free, at least for that moment. Shinkichi Miyoshi, the head of the Shinto shrine, was not immediately taken into custody, one of many examples of the arbitrary nature of the roundups.

As the telegram from the Dies Committee investigators indicated, the Issei were being watched, even months before the bombing of Pearl Harbor and America's official entry into World War II. For instance, as early as October 1941, Gongoro Tonai, a produce man in San Pedro, found himself being questioned by authorities regarding twenty-five dollars that he had given to the Japanese Navy. That donation had been given to quiet a prominent community member's wife who had been on a fundraising team. And for that, Tonai found himself under arrest on December 7.

A December 8 article in the *Los Angeles Times*, "Japanese Aliens' Roundup Starts: F.B.I. Hunting Down 300 Subversives and Plans to Hold 3000 Today," confirmed that plans to detain Japanese Americans had

Individuals rushed to get their children's birth certificates from safety deposit boxes and funds from accounts at California Bank.

been in the works prior to the bombing of Pearl Harbor. "It was known that Federal officials planned to hold persons rounded up at various outlying police stations, according to plans formulated months ago, until a concentration camp is decided upon."

The article stated that one official admitted, "Although we had our plans set, the Japanese attack caught us a little early."

School as Usual

The day after the Pearl Harbor bombing was a Monday, which meant the Nisei students had to cross the channel on the ferry to attend Dana Junior High School or San Pedro and Banning High Schools.

Despite her father being taken into custody in the middle of the night, Fusaye Mio and her younger sister, Kyoko, made their way to the ferry landing just like any other school day. But it wasn't an ordinary day. All the Japanese American students were denied entry unless they showed proof of their U.S. ancestry. Parents had to provide their children's birth certificates—many had to be removed from safe deposit boxes. William Goodwin, San Pedro High School principal, seeing that a sizable population of his student body, two hundred, was absent, actually went to Terminal Island, according to the *San Pedro News Press*. School identification cards, even for those born in Japan, eventually made it possible for students to travel back and forth on the ferry without incident.

Reactions to the presence of Nisei Terminal Islanders at school was mixed. Min Tonai, Gongoro Tonai's son, was relieved to find that his school friends did not seem to view him as the enemy. Living in San Pedro at

the time, he was sitting in homeroom at Dana Junior High School when he saw a group of Terminal Islanders coming in late. "The kids in my class stood up and clapped, because they were so glad to see them be able to come to school," he recalled.

Fusaye Mio also remembered that her favorite teacher at San Pedro High School vocalized her support: "You have nothing to be sorry about, and if you hear any remarks from any of the students, just let me know."

Others found that their fellow classmates started to look at them differently, while certain teachers seemed less than enthusiastic to have them in their classes.

Terminal Island Becomes an Interrogation Center

Meanwhile, the roundup of "Japanese aliens" throughout California continued—ninety-three men and eight women were booked, fingerprinted, and photographed in Los Angeles County Jail by December 9, 1941, according to the *Los Angeles Times*. They were transported to the Terminal Island Immigration Station, where more than three hundred Japanese were being interrogated.

Some could not take the pressure of detention. A forty-eight-year-old doctor from Gardena, reportedly having served in the Japanese Army medical corps in the past, slashed his wrists with a razor blade while being held at Terminal Island and bled to death.

Virginia Swanson went to the station to vouch for the good character of the men whom she knew at Terminal Island. Some, thankfully, were released. The rest were on their way to destinations far away, some not to be seen by their families for three years.

Armed guards were assigned to certain shuttered stores like Hama and Hashimoto chandleries in Fish Harbor; families, now without their patriarch, wondered what to do next.

Tomitaro Marumoto, along with other men, was to be moved to Tuna Canyon Detention Station in Tujunga. Formerly a Civilian Conservation Corps (CCC) camp, Tuna Canyon was taken over by the U.S. Department of Justice, so its Immigration and Naturalization Service would have a secure place to identify and detain "enemy aliens," including Japanese, Germans, and Italians. Its first prisoners were received on December 16, 1941.

The Marumoto family gathered together to see their patriarch off on a bus to Tuna Canyon. Upon seeing her father outside the Terminal Island Immigration Station, the youngest daughter, Junko, about four, called out, "Father, don't get on that machine. You won't be able to come home, so don't get on it!"

The Mio children were also able to visit their imprisoned father, who was apparently going to be sent to a place that required warm clothing. Only two members of the family were allowed to see him. They reported he was wearing a prison uniform and was under armed guard. The children, shocked to see their father in such a state, broke down.

The military, meanwhile, had descended on the island. No one could enter or leave the area without first being checked by the soldiers. A blackout was temporarily instituted, and boats were allowed to leave and enter the harbor only during daylight hours in the beginning. Italian, German, or Japanese aliens were all barred from going out to sea "under any conditions."

Even model airplanes were considered possible contraband and were confiscated.

Sardine fishing was immediately affected, as vessels were not allowed to fish at night. One cannery reportedly released all of its Japanese American cannery workers, but other women continued employment. When there was talk of the Cannery Workers' Union possibly ousting its Japanese members, Iku Yamashita and Chizuru Nakaji Boyea drove to the union meeting in Wilmington. Signing in with the names of their mothers, who were members, these young Nisei women sat in the meeting. According to Boyea, Yamashita stood up to give an impassioned speech on behalf of the Japanese workers, effectively shutting down any consideration of excluding them from membership.

Stores, including Hashimoto Company, were padlocked for a month and kept under military watch. Jeeps with uniformed military police were a common scene. Storekeepers with perishable food saw their investment literally rot away. Due to a mixup, one Issei woman, whose husband had been taken away, was trapped in her upstairs apartment above their locked business. Her phone was disconnected. A next-door neighbor delivered food to her through a window every day. One white friend finally confronted authorities, who admitted that her confinement had been a case of misunderstanding.

The war caused frenzy and inexplicable behavior. Homes were turned upside down. Seemingly harmless items—a boy's Morse code telegraph key, amateur radio components, kendo certificates—were confiscated. Shortwave band radios, many that Nisei boys had made in junior high school, were considered contraband, as were flashlights, cameras, and, of course, guns. (The two chandlery stores, in addition to selling heavy-duty fishing equipment, sold guns; sixty firearms and twenty thousand rounds of ammunition were immediately confiscated.) The JACL made arrangements for the contraband to be turned in to the Fishermen's Hall, even as the FBI continued their inspections, sometimes nightly at late hours.

Before Christmas, sheriff's deputies and FBI agents barged into the home of Kuniko Okumura. "Some of them broke Christmas ornaments on the trees. Their excuse being—there might be explosives in them. Of course, there weren't any. For if they truly believed there were any explosives they surely wouldn't have jeopardized their own lives," she stated.

New Year's Eve and Day, the most festive time in Fish Harbor, were somber. Virginia Swanson of the Baptist church conducted a financial census and came up with these results: eighteen families needed immediate financial aid; sixty-three families could manage one month; seventy-six families, two months; ninety- three families, three months; thirty-four families, four months; and twenty-three families, five months. Surprisingly, 143 families reported that they could survive six to twelve months, and 111 families, one year. Although the situation was desperate and dire for some, more families believed that they could somehow economically weather this enormous setback despite of money being frozen in Japanese banks. JACL had seven hundred dollars in its welfare fund and gave it to Swanson to distribute as necessary for food and financial aid.

In spite of all this uncertainty, the harbor commissioners made no mention of the future of Fish Harbor or the Japanese American community in the Harbor Commission minutes. In fact, the January 20, 1942, minutes noted that the historic Nanka Company had applied for a permit to alter its structure at 700 Tuna

Street, which was approved by the harbor engineer and general manager. Within a month, this request would be completely moot.

On Saturday, January 24, 1942, a handpainted sign was on display outside of Fishermen's Hall. It announced that photographs of Issei would be taken for identification cards at the hall on the next day, Sunday, at 9:30 p.m. Apparently the local chapter of the JACL was assisting in this effort. Later, the national JACL would be heavily criticized for being too accommodating to the U.S. government during World War II at the expense of certain segments of the Japanese American community, including the Issei, Kibei Nisei, and wartime dissenters.

February 2, 1942

On Monday, February 2, the FBI agents—reportedly 150 strong—returned to the island. They were not after radios or so-called contraband this time. They were after men again.

This time, it was all remaining Japan-born men with commercial fishing licenses. The number was estimated to be four hundred.

"Hey, we got a young one here," one of the agents said as he picked up eighteen-year-old Charlie Hamasaki at home. "Get your coat, shoes, and everything."

"It's too hot."

"No, put on your coat."

Hamasaki and the other men were taken to the

The federal prison, which once incarcerated Al Capone, received its first inmates in June of 1938. The immigration station was one of the buildings on the left. Both Reservation Point facilities held Japanese Americans on December 7, 1941, and days afterward.

Terminal Island Immigration Station. He was surprised to see his childhood friends James and Ann Kaseroff also there. Recruited for their bilingual abilities, they were serving as interpreters. "What are you doing here?" they asked Hamasaki, assuming that he was American born.

"I'm an enemy alien," he replied with ironic sarcasm.

Other Nisei, including Toshiro Izumi, also arrived to help translate, so Hamasaki stepped in as an interpreter for his elders. When it was getting late, he told the authorities. "I'm going home."

An unsuspecting official thanked him for his help, and as Hamasaki headed for the door, he was stopped. "He belongs in here," the authorities said.

At Mildred Obarr Walizer Elementary School, the announcement was made: students' fathers were being taken away. The affected children were allowed to leave to say good-bye. One fifth-grade boy opted not to and stayed in his seat.

Tom Yamamoto, the proprietor of a market on Tuna Street, got word that some of the detained fishermen were requesting personal items and clothing from their homes. Yamamoto volunteered to collect them and was driving his Yamamoto Company truck, filled with the fishermen's suitcases, when he heard yelling from the second floor of the holding facility. "Yamamoto-*san*! Yamamoto-*san*!" Hands waved through the prison bars.

The grocer bent his head to see if he could recognize the men and then—crash! He had hit a parked car. It happened to be owned by one of the authorities. *Surely I will go to jail now*, thought Yamamoto, an Issei. But after trading insurance information, he was free to leave.

After about three days at the immigration station, Hamasaki and the others, including men from Imperial Valley, were taken to Union Station in downtown Los Angeles. The Japanese men were escorted onto a train. Hamasaki had no idea where they were heading. The blinds were drawn, but that didn't stop him from stealing looks. Stops in Bakersfield, Fresno, Marysville, and then out of the state—Eugene, Oregon and Seattle, Washington. When they were fed a meal including steak, a rare treat, some became panicked. *They are going to kill us in the middle of nowhere.*

Finally, they stopped in Missoula, Montana, where half of the passenger cars remained. Hamasaki rode until the end of the line: Bismarck, North Dakota. He had never seen snow before. It was cold as hell, he remembered, maybe thirty degrees below zero.

Another Terminal Islander who found himself in Bismarck was Henry Murakami, a fisherman for Van Camp and a devout member of the Baptist church, who had a pregnant wife and four young children. When he was taken, he was not given a chance to put on his shoes and socks, so arrived in Bismarck in *zori*, Japanese slippers. He begged for the guards to get him a pair of shoes, but Murakami's pleas were ignored, so that he had to instead wrap clothes around his feet to stand in line to get into the mess hall. By the third day, his feet were frostbitten.

The men stayed in approximately twenty-five barracks, forty in each room, twenty beds lining each side. Some became depressed, withdrawn, yet Hamasaki, known for his outspokenness, would not be silenced. The food was lousy, so he complained. Not to the detention camp's director, but to the Spanish consulate. Spain, neutral during World War II, was supposed to represent the Issei prisoners' interests.

The Bismarck camp was officially called the Fort Abraham Lincoln Detention Camp, and was actually

Many Issei Terminal Islanders spent the war years in all-male alien detention camps in locations like Bismarck, North Dakota, and Santa Fe, New Mexico. Here in Santa Fe in 1945 were, from left, back row: George Yamanishi, unidentified, Tadashi Hiromoto, Minoru Kuwabata, Tsutomu Fujii, unidentified, Yasuo Seko, Masuto Seko (wearing a *Yogore* T-shirt), Hideo Kimura, Yutaka Hiromoto, Tokio Tsuji. Middle: Masao Hamachi, Yoshiichi Shibanaka, Frank Ego, unidentified, Hiroaki Kamemoto, Kiyoshi Matsuno, Yoshiharu Yamanishi, Hideo Wada, Ichiro "Art" Miyamoto. Front row: Yurao Kobata, Akira Kaino (wearing a San Pedro Pirates T-shirt), Shigeru Ozawa, Kisaburo Ochi, Gunpe Honda, and Osamu Kamemoto.

located four miles southwest of Bismarck, according to Tetsuden Kashima in his comprehensive work *Judgment Without Trial: Japanese American Imprisonment during World War II*. Both Italians and Germans were initially held there by the Immigration and Naturalization Service before America's entry into World War II. After the bombing of Pearl Harbor, it became a detention center specifically for Germans and Japanese nationals. *Judgment Without Trial* documents that by February 1942, there were 1,129 Issei, 282 German seamen, and 107 German nationals. (Hearings were eventually held, and Murakami, who was bilingual, agreed to stay in Bismarck an extra three months to interpret for the Japanese prisoners. Most people, like Henry and Charlie, were released into other camps.)

Meanwhile, rumors ran rampant on the once conge-

nial island. *Japanese were being stabbed, raped, and killed.* A community meeting was held on the baseball diamond where the Skippers once ruled. *What was going to happen to them?* People were angry; some even expressed support for Japan. So many of the men had been taken away, leaving women, children, and young Nisei men and women to navigate their fate. Hawaii-born Kikue Furutani, the Japanese-school teacher and one of the few English-speaking mothers of her age, was one of the few women who spoke out.

The islanders felt that they could not rely on the media to accurately represent their interest. Virginia Swanson already said she had been deceived by *Life* magazine, which had sent a sociologist to come to Fish Harbor before the war and assured the missionary that the weekly journal intended to give "a fair representation of the Japanese people." Swanson, however, charged that the resulting article lacked photographs that were "favorable" toward its residents.

After the bombing of Pearl Harbor, Swanson convinced a cameraman at Paramount Pictures to take footage of the children of Fish Harbor. A cameraman apparently did come, but reportedly told Virginia: "[The images] aroused sympathy, and that's not what we want in war times. We must stir hatred. These Japanese people are more loyal than I am, but we don't want to put that on the screen. Our pictures must show that the Japanese are a menace."

Dave Yutaka Nakagawa was a victim of false identification. Apparently, a wartime newsreel playing in a San Pedro theater showed a young Japanese officer pointing to warplanes. "Hey, that's Yutaka," someone exclaimed. Afterward, an effigy of Nakagawa was hung on the rafters at the ferry landing with a sign, "Traitor." Decades later, he would discover that people had said that he had boarded a Japanese submarine while fishing on his father's boat, puzzling him because he saw himself as "American as apple pie."

The rumors were relentless. They would have to evacuate in days. They would have to evacuate in hours. Sirens and the sound of machine guns rang out in the middle of night. The Mio women began to get dressed, lights were turned on, only to receive a message from downstairs: "Put that light out or I'll shoot!" a soldier shouted. They had forgotten that the siren was used to indicate blackout, or total darkness.

It was clear that the navy was taking over the island.

Private Ed Collinash presents orders to Shiro Matsushita of 218B Terminal Way demanding that he and his family move out in forty-eight hours. February 1942.

The prison cells had been cleared out of "enemy aliens" to make way for receiving sailors on their way to ships or other stations.

Swanson contacted the navy to get clarification but received no clear information. On February 14, a notice had gone out giving a thirty-day deadline for ninety-five Japanese American businesses and residences leasing land from the Harbor Department to evacuate the area, although Fish Harbor had not yet been designated as prohibited territory. None of the canneries, which controlled three hundred houses inhabited by Issei families, had received that evacuation notice. "No instructions have been

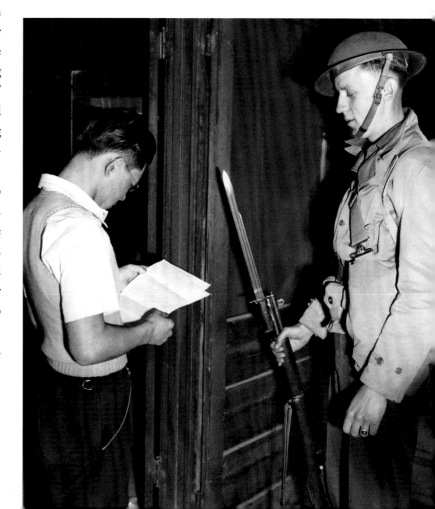

Issei on bus headed to the Terminal Island Immigration Station during the roundup of fishermen on February 2, 1942.

The Daijin-Gu minister, Shinkichi Miyoshi, cleaned the Shinto shrine in preparation for the move. On the altar are the enshrined images of two American presidents, George Washington and Abraham Lincoln.

received, the harbor department said, on removal of three fishnet lockers on land leased to Italians," the *San Pedro News-Pilot* reported in its February 14, 1942, issue.

Four days later, on February 19, President Franklin D. Roosevelt signed Executive Order 9066, which allowed for the creation of military zones, and thereby opened the way, for the mass incarceration of Japanese Americans.

On February 22, the news was out: the navy had filed legal proceedings in federal court to take over "a strip of land on Terminal Island fronting on the Naval Operations Base and Reeves Field, Fleet air base, which is occupied chiefly by Japanese." According to the *San Pedro News-Pilot*, "Roughly the area to be taken over comprises a strip varying in width from one to two or more blocks from a point near the ferry terminal on Terminal Island in Los Angeles, to the Los Angeles River channel on Terminal Island in Long Beach, a distance of nearly two miles."

Soldiers, in full uniform with bayonet rifles, went door to door in Fish Harbor with official letters. All residents of Terminal Island were given forty-eight hours to leave the island by February 27.

Diaspora

The evacuation affected residents of Fish Harbor, Terminal, and Brighton Beach, and not only Japanese Americans. Apparently, since the focus had been on those of Japanese ancestry, non-Japanese residents had not taken the eviction orders seriously until the last minute.

Packing a lifetime of possessions in forty-eight hours was overwhelming, and the process especially took its toll on mothers with young children.

Motoyoshi Murakami optimistically revealed the vegetables he would take with him during his exile from Terminal Island. He would never return to his home.

Below: The press was in full force to cover the last days of the Fish Harbor community. February 1942.

A truck from Seiichi Nakahara's Pacific Coast Fish Company in San Pedro was used to help displaced residents of Fish Harbor.

Non-Japanese residents of Terminal Island also were given forty-eight hours to leave their homes. February 1942.

Arnold Esparza's mother, Marie, hired some trucks to move her grocery store inventory and equipment to Star Grocery on Third Street in San Pedro. There, the Esparzas relaunched their business.

All the other non-Japanese, including Filipinos in the neighborhood of Terminal, would have to find a new place to live. Mobilizing to support the U.S. Armed Forces and the Philippines, which had been invaded by Japan on December 8, 1941, the community created a new organization, Filipino Community of Los Angeles Harbor District. (In response to the Japanese invasion, Filipinos stopped frequenting Issei-owned businesses on the island.) The businesses, including the canneries, remained on the island, so Filipinos were able to replace the absent Japanese female cannery workers.

As soon as they received the news, George Mio rushed to Los Angeles to find housing for his mother and sisters. He returned with bad news. The hotels in Little Tokyo were filled to capacity. Responses from other locations: "No room for Japs" or "Families with Children Not Allowed."

Fortunately, various community members, anticipating the worst, had been working to secure emergency housing. Virginia Swanson had been taking down names of families who had no place to go if a full evacuation was called.

Besides Swanson, members of the Baptist church, including Reverend Kichitaro Eric Yamamoto, the Terminal Islander who had served on the island a year earlier, found locations for potential hostels. With additional

Terminal Island: Lost Communities on America's Edge

help from the American Friends Service Committee, space was secured in three Japanese-language schools in El Monte, Norwalk, and East Whittier. Through Reverend Julius Goldwater's efforts, Buddhist temples in the area opened their doors to the Terminal Islanders. The Forsythe Memorial School in Boyle Heights was another hostel site.

Officers of the local JACL chapter reportedly called on various Japanese American businessmen and wholesale produce markets on the mainland. More than one hundred trucks were on their way to assist—pack and move large items and transport both property and people to their next destinations.

Not leaving the island were the fifty small *ken-ken* boats. They would have new owners, namely "American, Jugoslav, and Italian fishermen," stated Kiyoshi Sakimoto, the new secretary of the Fishermen's Association.

Since many of the men were gone from households, it was up to the resourcefulness of women to sustain their families. Some Issei women whose husbands were gone for days, weeks, or even months on fishing expeditions were at an advantage. They knew what it was like to be in charge.

Fumi Marumoto, mother of five, took spare boards and began hammering them into boxes. Otane Shibata, whose husband was recovering from illness, began

Certain jig boats owned by Japanese fishermen were impounded by the government. The owners were eventually compensated for their loss, but only for a fraction of what their property was worth. February 1942.

making five duffel bags for herself and four children. Her son, Mas, put their names on each one.

Of course, not all could handle this life-changing stress. There was much crying and weeping. A mother of seven children—the oldest fourteen—was left to fend for the family. She was inconsolable. Young men came to her aid, packing and boxing everything that the family would need.

Fred Fujikawa, a doctor whose hospital privileges were stripped away, worked day and night to dismantle his medical equipment from his second-floor office and pack it in boxes. His wife and parents worked on their residences. Luckily, the doctor was able to make arrangements to put their property in the Bekins storage warehouse. Still, they could not take everything. His Issei mother, seeing the "unscrupulous" strangers badgering housewives, decided instead to make a bonfire. "With tears streaming down her face, [she] burned articles that I had made in woodshop, such as a footstool, a small side table, as well as her kitchen table and chairs," reported the doctor. Others did the same, breaking dishes and choosing to destroy precious items rather than let strangers profit from their misfortune.

The Mios had the tremendous task of getting rid of items from their two popular restaurants as well as their home. They had recently remodeled and re-equipped the store for a sizable amount of money. Now buyers were offering less than a third of its worth for everything. No, Orie Mio said. She could not sell for that price.

"It was the most stressful, traumatic period of my whole life, being left with four children and no husband to help disburse restaurant supplies within that ridiculous time frame," stated Orie Mio. "Businessmen from all over came swarming around like vultures to take advantage of the dirt-cheap goods we were forced to sell."

Inventory—nonperishable food and equipment for two stores—was stacked ceiling high. So many articles had accumulated after living in the same unit above their store for seventeen years. Now they had forty-eight hours to pack, store, and move those items.

The Mios began breaking up perfectly good furniture to make wooden boxes. They picked up discarded boxes, only to later be chased down by someone who demanded payment for them. Strangers streamed into the store to buy supplies and equipment at cut-rate prices. They chased the "vultures" out of the front door, only to discover valuable items—an electric wall clock, a milkshake motor—stolen. Items from the back, plants nurtured and tended over the years, and even the water hose, were gone.

The entire family worked without stopping, only sleeping for a couple hours. During this time they were visited by someone from the state equalization board who wanted to calculate tax from any sales.

Before leaving, Fusaye Mio took one last glance at the disheveled rooms, her home for practically her entire life. She wanted to cry, but could not.

Five hundred Japanese Americans and one hundred white families had waited until the final day to leave. In the darkness, Fusaye traveled with her family toward Wilmington. "This was our last ride on the beloved soil of Terminal Island, once a hustling, bustling harbor; now a ghost town," she remembered. "The only souls around were the soldiers and the prowlers who were going through the empty homes. Downhearted, we crossed the bridge just in the nick of time, at twelve o'clock midnight."

The Takeuchi and Yoshizumi families stayed at

a hotel in Los Angeles. From there, they joined about six other families, including the Yamamotos, in a now-defunct Japanese school in Whittier, an area referred to as Blue Hills because of its blue lupine. The females slept in the main hall, while the males took residence on stage. A Japanese American flower grower who lived up the hill offered his shed space for additional storage. He also gave them use of his bathhouse.

A day after their move, the Yamamotos realized they had forgotten all about their cat, a golden-haired female with six toes on each paw. She was nursing her recent litter—coveted baby kittens. Roy Yamamoto and his siblings received a special pass back on the island to find her. "The island was deserted, like a ghost town. We couldn't find our cat. Even our cat knew that she no longer had a home."

By April of 1942, cannery housing was uninhabited.

Epilogue

The Terminal Islanders, now largely organized by the former residents' children, produced this *happi* coat in June of 2013. This type of coat is often worn at Japanese American summer festivals in Southern California.

The Terminal Islanders resettled after receiving the notice to vacate the island in forty-eight hours, but another notice came in March. All people of Japanese ancestry—alien and "non-alien"—had to leave certain military zones on the West Coast.

Writer Olive Percival, a frequent visitor to Idah Meachum Strobridge's Wickieup on Terminal Island, had actively protested the 1920 Alien Land Law, so now she attempted to do what she could for Japanese Americans near her Garvanza home. Like others sympathetic to the plight of their outcast friends and neighbors, she agreed to store items belonging to Japanese American families.

Some islanders with outside contacts and capital were able to voluntarily relocate to the nation's interior—to places like Utah—during a short window of time given by the government. Most households, however, were still without their patriarchs, and the families had little choice but to go to assembly centers and War Relocation Authority (WRA) camps.

Former Terminal Islanders were scattered into different camps, although a majority ended up in the Manzanar WRA center in the shadow of the Sierra Nevada mountain range. They were concentrated within three adjoining camp blocks, comprising approximately eight hundred people. The Terminal Islanders' prewar rambunctious and close-knit reputation preceded them. Young men embraced this image, even proudly wearing T-shirts claiming them as *Yogores*, or "dirty ones." Nisei Minori Hinoki even penned a "Terminal *Yogore* Song," according to an essay written by Hayato Sakurai in the booklet *Taiji on Distant Shores*, published by the Taiji Historical Archives.

Stanzas of the song, sung to the tune of the 1938 Japanese hit song "Shanghai *Dayori*" (Shanghai News), included the following:

They point and call us Yogore, Yogore
These bodies were polished by the tides
We're proud of our dark Yogore
Our hands and feet are strong
We live with a mariner's will

We risk our lives on the sea
The spirit forged into our bodies
These hands and feet come quick
Rough words and deeds have become our way

Meanwhile, back on Terminal Island, the last squatters were forced out. Leases for the cannery housing and Mildred Obarr Walizer Elementary School were pulled, but the canneries themselves remained open for operation. The navy took over a large portion of the island, and soon houses and the school were bulldozed—flattened, as if they had never existed.

Japanese were still being brought to the Terminal Island Immigration Station on Reservation Point during this time, notably Issei women from various locations, many of them Japanese-language school teachers, who had been taken into custody.

According to Professor Tetsuden Kashima in *Judgment Without Trial*, on October 10, 1945, Issei and Nisei segregants were transported to the immigration station from a secret segregation camp in Fort Stanton, New Mexico. The camp apparently held a select number of "troublemakers," including at least one Terminal Islander, a forty-four-year-old Nisei who had spent time in Japan. Redesignated "Segregation Camp No. 1 for Japanese," the building was used as a holding station while

the United States prepared to deport the prisoners to Japan. A number of Terminal Islanders eventually repatriated to Japan, including some of their Nisei children, minors who had little say in the matter. Many eventually returned to the United States.

The resettlement period after World War II was an especially challenging time for Terminal Islanders. No one had homes to return to, but they were still called to the sea breeze and salt air and moved to places like Long Beach. A few, including fisherman Torao Takahashi, attempted to return to their prewar occupations, but soon encountered the ultimate roadblock. In 1943, during the mass incarceration of Japanese Americans, the California legislature amended Fish and Game code Section 990 to read: "A commercial fishing license may be issued to any person other than an alien Japanese." Language also prohibited companies that were majority owned by Japanese from receiving a license. In 1945, when the government began releasing Japanese Americans from WRA camps, Section 990 was amended again to replace "alien Japanese" with "ineligible for citizenship" to avoid any possible court challenges.

That didn't stop Takahashi, a pioneer who had been fishing since 1915, from filing a lawsuit against the Fish and Game Commission in 1947 for refusing to issue him a license. The case eventually went to the United States Supreme Court, which reversed a California Supreme Court decision that had earlier upheld the Fish and Game Commission exclusionary amendment. Takahashi and other Issei were now eligible for commercial fishing licenses.

In a blistering majority opinion in *Takahashi v. Fish and Game Commission* (334 U.S. 410) on June 7, 1948, Justice Frank Murphy wrote: "For some years prior to the Japanese attack on Pearl Harbor, these protagonists of intolerance had been leveling unfounded accusations and innuendos against Japanese fishing crews operating off the coast of California. . . . Yet full investigations by appropriate authorities failed to reveal any competent supporting evidence."

That same year, President Harry Truman signed a bill, H.R. 3142, the Japanese Evacuation Claims Act of 1948, which was created to compensate Japanese Americans for financial losses sustained by their forced removal and incarceration. However, compensation was capped at $2,500, less than ten cents for every dollar lost. Certain former internees, figuring something was better than nothing, took the $2,500 and attempted to rebuild a new future.

Meanwhile, cannery work continued on Terminal Island. During World War II, Filipinos and Latinos largely replaced the displaced Japanese workers. The Bogdanovich family's French Sardine Company grew, according to the *Los Angeles Times*. By 1946, Los Angeles Harbor was the largest fish-canning center in the world. In the 1950s, the harbor contributed approximately 80 percent of the tuna canned in the United States, employing more than five thousand people. In 1952, French Sardine's new expanded tuna-packing facility along Fish Harbor was the largest of its kind in the world. The same year, French Sardine became Star-Kist Company, named after its most popular product line.

Despite this economic growth, challenges followed. As in the Fish Harbor era, strikes over pricing disagreements occurred frequently. In 1950, Van Camp, which was still in operation, announced that the cannery was

unable to accept more local fish due to the rise of imports—ironically, from Japan. Throughout that decade, the cannery was able to remain a family operation, according to Andrew F. Smith's *American Tuna*. As the world's largest tuna packer, it had the Chicken of the Sea and White Star brands, and in 1955, the mermaid with long blond hair became its logo. The company was finally sold in 1963 to Ralston Purina, with various sales and mergers following.

With its iconic Charlie the Tuna character, Star-Kist, too, went from family ownership to being acquired by the large conglomerate, H.J. Heinz Company. As more tuna was being caught in Atlantic waters in the 1960s, production began to move overseas to places like Puerto Rico and, later, Samoa. In the fall of 1984, Star-Kist shut down its presence on Terminal Island. Chicken of the Sea remained on the island until 2001.

Another Terminal Island industry experiencing extreme highs and lows has been shipbuilding. Pacific Wharf and Storage, a company that once battled with squatters over land, was sold to Southwestern Shipbuilding Company for use as a shipyard in 1918. Bethlehem Shipbuilding Corporation (BSC), a division of Bethlehem Steel, acquired the yard at 985 South Seaside Avenue in 1922. After World War II, BSC continued to grow, reporting four million dollars of sales in the repair of 280 ships in 1956. While revenues increased to seven million dollars in 1966, the volume of repairs plummeted to 120 ships. With the reduction of government contracts and labor strikes, BSC closed its shipyard in 1980 and sold its property to Southwest Marine in 1981. Shipyard operations ceased at this site in 2004.

On May 27, 1971, twenty-three Japanese Americans, all former residents of Terminal Island, got together in Gardena, California, to form a new group, Terminal Islanders. A week later, on June 6, a reunion was held for all Terminal Islanders at the Golden Palace Restaurant in Los Angeles's Chinatown. People traveled from as far as Chicago and Seabrook, New Jersey, to attend the inaugural event in downtown Los Angeles. Educators such as former principal Dr. Burton E. Davis and teacher Katherine Chan were present. The Baptist minister Eric Kichitaro Yamamoto came with his wife, missionary Virginia Swanson, the couple having wed after World War II. More than seven hundred guests filled the banquet hall.

Even though their Fish Harbor homes, Shinto shrine, and schools were all decimated, their spirit of home and family was still intensely felt. They shared old stories and toasted each other. They made plans to meet annually and eventually even more often.

Ten years after the group's establishment, more stories from Terminal Islanders were told, this time to the presidential Commission on Wartime Relocation and Internment of Civilians (CWRIC) regarding the forced removal of Japanese Americans. Among those to speak was Kanshi Stanley Yamashita, who had become a colonel in the United States Army and would later write his doctoral dissertation on Terminal Island.

Yamashita made an impassioned speech, highlighting attitudes, both past and present, regarding Japanese Americans. He quoted from a 1942 memorandum from General DeWitt to the secretary of war: "The Japanese race is an enemy race and while many second and third generation Japanese born on United States soil, possessed of United States citizenship, have become

Terminal Islanders, circa 1971. The group officially formed in the 1970s and meets at least twice a year.

'Americanized,' the racial strains are undiluted."

"Had I been aware of such twisted and rampant, racist views, I doubt whether I would have volunteered for the United States Army and served in the Pacific theater during World War II as I did," Yamashita said.

On August 10, 1988, President Ronald Reagan signed H.R. 442 into law, awarding redress and reparations of twenty thousand dollars to each Japanese American survivor of the camps. Upon signing, he said, "Yes, the nation was then at war, struggling for its survival, and it's not for us today to pass judgment upon those who may have made mistakes while engaged in that great struggle. Yet, we must recognize that the internment of Japanese Americans was just that: a mistake. For throughout the war, Japanese Americans in the tens of thousands remained utterly loyal to the United States."

More redemption followed. On June 8, 1994, a special ceremony was held to finally give diplomas to the thirty-six Nisei who were in the class of 1942 at the San Pedro High School. "We haven't been forgotten," expressed Frank Endo, one of the honored graduates.

On Terminal Island today, the most noticeable sound is not the whistles of canneries but of locomotives traveling over tracks. Since 1921, the Union Pacific Railroad, the successor company to the Los Angeles and Salt Lake Railroad, has provided daily service to Los Angeles Harbor. On Seaside Avenue is Al Larson Boat Shop, which reopened a boatyard operation in Fish Harbor not far from where the shop had originally been located. The operation is one of the port's longest remaining tenants.

Just south of the boat shop and across from a vacant shipyard site on 1124 South Seaside Avenue is a relatively new addition. Financed by the Terminal Islanders and formally dedicated in 2002, the Terminal Island Memorial Monument features bronze statues of two Issei fishermen, a replica of Terminal Island's Daijin-Gu, and calligraphy by then Terminal Islander Club president Yukio Tatsumi.

Further northeast is the once-bustling Tuna Street, the heart of the Japanese fishing village. Two altered buildings, unrecognizable as the pre–World War II stores that once served Issei and Nisei, still stand. Both structures have been placed on the Los Angeles Harbor Department's historic inventory, as part of its recently adopted historic architectural and cultural resource policy. Stucco covers the exteriors, and all the doors and windows have been replaced. Only their basic forms exist, yet like the enduring Terminal Islanders, who continue to gather two times a year, they represent a persevering and undefeated spirit.

The building at 700–702 Tuna Street is actually one of the earliest businesses on Fish Harbor. Nanka Company, also known as *Nanka Shoten*, opened in 1918. Port minutes report that a K. Oku from 233–235 East First Street in Little Tokyo had applied for right to use two thousand square feet for a dry-goods business in April 1918.

According to *San Pidoro Doho Hattenroku* (1937), Masayoshi Tokunaga and Iwajiro Asai managed the Nanka Company. Tokunaga arrived in the United States in 1903, worked on the Santa Fe Railroad, and then managed a noodle factory in Los Angeles. In 1907, he cofounded Coast Fishing Company in Wilmington.

Tokunaga was extremely entrepreneurial, managing a number of residential hotels while co-owning Nanka

Company. Besides being enterprising, Asai was also well connected. The *San Pidoro Doho Hattenroku* mentioned that he accompanied former California Governor and United States Minister Henry Gage on a diplomatic mission to Europe.

Asai and his family lived in Little Tokyo, where he and two other men formed a partnership and ran dry-goods stores in three different locations, including the Los Angeles produce market. Afterwards, the Asais moved to Terminal Island to be close to Nanka Company.

The Asais eventually were incarcerated in Poston War Relocation Center in Arizona, where their son, Sadaichi, met his future wife, Shizue Marian Tsumura. In Poston, Sadaichi served as assistant pastor of a church camp and worked under Reverend Jitsuo Morikawa, one of the past ministers of the Baptist church on Terminal Island. Through a program administered by the Japanese American Relocation Committee, the Asais were able to leave Poston for Buffalo, New York, where Sadaichi was assigned to work as youth program director at a Baptist church. He eventually came to lead congregations in Kansas and Vermont in communities where the Asais were the only people of Japanese ancestry.

"One of the saddest moments in my life was experienced on the drawbridge near the Ford plant in Wilmington when we were leaving Terminal Island on that dark February day in 1942," Sadaichi expressed in a 1994 sermon. "Being evicted from our business place was in itself a great financial loss, but to be torn asunder from our home, our church, and our community was a cataclysmic emotional experience."

The other surviving building at 712–716 Tuna Street housed the A. Nakamura Company, one of the several grocery stores on Fish Harbor. The store's namesake and founder, Akimatsu Nakamura, had come to the United States from Kanagawa Prefecture, Japan, in 1910. He worked for a couple of electric companies in Los Angeles before laboring in fruit orchards in Riverside. He worked in various Los Angeles businesses before launching his store in 1925.

Nakamura's daughter, Hideko, and Kenji Yamamoto, another Terminal Islander, married while in Manzanar. Both in their nineties and living in their son's home, the couple celebrated their seventy-year anniversary in 2013. They had been classmates at the grammar school in Fish Harbor; Hideko was then sent to Ehime Prefecture for her education and returned to Terminal Island as a young woman in 1940. Kenji, meanwhile, was selling produce from a truck for Murakami Company. In a July 2, 2013, article in the *Rafu Shimpo* by Ryoko Ohnishi, Hideko recalled that Kenji drove by one day in 1940 and gave her a large peach.

At either the New Year's celebration or the summer picnic of the Terminal Islanders, Kenji often plays the harmonica, a skill he apparently learned from someone at the Baptist church on Fish Harbor. At some point during the afternoon, emcee Charlie Hamasaki, who once described Terminal Island as an "enchanted island," attempts to get children and grandchildren of Terminal Islanders to join in the singing of the "Terminal *Yogore* Song," including this last stanza:

> *No matter if our bodies are Yogore*
> *This is the San Pedro we love*
> *Our hearts are clean*
> *Take a look everyone*
> *At the spirit of a Terminal Yogore*

Afterword

by George Takei

In 1941, when I was a little boy, the Japanese military attacked Pearl Harbor. It was a surprise attack, and thousands of U.S. service members and civilians perished. As a nation, we were stunned. And we vowed to strike back. Revenge was on everyone's mind. However, a large number of immigrants from Japan were fishermen who had settled in the fishing villages of Terminal Island and Bainbridge Island across from Seattle, contributing their skills and expertise to the local economic vitality.

In its zeal to exact revenge, the U.S. government overreacted, out of fear and bigotry. They targeted everyone who happened to look like the people who had carried out the attack. Japanese Americans on Terminal Island and Bainbridge Island were the first to be removed from their homes. By February 1942, most of the fishermen from Fish Harbor were arrested and sent to Japanese American internment camps set up by the Department of Justice. The Bainbridge Islanders were the earliest to be rounded up and sent to Manzanar, the dusty, landlocked, barbed-wire prison camp in the Owens Valley of California.

Those of us who had done nothing wrong were forced to suffer the consequences for the decisions of others far away and disconnected from us. We were interned for years, in these open-air prisons, while young Japanese American men and women went off from behind barbed wire fences to fight Japan, Germany, and Italy.

It's so important that we carry the lessons of the past through to today. Merely because one group commits atrocities and acts with depravity does not mean vast hundreds of thousands or even millions of others should be lumped together with them and made to suffer. We must never paint with the brush of retaliation, or the toll of human suffering will again rise immeasurably.

The story of Terminal Island, a lost community of Los Angeles, should never be forgotten.

Acknowledgments

謝辞

I am grateful to the Los Angeles Board of Harbor Commissioners, who supported the research and publication of this work. Commissioner Dave Arian and former Commissioner Doug Krause were the first to suggest writing a book documenting the story of the Japanese village on Terminal Island after we spent several hours at the Fisherman's Village memorial on the island with former resident Minoru "Min" Tonai. The current board, under the leadership of Ambassador Vilma Martinez, carried the project through to completion.

Publishers Paddy Calistro and Scott McAuley of Angel City Press brought with them the exceptional talents of graphic designer Amy Inouye and photographic researcher Eric Lynxwiler. I will be always grateful to Paddy and Scott for the introduction to my coauthor Naomi Hirahara; it has been my honor to work with her.

I also am indebted to William Deverell for his thought-provoking and gracious Foreword to *Terminal Island*. I admire his work and am gratified by his response to this book. As he always does, Bill provides great perspective to an important aspect of Southern California history.

Tara Fansler, archive director for the Port of Angeles, supervised the book project, provided guidance, critique, and photographs. Nick Beyelia and Andrea Serna searched for records online and in the archives, and Andrea even braved the freezing basement of the County of Los Angeles Hall of Records to search for deeds and visited the National Archives in Riverside. Neca Alves and the Port of Los Angeles Construction Division worked with Port Archives to scan historical photographs. Cynthia Ruiz, Theresa Adams-Lopez, Arley Baker, and Michael Hale oversaw the project for the External Relations Bureau. Bob Henry, formerly of the Port of Los Angeles, was a kindred spirit in support of this project and collected information on the squatters, which he generously passed onto me. I thank all of these people.

I also want to thank Todd Gaydowski and Michael Holland of the Los Angeles City Archives for providing a listing of Los Angeles City Council actions related to Terminal Island. San Pedro resident Randall Taylor, a descendant of ferryman Michael Duffy, provided pictures of Mr. Duffy and information about his daughter Elsie. Liza Posas, archivist and head librarian at the Braun Research Library, offered invaluable help by introducing me to the Braun Collection at the Autry National Center and sharing its materials. Gail Wasil of the Port of Long Beach helped to obtain leases from the Long Beach City Clerk's office for the period when Long Beach controlled all of Terminal Island. Joy Crose of the Los Angeles City Attorney's office provided cases associated with the annexation of Terminal Island by the City of Long Beach. James H. McLean, curator emeritus of mollusks at the Los Angeles County Museum of Natural History, supplied the photo of the shell named for M. Burton Williamson. Edward Squires, great-grandson of Borden employee Edward Hodgson, provided photographs of the Borden house. My new friend, Stephen Dudley, a descendant of the Bixby family of

From left, Akimatsu Nakamura, Jitsuji Hori, and Murao Kobata standing in front of A. Nakamura Company. Circa 1925. Nakamura founded the grocery store after working in retail stores in Los Angeles.

Long Beach, who has a keen interest in the history of this area, taught me about the art that emerged from the region and discovered numerous paintings of Terminal Island and the harbor which were created during the period covered by this book. He graciously allowed us to publish a photograph of his painting by Albert H. Slade. How wonderful it would be to discover where all the artwork is today.

The 1901 *Annual Publication of the Historical Society of Southern California* was a gift to me from former port employee Jan Green-Rebstock. It included an article by M. Burton Williamson about the Marine Biological Station at Terminal Island, which was the first inkling I had that such a laboratory existed. Peter Brueggeman, the archivist for the Scripps Institution of Oceanography, got as excited as I did upon learning about the Marine Biological Laboratory on Terminal Island, and delved into records at Scripps to uncover photographs and information about the laboratory. I am especially indebted to Anne Hansford, archivist for the San Pedro Historical Society, whose listening skills picked up my mention of Miss Sarah P. Monks, which reminded her of a photo album given to the society about Miss Monks. I feel as though the nineteenth-century women scientists Miss Sarah P. Monks and M. Burton Williamson were waiting for me to find them. They deserve more than the short space given to them in these pages.

Finally, I thank my dear friend and officemate at the Port of Los Angeles in the 1970s, Lillian Kawasaki. Lillian told me about her family who lived in the Japanese village on Terminal Island and were removed to Manzanar, a story I had a hard time believing could have ever happened in America. Lillian passed away while Naomi and I were completing *Terminal Island*. All of my efforts on this book are dedicated to her memory and to the Terminal Islanders, who once lived in the Japanese village and who continue to ensure that this story will never be lost.

—Geraldine Knatz
June 2014

Conversations with and material from Kanshi Stanley Yamashita's widow Dorothy and sister-in-law Yuki Yamashita, helped to gird this history of Terminal Island in its infancy.

Another invaluable source was Marie Masumoto, who has been doing extensive research on Terminal Island and its immigration center. Marie also provided an important contact at Los Angeles Harbor College, the institution's librarian Traci Liley, who opened an archive into another world for us.

Kazu Shimasaki, the great-grandson of Kihei Nasu, shed important light on this historic figure whose role in fighting for the fishermen of Terminal Island has been hidden for decades.

Needless to say, Terminal Islanders were integral to the success of this project. Special thanks to President Minoru Tonai, Yukio Tatsumi, Kisaye (Nakasaki) Sato, Charlie Hamasaki, Lynn Yoshiko Hori, Chizuru Nakaji Boyea, and Kenji and Hideko (Nakamura) Yamamoto. Children of Terminal Islanders—Sue Shackelford, Mel Tatsumi, and Tim Yuji Yamamoto—provided digital images of key photographs from personal collections. Evelyn Kita and Marlene Yamada shared their valuable scrapbooks from the Mio and

Although severely altered, the structure still remains at the original location at 712 Tuna Street. The store was in the building with two blue doors.

Terminal Island: Lost Communities on America's Edge

Hashimoto families.

Takashi "Tash" Kushi offered invaluable help from the very start of the research, providing information about the links to Wakayama, as well as securing a better copy of the map created by Shoji Hirami and five other Terminal Islanders.

Appreciation also goes to Richard Chikami, Arnold Esparza, and Warren Furutani for sharing information and photographs. Cal Walters shared clippings related to the disappearance of the *Belle Isle*.

We are amazed by the beautiful Foreword written by scholar William Deverell and thank him for taking the time from his own academic work to review the text. Another Southern California history expert, Donald Hata, also generously reviewed an early outline of the manuscript and provided invaluable feedback. University of Southern California Professor Duncan Williams kindly reviewed the section on religion on the island.

The San Pedro Historical Society, led by archivist Anne Hansford, was helpful in gaining access to back issues of the *News-Pilot* as well as its amazing collection of photographs. Appreciation goes out to the group's volunteers, including Sonja Ulrich.

Richard Chikami, who is related to the Fukuzaki family, was extremely helpful because he was an active fisherman after World War II and worked alongside some former residents of Terminal Island. Richard is working in conjunction with Craig Heberer of the National Oceanic and Atmospheric Administration (NOAA) Fisheries to create a documentary on tuna fishing, in association with the Aquarium of the Pacific.

Special thanks to Mayumi Hirahara and Yuki Nagashima for their translation assistance.

Librarian Linda Fernandes of Rosemead Library's Asian Pacific Resource Center was able to facilitate microfilm access to past issues of the *Rafu Shimpo*, dating back to 1919.

Thomas Philo of the California State University, Dominguez Hills Archives and Special Collections Department gave full access to a master's thesis written by Richard R. Perkins. Yuko Konno kindly shared a chapter prepared for her doctoral dissertation before its publication. In addition to sending an exhibition catalogue, Hayato Sakurai, of Taiji Historical Archives, enabled the use of a photograph of teacher Mildred Obarr Walizer in Wakayama. Also giving guidance were the late Karin Higa, Tetsuden Kashima, and Minoru Kanda.

Specific photo assistance was provided by Debra Kaufman and Mary Morganti from the California Historical Society; Christina Rice, Los Angeles Public Library; Erica Varela, *Los Angeles Times*; Brandon Barton, UCLA Special Collections; Maggie Weatherbee, Lauren Zuchowski, and Tomi Yoshikawa, Japanese American National Museum; Kathleen Correia, California History Room of the California State Library; Liza Posas and Marilyn Van Winkle, Autry National Center's Braun Research Library; Beverly Patterson, U.S. Army Corps of Engineers; Randall Taylor; and Erin Chase, the Huntington Library, San Marino.

Last, and perhaps most essential, were the Port of Los Angeles, initiator of this project, and the members of our book team. Again, Tara Fansler for her consummate professionalism, and the staff of the Port of Los Angeles Archives, including Andrea Serna and Nick Beyelia, for unearthing material that has never been published before. Amy Inouye was the design magician who presented the many elements of this book in a beautiful, highly visual way. And to everyone at Angel City Press, especially Paddy Calistro and Scott McAuley, for continuing its mission of producing great books committed to the wonder and power of history.

—Naomi Hirahara and Eric Lynxwiler
June 2014

Bibliography

Chapters 1–3

David E. Bertão's book on *The Portuguese Shore Whalers of California, 1854–1904* was the source of the information on whaling operations on Deadman's Island. Richard Henry Dana in his *Two Years before the Mast* provided the haunting description of the island in 1840. Information on burials on the island came from the *Los Angeles Times* and *Los Angeles Herald*. Other written work provided additional information about Deadman's Island, including: papers published in the *Annuals of the Historical Society of Southern California* by M. Burton Williamson and J.M. Guinn, and J. Duncan Gleason's book *The Islands and Ports of California*.

The San Pedro Bay Historical Society devoted an entire issue of its publication *Shoreline* (24, No. 2, 1997) to the "Islands of San Pedro Bay" written by Reverend Arthur Bartlett and another (19, No. 1, 1991) to "Terminal Island History" by Mary Zangs. Several other issues of *Shoreline* also proved extremely valuable: Volume 14, Number 1, dated July 1987, was an entire issue entitled "Nostalgia and Remembrance," which included an interview with Allen Atchison by Flora Baker, editor of *Shoreline*; Volume 15, with no sequential number, dated December 1988, and Volume 18, Number 1, dated February 1990, contained Parts I and II, respectively, of William Olesen's fine article "Harbor Memories."

The Los Angeles-Long Beach Harbor Areas Cultural Resource Survey produced by Lois J. Weinman and E. Gary Stickel in 1978 for the U.S. Army Engineer District in Los Angeles was the source of information about the Native American population in the harbor area.

The memoirs of Captain Amos Fries detailed the construction of the East Jetty and the difficulty in maintaining it. Those memoirs were published in Volume IV of the 1912 edition of *Professional Memoirs, Corps of Engineers and Engineer Department at Large* and the *Annual Reports Upon the Survey and Improvements of Harbors in California* beginning in 1873 through

1907. Records of U.S. Army Corps of Engineers from the Office of the Chief of Engineers (RG77), Box #10, files W-10 a,d,e, and f, in the National Archives Regional Center at Riverside holds the correspondence between the squatters living in East San Pedro and the army engineers. I found detailed information concerning litigation over the Long Beach Annexation of Terminal Island in court records of *People (ex rel E.T. Scholler) v. City of Long Beach (1909)*.

I relied heavily on the diary of Charles Lummis and his files on Tommy Leggett and Terminal Island available for study in the Braun Research Library of the Autry Museum. Period diaries in the Huntington Library written by Olive Percival helped to chronicle her time in East San Pedro and the activities of many of the Arroyo bohemians. Also at the Huntington are Percival's photos of East San Pedro and letters written by Charles Dwight Willard to his father. These firsthand accounts of island life made the story of the island people come to life.

Hundreds of newspaper clippings from the *Los Angeles Herald*, *Los Angeles Star*, *Los Angeles Times*, and *Sacramento Daily* from the 1870s though 1910 were used to track daily details of the construction of the East Jetty and the trials and tribulations of the

San Pedro Harbor, Cal., in 1857.

squatters who resided in East San Pedro. The society pages of the *Los Angeles Times* chronicled the comings and goings of Los Angeles visitors to Terminal island, and those pages also reported the activities and art showings of the California artists and writers who worked on Terminal Island.

Marco R. Newmark published a paper entitled "Early Resorts in California" in the *Annual Publication of the Historical Society of Southern California*, 1953. *The Sunset Club of Los Angeles* by Fred Alles and Louis Vetter, published in 1916, details the club members' activities and outings to the resorts at Terminal Island. Jackson Graves's *My Seventy Years in California* includes a chapter about his home on Terminal Island. Clarence Henry Matson was a key witness to many of the events in this book, and his 1945 book *Building A World Gateway: The Story of Los Angeles Harbor* provided significant background.

Several doctoral papers provided insightful commentary on relevant topics. Richard Webster Barsness's "The Maritime Development of San Pedro Bay, California, 1821–1921," for the University of Minnesota in 1963, described the port development efforts that were ongoing during the period of residential occupation of Terminal Island. Sharyn Wiley Yeoman's thesis for the University of Colorado at Boulder in 2003, "Messages from the Promised Land: Bohemian Los Angeles, 1880–1920," gives an excellent review of the Arroyo Seco artists and writers. Finally, Donald Ray Culton's 1971 dissertation for the University of Southern California, "Charles Dwight Willard: Los Angeles Booster and Professional Reformer, 1888–1914," covered the precise period of interest for this book and is comprehensive and thorough.

Using the papers of William Ritter, founder of the Marine Biological Laboratory at Terminal Island and the first director of the Scripps Oceanographic Institution at the Scripps Oceanographic Institution Archives, as well as articles from the *Los Angeles Times* and *Los Angeles Herald*, I was able to piece together the story of the lab's establishment and its relocation to San Diego.

Martha Burton Williamson took great pains to leave written records of her own work, and Eugene V. Coan published a review of the malacological papers and taxa of Martha Burton Woodhead Williamson, 1843–1922, and the Isaac Lea Chapter of the Agassiz Association in the July 3, 1989, edition of the journal *Veliger*. *Sunset* magazine published a profile on Williamson in Volume 44 in 1920. Yearbooks and annuals from the Marine Biological Station at Woods Hole and the Normal School were useful in confirming when the scientists were at these locations.

The research efforts of the husband-and-wife team of Anna Marie Hager and Everett Gordon Hager published in various publications including the Westerner's *The Branding Iron*, the *Downey Historical Society Annual* from 1968–69, and their own booklet *San Pedro Harbor Highlights* published by La Siesta Press in 1968. These works were the source of information about island life, and the interior of the island homes. Anna Marie Hager's article, "A Salute to the Port of Los Angeles from Mud Flats to Modern Day Miracle," published in the *California Historical Society Quarterly* in 1970, was my first lead to the names of artists working on the island, and in the course of doing research for this book, I discovered others. Information about Idah Meacham Strobridge and her Wickieup came from her Sagebrush Trilogy, published by the University of Nevada Press, news clippings, and the Lummis and Percival diaries. Linda Popp DiBiase's paper "Forgotten Woman of the Arroyo: Olive Percival," from the Fall 1984 edition of the *Southern California Quarterly*, provided background information about Percival. Significant information about the homes on Terminal Island came from the research work done by Camille Baxter available at the Harbor College Library. Baxter documented residents and their homes on the island, including a significant collection of photographs with caption data.

Census data from ancestry.com and city directories from the Long Beach Public Library website were instrumental in determining information about permanent residents on the island, particularly their occupations. The Harbor Commission minutes perused at the Port of Los Angeles Archives also provided key information and dates.

Bill Olesen, (1904–2003) a longtime member of the San Pedro Historical Society and a "Tom Sawyer of Terminal Island," left many stories of his days growing up amid the "old salts" who hung on as squatters on Terminal Island. In addition to appearing in various editions of the San Pedro Historical Society *Shoreline*, his work was published many times in the *San Pedro News-Pilot*.

My primary sources for information about the railroads on Terminal Island were John R. Signor's 1988 Golden West Book, *Los Angeles and Salt Lake Railroad*; Franklyn Hoyt's paper "The Los Angeles Terminal Railroad" published in the *Southern California Quarterly*, Vol. 36 in 1954; William Deverell's *Railroad Crossing: Californians and the Railroad 1850-1910*; and Richard Barsness's thesis.

—Geraldine Knatz
Long Beach, 2014

Colonel Kanshi Stanley Yamashita's 1985 University of California, Irvine doctoral dissertation, "Terminal Island: Ethnography of an Ethnic Community: Its Dissolution and Reorganization to a Non-Spatial Community," provided a strong foundation for inquiry and organization regarding the Japanese fishing village.

The first known English-language paper, "The Japanese Community of East San Pedro, Terminal Island, California" was produced in 1931 by University of Southern California master's student Kanichi Kawasaki, who relied heavily on interviews. Richard R. Perkins of California State University, Dominguez Hills wrote an impassioned master's thesis in 1992, "The Terminal Island Japanese: Preservation of a Lost Community," which advocated for the historic preservation of Fish Harbor.

"A Transpacific Community," Yuko Konno's chapter in her USC doctoral dissertation (2012), "Trans-Pacific Localism: Emigration, Adaptation, and Nationalism among Japanese Immigrants in California, 1890–1940," traced the connection of Terminal Islanders to the town of Taiji in Wakayama Prefecture, Japan. It also included the ethnic breakdown of residents living in Fish Harbor versus Terminal. Another important academic work was Mary Carmel Finley's 2007 University of California, San Diego dissertation, "The Tragedy of Enclosure: Fish, Fisheries Science, and U.S. Foreign Policy, 1920–1960."

As many former Fish Harbor residents had already passed away as of 2013, I depended on oral histories conducted mostly in the 1970s and 1990s.

California State University, Long Beach was the first academic institution to undertake a large archive of interviews with individuals who lived on Terminal Island. Transcripts used for this manuscript included interviews with Fred Fujikawa (May 14, 1973), Chuck Furutani (May 14, 1973), Miyo Higashi Ida (November 4, 1979), Sonoko Katsuyama (March 5, 1973), Dave Nakagawa (November 15, 1975), Mitsuyo Nakai (undated), Helen Robello (October 12, 1979), Mas Shono (undated), and Aiko Takeshita (November 26, 2001).

San Pedro Harbor, Los Angeles, Cal.

Under the leadership of former Terminal Islander President Yukio Tatsumi, an oral history project was initiated in conjunction with an exhibit at the Japanese American National Museum from July until November 1994. Many transcriptions of these interviews are on the Japanese American National Museum website, while the original tapes of the interviews are housed in the museum's archive. The transcriptions include Kimiye Okuno Takeuchi Ariga (June 1994), Sadaichi Asai (1994), Frank Endo (1994), George and Ben Fukuzaki (1994), Charlie Hamasaki (March 2, 1994), Min Hara (1994), Hideyo (Ono) Ikemoto (February 8, 1994), Yoshio Iwamae (May 1994), Kuichi Izumi (February 6, 1994), Yurao Kobata (February 15, 1994), Frank and Mitsuyo Manaka (April 5, 1994), John Marumoto (1994), Tomitaro Marumoto (March 10, 1994), Orie Mio (February 3, 1994), Eiichi Miyagishima (May 1994), Yutaka Dave Nakagawa (1994), S. John Nitta (June 7, 1994), Teruko Miyoshi Okimoto (June 2, 1994), Joe Ozaki (May 3,1994), Takao Shintani (1994), Frank and Nakako Takeuchi (April 18, 1994), and Mas Tanibata (March 2, 1994). Included in this collection is an account written by Fusaye (Mio) Hashimoto on February 18, 1944 while she was working as a stenographer in Manzanar for the University of California, Berkeley sociological study, Japanese American Evacuation and Resettlement Study.

More interview transcriptions were included in the book *Terminal Island: An Island in Time, Collection of Personal Histories of Former Islanders, 1994–1995.* Toshiro Izumi, who also contributed many essays about daily life in Fish Harbor, conducted most of the interviews, with Mary Tamura transcribing. Material from this book included the following: essays written by Toshiro Izumi (February 1995), John Marumoto (December 1979, Holiday Supplement, *Kashu Mainichi*), John Oka (undated); and the following interviews: Tadao and Toshiye Kobata (May 27, 1994); George Mio (undated); Yukizo Ryono (May 16, 1994); Katsuyemon Shibata (November 1994); Otane Shiga (undated); Kazuye Shibata Kushi (undated); Roy Hideo Yamamoto (September 17, 1994); Virginia Swanson Yamamoto (June 1994); Virginia Swanson Yamamoto regarding her husband, Eric Kichitaro Yamamoto (June 1994), and her own life (June 1994); and Kiyoo Yamashita (March 1995).

As part of its Centennial celebration, the Port of Los Angeles also did interviews. Utilized for this book were those with John Marumoto, Minoru "Min" Tonai, Haruye Sakamoto, Yukio Tatsumi, and James Yamamoto.

With the help of current Terminal Islander President Minoru Tonai, I did follow-up interviews with Yukio Tatsumi (September 12, 2013), Kisaye (Nakasaki) Sato (September 17, 2013), Charlie Hamasaki (October 17, 2013), Lynn Yoshiko Hori (November 12, 2013), and Chizuru Nakaji Boyea (November 13, 2013). More informal interviews were done at Terminal Islander picnics. I conducted additional interviews with Richard Chikami (October 10, 2013), Arnold Esparza (October 18, 2013), and Warren Furutani (October 23, 2013). Another oral history source was my interview with Dr. Fred Fujikawa (April 1, 1989), transcribed by Paul Tsuneishi.

The booklet, "Terminal Islander 25th Anniversary, 1971–1996," contained details of the club's early activities.

While writing a regional history when many are not available for interviews has distinct disadvantages, the twentieth-century has brought one benefit—digital technology and faster access to primary documents. Early issues (1903–1911) of the Seattle-based fishing industry journal, *Pacific Fishermen*, are part of the digital collection of the University of Washington, found at www.content.lib.washington.edu/pacfishweb/. Digital archives of the Japanese American Citizens League house organ, *Pacific Citizen*, are available on the website, www.pacificcitizen.org.

Of course, since this is a Los Angeles Harbor Department project, the first source of information was the Port of Los Angeles Archives. Digitized Harbor Commission minutes, dating back to the early 1910s, were important, especially about the establishment of Fish Harbor and its related businesses and organizations.

Regarding dates of the removal and arrests of Terminal Islanders, 1941 and 1942 clippings from the *Los Angeles Times* and *San Pedro News-Pilot* were vital.

More in-depth information about the alien detention centers in San Pedro, Tujunga, and Santa Fe were found in Tetsuden Kashima's *Judgment Without Trial: Japanese American Imprisonment during World War II.*

Annie Garcia, whose photo collection was the inspiration behind Maggie Shelton's *Red Lacquer Bridge* (2006), donated her albums to Harbor College, where she had worked years after serving as an educator for the grammar school at Fish Harbor.

Census records as well as the transcripts of the Commission on Wartime Relocation and Internment of Civilians testimonies were accessed online on the County of Los Angeles Public Library's website, www.colapublib.org.

Another invaluable resource was provided by Lynn Yoshiko Hori, whose mother had dutifully packed certain historic sources when they were forced off the island in 1942. It is amazing that this mother of four could have considered the importance of history as she packed her family's belongings.

One of the items that Hori packed was Kosuke Takeuchi's Japanese book, *San Pidoro Doho Hattenroku: Record of the Development of the Japanese in San Pedro* (1937), which provided specific histories of leading individuals and organizations. That information was integral in checking oral history accounts and providing concrete detail to make photo captions come alive.

Another Japanese-language resource is the *Rafu Year Book and Directory, 1939–1940*, published by the *Rafu Shimpo: L.A. Japanese Daily News*. The directory was extremely helpful in verifying the addresses of various businesses and families in Fish Harbor and Terminal. Also significant was a 1927 Southern California directory of Wakayama Kenjinkai, provided by Takashi "Tash" Kushi. "Warera Shin Sekai ni Sankasu," a 2004 booklet produced JICA's Japanese Overseas Migration Museum in Yokohama, Japan, provided some statistics about historic Japanese emigration.

University of California, Los Angeles Special Collections has a treasure trove of intimate details about Japanese Americans in Terminal Island in its papers from Masaru Ben Akahori, who maintained a legal office on the island in the 1920s. Within the collection are a sketch of the Shinto shrine and legal documents that clarify the origins of the shrine. Also at UCLA are microfilm of *The Southern*

Coast Herald (*Minami Engan Jiho*), July to November 1941. Originally called *The San Pedro Times* (*San Pidoro Taimasu*) in 1915, the Japanese-language publication changed its name in 1927.

C. Robert Ryono's booklet, "Although Patriotic, We Were Drydocked," which also has an online version at ryono.net/terminal-island/terminalisland.html, contains wonderful anecdotal accounts, as well as translated information from Takeuchi's work. Copley Los Angeles Newspapers' News-Pilot/The Daily Breeze produced a special centennial publication, *San Pedro: The First 100 Years*, on March 24, 1988, edited by Robert F. Beck, Timothy T. Lemm, and Sandra Radmilovich. Finally, Lillian Takahashi Hoffecker wrote a riveting account of Terminal Island in the context of her grandfather, Torao Takahashi, in "A Village Disappeared" in the *American Heritage*, November/December 2001 (Volume 52).

—Naomi Hirahara
Pasadena, 2014

Alles, Fred Lind, and Louis Fisher Vetter. *The Sunset Club of Los Angeles*. Los Angeles: G. Rice & Sons., 1916.

Annual Report Upon the Surveys and Improvements of Harbors in California. Washington: U.S. Government Printing Office, 1873–1907.

Apostol, Jane. *Duncan Gleason: Artist, Athlete, and Author*. Los Angeles: Historical Society of Southern California, 2003.

Apostol, Jane, Judy Harvey Sahak, and Dan Luckenbill. *Olive Percival, Los Angeles Author and Bibliophile*. Los Angeles: Dept. of Special Collections, University Research Library, University of California, 1992.

Beck, Robert F., Timothy T. Lemm, and Sandra Radmilovich, eds. *San Pedro: The First 100 Years*. San Pedro, California: Copley Los Angeles Newspapers, 1988.

Bertão, David E. *The Portuguese Shore Whalers of California, 1854–1904*. San Jose, California: Portuguese Heritage Publications of California, 2006.

Bradford, Russell R. *Historic Fishing Industry of San Pedro Bay*. Denver: Outskirts Press, 2009.

Broom, Leonard, and Ruth Riemer. *Removal and Return; the Socio-Economic Effects of the War on Japanese Americans*. Berkeley: University of California Press, 1949.

Chuman, Frank F. *The Bamboo People: The Law and Japanese-Americans*. Del Mar, California: Publisher's Inc., 1976.

Croker, Richard Symonds. *The California Mackerel Fishery*. Sacramento: California State Printing Office, 1933.

Dana, Richard Henry. *Two Years Before the Mast: A Personal Narrative of Life at Sea*. New York: Harper & Brothers, 1840.

Deverell, William Francis. *Railroad Crossing: Californians and the Railroad, 1850–1910*. Berkeley: University of California Press, 1994.

Erie, Steven P. *Globalizing L.A.: Trade, Infrastructure, and Regional Development*. Stanford, California: Stanford University Press, 2004.

Gaffey, John T. *Nets, Hooks and Boats: The San Pedro Bay Fishing Industry, 1850–2000*. Irvine, California: John T. Gaffey II, 2010.

Gleason, J. Duncan. *The Islands and Ports of California: A Guide to Coastal California*. New York: Devin-Adair, 1958.

Graves, Jackson A. *My Seventy Years in California, 1857–1927*. Los Angeles: Times-Mirror Press, 1928.

Guinn, James Miller. *A History of California and an Extended History of Los Angeles and Environs: Also Containing Biographies of Well-Known Citizens of the Past and Present*. Los Angeles: Historic Record, 1915.

Hayashi, Brian Masaru. *For the Sake of Our Japanese Brethren: Assimilation, Nationalism, and Protestantism Among the Japanese of Los Angeles, 1895–1942*. Stanford, California: Stanford University Press, 1995.

Hosokawa, Bill. *JACL in Quest of Justice*. New York: William Morrow, 1982.

Ibanez, Florante Peter and Roselyn Estepa Ibanez. *Filipinos in Carson and the South Bay*. Charleston, South Carolina: Arcadia, 2009.

Ichioka, Yuji. *Issei: The World of the First Generation Japanese Immigrants, 1885–1924.* New York: Free Press, 1988.

Japanese Immigration. Hearings before the Committee on Immigration and Naturalization. Washington, D.C.: House of Representatives, Sixty-sixth Congress, Second Session, 1921.

Kashima, Tetsuden. *Judgment Without Trial: Japanese American Imprisonment During World War II.* Seattle: University of Washington Press, 2003.

Leonard, Bill J. *Baptists in America.* New York: Columbia University Press, 2005.

The Lost Village of Terminal Island. By David Metzler and Elizabeth Michalak. Produced by Allyson Nakamoto. Culver City, California: Our Stories, 2007. DVD.

Maki, Mitchell T., Harry H.L. Kitano, and S. Megan Berthold. *Achieving the Impossible Dream: How Japanese Americans Obtained Redress.* Urbana, Illinois: University of Illinois Press, 1999.

Marquez, Ernest. *Santa Monica Beach: A Collector's Pictorial History.* Santa Monica, California: Angel City Press, 2004.

Marquez, Ernest, and Veronique de Turenne. *Port of Los Angeles: An Illustrated History from 1850 to 1945.* Santa Monica, California: Angel City Press, 2007.

Matson, Clarence Henry. *Building A World Gateway: The Story of Los Angeles Harbor.* Los Angeles: Pacific Era Publishers, 1945.

McWilliams, Carey. *Prejudice: Japanese-Americans: Symbol of Racial Intolerance.* Hamden, Connecticut: Anchor Books, 1971.

Mears, Eliot Grinnell. *Resident Orientals on the American Pacific Coast: Their Legal and Economic Status.* New York: American Group Institute of Pacific Relations, 1927.

Roberts, Lois W., and E. Gary Stickel. *Los Angeles-Long Beach Harbor Areas Cultural Resource Survey.* Los Angeles: U.S. Army Corps of Engineers, 1978.

Ryono, C. Robert. *Although Patriotic, We Were Drydocked.* Los Angeles: Terminal Islanders, 1994.

Sakurai, Hayato. *Taiji on Distant Shores* [exhibition catalog]. Taiji, Wakayama, Japan: Taiji Historical Archives, 2014.

San Pedro–Terminal Island Tube; a Preliminary Report to the Legislature on the Feasibility of a Highway Tunnel beneath the Main Channel of the Los Angeles Harbor. Sacramento: California Division of Highways, 1953.

Shelton, Maggie, and Lucile Cattermole Regan. *The Red Lacquer Bridge.* Bloomington, Indiana: AuthorHouse, 2006.

Shirai, Mari, editor. *Nanka Wakayama Kenjinkai, Celebrating 100 Years, 1911–2011* [anniversary booklet]. Los Angeles: Nanka Wakayama Kenjinkai, 2011.

Signor, John R. *The Los Angeles and Salt Lake Railroad Company: Union Pacific's Historic Salt Lake Route.* San Marino, California: Golden West Books, 1988.

Smith, Andrew F. *American Tuna: The Rise and Fall of an Improbable Food.* Berkeley: University of California Press, 2012.

Strobridge, Idah Meacham. *Sagebrush Trilogy: Idah Meacham Strobridge and Her Works.* Reno: University of Nevada Press, 1990.

Takemoto, Paul Howard., Alice Takemoto, and Kenneth Kaname Takemoto. *Nisei Memories: My Parents Talk About the War Years.* Seattle: University of Washington Press, 2006.

Takeuchi, Kosuke. *San Pidoro Doho Hattenroku: Record of the Development of the Japanese in San Pedro.* Terminal Island, California: K. Takeuchi, 1937.

Terminal Islanders, *Terminal Islander 25th Anniversary, 1971–1996.* Long Beach, California: Terminal Islanders, 1996.

A Time Remembered: The Terminal Island Story. Directed by Trevor Greenwood. Los Angeles: Churchill Media, 1994. DVD.

Uchima, Ansho Mas, and Larry Akira Kobayashi. *Fighting Spirit: Judo in Southern California, 1930–1941.* Pasadena, California: Midori Books, 2006.

Willard, Charles Dwight. *A History of the Chamber of Commerce of Los Angeles, California from Its Foundation, September 1888.* Los Angeles: Press of Kingsley-Barnes & Neuner, 1899.

Index

画像提供者

Image Credits

Thanks to these individuals and families for contributing images from their personal collections: Steve Dudley (38); Arnold Esparza (230, 233); Warren Furutani (168, 193); Charlie Hamasaki (185); Naomi Hirahara (157); Shoji Hirami (172); Ed Hodgson (88, 100 top left, 107); Amy Inouye (268); Geraldine Knatz (4, 33 left, 54 all, 89 all, 90, 104 top, 106, 110, 114 top, 118, 122 top, 136 all, 159 inset, 239, 278, 280); Takashi "Tash" Kushi (256); Mio Family Archive (231); Mio-Hashimoto Family Archive (155, 156, 177, 189, 214 top, 215 all); John Mulvey (274 bottom); Hayato Sakurai (208 top); Kisaye Sato (271); Sue Shackelford (154, 198); Kazu Shimasaki (162, 164); Yukio Tatsumi (212); Ansho Mas Uchima (216); Kenji and Hideko (Nakamura) Yamamoto (222, 274 top)

The authors, photography editor, and publisher thank the following institutions for their cooperation:

Autry National Center, Los Angeles: Braun Research Library Collection: P.15603 (52 inset), P.15603 (64), OP.380 (64 inset); Charles Fletcher Lummis Manuscript Collection: MS.1, Box 229, Series 1.9 (65, 79)

California Historical Society: CHS2013.1183 (14), CHS2013.1184 (20), CHS2013.1186 (31 bottom), CHS2013.1187 (44), CHS2013.1185 (45), CHS2013.1188 (48); California Historical Society Collection at the University of Southern California. Title Insurance and Trust, and C.C. Pierce Photography Collection: CHS-32718 (22)

California State Library (17, 35, 51, 58)

The Huntington Library, San Marino, California (24, 42, 52 left, 55, 56, 57, 70, 83)

Japanese American National Museum (146, 158, 174 right, 197, 199, 200, 202, 217, 225 right)

Long Beach Public Library (137)

Los Angeles Harbor College Library, Archives and Special Collections (1 top, 5, 27, 33 right, 34, 59, 60, 91 all, 92, 95, 97, 98, 99, 100 bottom, 101, 102, 103, 104 bottom, 105, 108, 109, 111, 113, 114 bottom, 116, 148, 174 left, 203 all, 204, 206 all, 207, 208 bottom, 210, 211, 214 bottom, 218 all, 219 all, 238

Los Angeles Harbor Department Collection (16)

Los Angeles Harbor Department Historical Archives (1 bottom, 2, 8, 28, 29, 32, 43, 47, 75, 80, 121, 122 bottom, 126, 127, 132, 133, 134 top, 138, 139, 150, 160, 170, 171, 181, 209 bottom, 235, 254)

Los Angeles Maritime Museum Collection (36)

Los Angeles Public Library Photo Collection (96, 167, 221, 226, 237)

Los Angeles Times: Wayne B. Cave, photographer (257); Andrew Hugh Arnott, photographer (258). Copyright © 2012, Los Angeles Times reprinted with permission.

San Pedro Bay Historical Society (12, 18, 19, 31 top, 40, 46, 50, 61 all, 62, 71, 72, 76, 84, 86, 112, 123, 124, 128, 131, 134 bottom, 141, 142, 143, 153, 159 top, 166, 173, 176 all, 178, 179, 180, 183, 187, 190, 191, 195, 196, 201, 209 top, 224, 227, 228, 229, 232, 244, 246, 247, 249, 251, 252, 259, 261, 262 bottom, 263, 264, 265, 267)

Scripps Institution of Oceanography Archives (68, 69)

Smithsonian Institution Archives, Accession 06-121, Box 1, Folder: Martha Burton Williamson (82 all)

UCLA Charles E. Young Research Library Department of Special Collections (225 left, 243, 262 top)

United States Army Corps of Engineers (140)

University of Southern California, USC Libraries Special Collections (175)

Terminal Island: Lost Communities on America's Edge

By Naomi Hirahara and Geraldine Knatz • Eric Lynxwiler, Photography Editor
Amy Inouye/Future Studio, Design • Foreword by William Deverell • Afterword by George Takei

Copyright © 2015 by The City of Los Angeles

10 9 8 7 6 5 4 3 2 1

ISBN-13: 978-1-62640-127-3

Library of Congress Cataloging-in-Publication Data

Hirahara, Naomi, 1962-
  Terminal Island : lost communities of Los Angeles Harbor / Naomi Hirahara, Geraldine Knatz ; Eric Lynxwiler, photography editor ; foreword by William Deverell ; afterword by George Takei,
     pages cm
  Includes bibliographical references and index.
  ISBN 978-1-62640-127-3 (hardcover : alk. paper)
  1. Terminal Island (Calif.)—History. 2. Terminal Island (Calif.)—Social life and customs. 3. Terminal Island (Calif.)—Biography. 4. Japanese Americans—California—Terminal Island—History. 5. Japanese Americans—California—Terminal Island—Social life and customs. 6. Japanese Americans—California—Terminal Island—Biography. 7. Japanese Americans—Evacuation and relocation—1942-1945. 8. Japanese Americans—California—Terminal Island—Pictorial works. 9. Terminal Island (Calif.)—Pictorial works. 10. Los Angeles Harbor (Calif.)—History—Pictorial works.
  I. Knatz, Geraldine. II. Lynxwiler, J. Eric, 1973- III. Title.
  F868.L8H45 2015

  979.4'93—dc23
                              2014020011

Printed in Canada